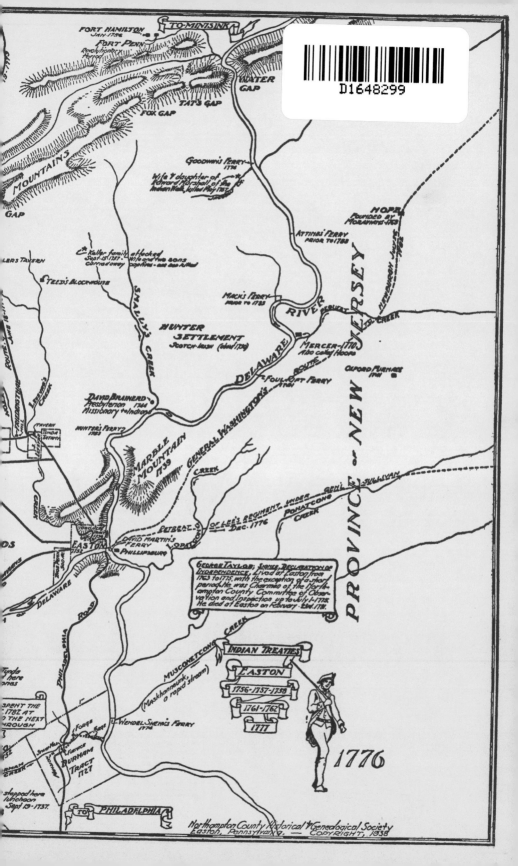

To Cousin Warren Parsley

Clyde LeFevre
5 JUN 1996

A Frontier Village

Pre-Revolutionary Easton

by

A. D. CHIDSEY, Jr.

President of the Northampton County Historical
and Genealogical Society
1931-33 and 1935-37

ILLUSTRATIONS, MAPS, AND TAIL-PIECE
BY THE AUTHOR

VOLUME III

in the publications of

The Northampton County Historical
and Genealogical Society

Easton, Pennsylvania

1940

Second Edition — 1966

PRINTED BY E. W. SCHLECHTER

Allentown, Pennsylvania

Contents

Illustrations

Illustrations, Maps, and Tail-Piece
by the Author

The thirteen eight-pointed star circle at the head of each
Chapter is taken from the first United States Flag to use
the Stars and Stripes, flown at Easton, Pennsylvania,
July 8, 1776.

Introduction

"A FRONTIER VILLAGE" records the history of Easton from seventeen thirty-five to seventeen seventy-six — from its first view by Thomas Penn when he selected its site as the most desirable in Pennsylvania for the city he visioned to its entry into the War of Independence.

Early local historians had frequently relied on tradition and hearsay for their narratives. Constant repetition by succeeding writers had given these every appearance of fact. The consequent need of a revision of Easton's history and the critical examination of statements made by former historians was early seen. In fact the first papers read before the Northampton County Historical Society in 1905 was devoted to the errors in Matthew Henry's "History of the Lehigh Valley."

The Society was fortunate in having a member who was fitted by inclination and training to undertake this work. He is A. D. Chidsey, Jr., the author of "The Penn Patents in the Forks of the Delaware," a native Eastonian, a graduate of Lafayette College, whose training and experience, both as a civil engineer and as an architect, combined to furnish the accuracy and imagination ideal for the examination and presentation of the results of his research.

No record has been accepted which can not be verified from original documentary sources. This painstaking investigation has disproved many erroneous statements, pricked legendary bubbles, and unearthed valuable information heretofore unknown.

The author's challenging attitude towards former recorded history has resulted in a series of essays and pen pictures of the leading personalities in this small community. The portraits of John Lefevre, the tavern keeper, William Parsons, the agent of the Penns, and Lewis Gordon, Easton's first lawyer, are given with an exactness and fullness of detail never attempted before.

The examination of manuscripts treasured in county archives and historical societies has enabled the author to portray the

5

complete life of characters prominent in the very beginnings of this village who played their brief part and then vanished as they came with but a short span of their career unrolled. There was Nathaniel Vernon, the tavern keeper, a prominent figure in the Indian treaties of the seventeen fifties, held at Easton. But no one before told of his earlier career in Chester County and his end as an expatriated loyalist in Nova Scotia. So it is with David Martin. History knew him formerly only as the owner of David Martin's ferry, yet was unaware of the fact that he never operated the ferry himself, that he was a large landed proprietor, a scholar, and the first Rector of the Academy, now the University of Pennsylvania. Even the University itself knew nothing of the details of his life as narrated in Mr. Chidsey's sketch.

The author's sturdy disregard of fireside tales and legend is best seen in the dethroning of Grace Parsons as a feminine Paul Revere. Her wild ride to bring aid to the helpless and affrighted villagers proved to be only the brain child of a fevered imagination.

The extent and minuteness of the author's delving into original sources is best illustrated by his property map of Easton in 1776. Here are definitely located the buildings then standing, with the names of their owners or tenants together with a brief biography of them. To secure complete accuracy in the plotting of the Easton of 1776, necessitated the indefatigable study of numerous court records, deeds, wills, and administrative papers.

Needless to say, this book, which is the outcome of many years of tireless research, will remain the definitive and authoritative work on this period of Easton's history.

HENRY F. MARX

Librarian, Easton Public Library, 1903-1936

John and Thomas Penn
Visit the Site of
Easton

John and Thomas Penn Visit the Site of Easton

Reprinted from
"Penn Patents in the Forks of the Delaware"

T H E R E is in the possession of the Historical Society of Pennsylvania a letter which Thomas Penn wrote to Richard Peters who was then Secretary of the Province of Pennsylvania. There are, in fact, many of these letters, all written in a fine hand with pale ink, most of them quite voluminous. The letter in which we are interested was written in London and is dated July 17th, 1752.

In this communication Thomas Penn requested Richard Peters to let William Parsons know the satisfaction which his appointment, as Prothonotary and Clerk of the Court of the new County of Northampton, gave the proprietaries, and also to tell him that they depended upon his prudence in the settlement and good government of Easton. It is apparent upon reading this letter that Mr. Peters did not have faith in the future of the town then building at the Forks of the Delaware.

Thomas Penn said:—"We shall hope for a better account of Easton from you on your return from thence, some of your arguments against its ever being considerable I think are not well founded. . . . The situation with regard to the River is certainly very advantageous and I have quite forgot the place if the land is very bad, when my brother and I were there we thought the place very proper to build a Town upon."

The important part of the quotation is "when my brother and I were there." Here we have Thomas Penn's own statement that he had been at the site of Easton. Fortunately he adds that his brother was with him. This information is not only interesting but it determines, within a narrow limit, the time when two of the Proprietaries personally inspected what, at that time, must have been a garden spot, but is now the City of Easton.

John was the brother who accompanied Thomas Penn on this trip into the hinterland, for Richard never placed foot on the soil of the Province. John Penn was born in Philadelphia on Jan. 29th, 1699, and on this account was called "The American." At an early age he was taken to England where he remained until 1734. In September of that year he returned to the Province of Pennsylvania. With him came his sister Margaret and her husband, Thomas Fraeme. John Penn remained in America just a year, returning to England in September of 1735. Thomas Penn had preceded his brother by two years, arriving at Chester in 1732. He remained nine years in the Province and returned to England in 1741.

With these facts and dates before us, the conclusion is obvious that Thomas and John Penn stood at the Forks of the Delaware and admired the beauty of the scene sometime between September of 1734 and September of 1735, most likely in the summer of the latter year. There were undoubtedly white men who had watched the waters of the Lecha flow into the waters of the Delaware long before these two Proprietaries stood at the confluence of these rivers and, in the vast solitude of the unbroken wilderness, visualized a town on the plateau between the two streams.

It would be interesting to know the personnel of the company which accompanied the owners of the Province on this trip. There must have been a guide, attendants to look after the horses and prepare camp, personal servants of the Penns, and no doubt some of the leading men of the Province. Undoubtedly there were Indians accompanying the party. Moses Tunda Tatamy quite likely acted as interpreter.

While it is to be regretted that so little is known of this excursion into the wilderness part of Bucks County, the principal fact stands out that the first white men of record to visit the site of Easton were the Proprietaries, John and Thomas Penn. At this time there were some Scotch-Irish settlers in the valley of the Monocacy Creek, but the Walking Purchase had not been perpetrated. The Moravians had not arrived. David Brainerd had not entered this territory and the forced exodus of the Delaware Indians from the Forks did not take place until seven years later.

It does not require a stretch of the imagination to conclude that this visit of the Penn brothers to the Forks was a momentous one that had a definite bearing on the subsequent history of the Province. The beauty of the hills and the streams must have made an indelible impression upon Thomas Penn, who immediately after the visit gave orders to have surveyed for his use one thousand acres at the Forks. The survey was made on Oct. 8th, 1736, and the survey book is marked "for the use of Thomas Penn." No patent was ever issued for the tract and when it was laid out the lots were sold by Thomas and Richard Penn as owners. John Penn had died in 1746. The favorable impression which Thomas Penn received at the time of his visit prompted him to give to our County and county seat names which had a sentimental value to him. Lancaster, Carlisle and Reading were not thus favored.

Is it not possible that this visit to the Forks made the Proprietaries extremely desirous of securing title to this land? It does not seem unreasonable to assume that this desire, thus nurtured, had its effect in the grasping manner in which the Walking Purchase was conducted. The same fostered desire may have hastened the expulsion of the Delaware Indians in 1742.

The impressions which Thomas Penn received in 1735 were lasting, for on March 18, 1752, seventeen years later, he wrote to Lieutenant Governor Hamilton that the county just erected was to be named Northampton and the town in the Forks, Easton, in honor of his bride whose home was at Easton-Neston, Northamptonshire, England.

Easton Before the French
and Indian War

Easton Before the French and Indian War

IN 1752 Easton was laid out and the sale of lots was begun. It had the distinction of being named the county seat of the newly erected county of Northampton. It is hard to conceive of any town starting out under less auspicious circumstances. A ferry across the Delaware and Lehigh Rivers, a healthful climate, and beautiful scenery were, with one exception, the chief and only assets of this new born community. The one exception was the fact that it had been made the county seat. I doubt that without this advantage Easton would have survived.

The growth of the town was slow. In September, 1752, there were but three houses, although during the following winter eleven families comprised the settlement. Notwithstanding the size of the town, its struggle for existence and its poverty, Easton in its first ten years secured a place in the history of our state and nation which it has never since reached. This was due to force of circumstances rather than to any inherent quality in the town or its inhabitants.

By this time settlers first penetrated the northern wilderness of Bucks county, William Penn had died and the Province had passed into the control of his sons, John, Thomas, and Richard. The high ideals which governed William Penn in his dealings with the Indians did not influence the conduct of his sons. To them the acquisition of the Province was a tremendous land transaction and their only interest was, I believe, a monetary one.

On October 25, 1736, the Proprietaries purchased from the Six Nations the northern part of Bucks County, as far north

as the Blue Mountains. This of course included the whole of
Northampton and Lehigh counties as they now exist. While the
Six Nations exercised an overlordship over the Shawnee and
Delaware Indians, they had no right or authority to convey their
lands. The Proprietaries therefore secured a questionable Indian
title and one which the Delawares refused to acknowledge. These
Indians continually complaining to the authorities that not only
were settlers moving into their lands at the Forks of the Delaware,
but that the Proprietaries were selling land in this territory. Their
complaints were well founded. The Scotch Irish had moved into
the Forks as early as 1728 or 1730 and occupied the valleys
of the Monocacy and Catasauqua Creeks. The Proprietors had
sold to William Allen 10,000 acres of land north of the Delaware
Water Gap. The 1,000 acre tract on which the town of Easton
was laid out was surveyed to Thomas Penn in 1736. There were
many other instances.

The Proprietaries in an attempt to pacify the Indians decided
to secure title to this land from the Delawares. They therefore conceived a plan which they hastened to put into operation.
The manner in which this was accomplished gave the transaction
the derisive name of "The Walking Purchase." It has also been
referred to as "the disgrace of the Colonies." This transaction
is a long story and can not be given at this time. It will be
sufficient to say that the manner in which this walk was carried
out, the interpretation which the authorities placed on the agreement, and the vast area which they included within the lines as
they laid them down, thoroughly disgusted the Indians and they
were greatly incensed. They realized that they had been cheated
and positively refused either to leave or to permit settlers to
remain in quiet possession of the lands which they occupied at
the Forks. The Delaware Indians declared that they would not
vacate or surrender possession, even though they should be compelled to go to war to protect their rights.

Having secured title to the land at the Forks as well as to
many thousand acres of land north of the Blue Mountains, it
became necessary for the Proprietaries to secure possession. The

white settlers were entering in ever increasing numbers and the Indians were restless and threatening. It was necessary to have them move out, but this they refused to do.

The Proprietaries having already stooped to questionable means to secure title did not hesitate to continue these same methods to secure possession. Under the guise of giving the Indians of the Six Nations presents for lands west of the Susquehanna River, a conference with these Indians was held in Philadelphia in July, 1742. The Delawares were invited to attend.

At this conference the Iroquois were easily persuaded to remove the Delawares from the Forks. As the conference closed, Canassatego, a Chief of the Six Nations, turned to the Delawares and said: "You ought to be taken by the hair of the head and shaked severely till you recover your senses and become sober . . . You act a dishonest part . . . We charge you to remove instantly. We don't give you liberty to think about it. You are women; take the advice of a wise man and remove immediately . . . We, therefore, assign you two places to go — either to Wyoming or Shamokin . . . Don't deliberate, but remove away and take this belt of wampum." This command of the Six Nations was too peremptory for the Delawares to disobey, so they immediately left the room. Soon after they left the Forks of the Delaware. Some went to Wyoming, some to Shamokin, while others went to the Ohio.

The exodus of the Indians from the Forks must have been rapid and complete. Four months after the Iroquois or Six Nations had delivered their ultimatum to the Delawares a petition was presented to the Provincial Council in Philadelphia. This was signed by Moses Tunda Tatamy, Captain John and sundry other Delaware Indians. The petition stated that as they had embraced the Christian religion and had attained a small degree of knowledge therein, they desired to live under the laws of the English and requested permission to remain in the forbidden land. Tatamy and Captain John were the only Indians present at the time the petition was presented. When questioned by the Governor concerning their knowledge of Christianity, the records state: "It appeared that they had very little if any at all." The result of the petition was that Tatamy and Captain John were given permission to remain, provided they secured the consent of the Chiefs of the Six Nations, but all the other petitioners had to move out. Thus, in 1742, ten years before the founding of Easton, that territory which now comprises Northampton and Lehigh Counties, was cleared of Indians. Locally speaking, the first step in the inevitable advance of civilization had been taken. The local Indians had started their westward march, and as the frontier was slowly pushed toward the setting sun, these Indians were irresistably carried before it, although their resistance at times was savage and bloodthirsty.

The white settlers could now enter this virgin territory without the fear of Indian depredations. With the Indian villages deserted and the savages several days' journey distant, the ever increasing immigrant, looking for a home, a haven of rest, a place to bring up his family, and an opportunity to share in the prosperity of the new world, crossed the Lehigh River with high hopes, and built his rude log dwelling. Now began another conquest: the battle with the wilderness — the taming of the land. Few, if any, of these first settlers had their hopes fulfilled.

As early as 1745 the division of the county of Bucks was discussed. The upper part of the county was almost exclusively peopled by Germans. These people affiliated themselves politically with the Quakers. This enabled the Society of Friends, who were opposed to the Proprietary Party, a controlling majority in the Provincial Assembly. The Proprietaries reasoned that if the support given the Quakers from the upper part of the county could be withdrawn, the control of the Assembly would be in their own hands.

The erection of a new county out of the northern or wilderness portion of Bucks might accomplish this object. The residents of this upper section were heartily in favor of the division. On May 11, 1751, a petition, signed by many, was presented to the Assembdy by William Craig, of the Irish settlement. The result of this petition was that on March 11, 1752, the act creating the new county was signed by Governor Hamilton.

In anticipation of the passage of this act, Thomas Penn had a town laid out on the 1,000 acre tract which had been surveyed to him in 1736. John Penn had died and Thomas Penn owned a three-quarter interest in the Province, his brother, Richard, owning the other quarter. On August 22, 1751, Thomas Penn married Lady Juliana Fermor. His bride was the daughter of Lord Pomfret and her home was at Easton-Neston, Northamptonshire, England. Names for counties, towns and streets must be secured in some manner and what was more natural than that the Proprietor who had the largest interest and had but recently returned from his honeymoon should not only select the names but should also choose those associated with his bride. If he consulted his brother Richard in regard to his choice of names, it is more than likely that Richard smilingly approved. Richard who was four years younger than Thomas, had been married for a period of twenty-four years. The county was named Northampton, the county seat Easton, and the streets were given the names of Juliana, Pomfret, and Fermor.

Some time in the spring of 1750, William Parsons and Nicholas Scull surveyed the site of Easton. It is evident that this attempt did not provide a satisfactory plan, for Thomas Penn requested Nicholas Scull, Surveyor General, and Dr. Graeme, Proprietary Commissioner, to visit the Forks of the Delaware and to inspect the place and the neighborhood where the town, then in Bucks county, was to be built. They were to make a draft of the town and submit it to Thomas Penn for his information, consideration and possible approval. It was on July 27, 1751, that these two gentlemen arrived at Bethlehem on their way to the Delaware at the Forks. William Parsons was not with them but John Okely of Bethlehem accompanied them from that place.

The report and recommendation of Scull and Graeme must have been favorably received, for on May 6, 1752, William Parsons and Nicholas Scull left Philadelphia for the Forks to lay out the proposed town. They traveled by way of Durham, crossed the hills south of Easton, and approached the Delaware River several hundred yards below the point where the Lehigh empties into it. As they rounded the base of Mount Ida,[1] they beheld the site of their labors and their future home.

Across the beautiful stream of pure mountain water, called by the Indians, *Lecha,* later corrupted into Lehigh, was a plateau of about 100 acres. The plateau was well wooded but in no sense a forest. After ferrying across the Lehigh, Parsons and Scull proceeded up the Lehicton Creek (now called the Bushkill) to the public house kept by John Lefevre, near the present borough of Stockertown. After the survey was completed Nicholas Scull returned to Philadelphia while William Parsons remained in Easton.

When Northampton County was erected, William Parsons was appointed Prothonotary and Clerk of the Court. He stood high in the esteem of the Proprietaries and was sent to Easton to look after their interests.

It had been planned to start the sale of lots on Monday, May 25, 1752, and William Parsons had everything in readiness. However, on the preceding Saturday, Richard Peters received a letter from Thomas Penn concerning the plan of Easton which upset the entire layout. The Proprietor proposed a square in the center of the town, which Nicholas Scull in his letter of transmittal to William Parsons said was too small for public use. He suggested that Parsons consider whether it might not be better to depart a little from the Proprietary scheme. Thanks to the decision of Parsons "to depart a little" the square is much larger than it would have been if Thomas Penn's plan had been followed.

The first election was held on October 1, 1752. John Burnside was elected member of the Assembly, William Craig, Sheriff, and Robert Gregg, Peter Trexler and Benjamin Showmaker, were chosen Commissioners. There was only one polling place in the county and that was at Easton. Every person who desired to vote was compelled to go to the county seat.

Politics had entered the county when William Parsons crossed the Lehigh with Nicholas Scull to lay out the town of Easton. It is not my intention to give in chronological order all the elections or other political events which took place. I will however cite one election which will show that the game of politics 180 years ago was similar to what it is today. The information in regard to this election is contained in a letter written by William Parsons to Richard Peters on October 2, 1754, immediately following the election at which James Burnside, a Moravian and a resident of Bethlehem, was elected a member of the Assembly. Mr. Burnside was a member of the Quaker political party. Mr. Parsons was very anxious to defeat him, and was quite upset over his election. It appears that he did all he could to stop the landslide for Mr. Burnside, who according to Parsons, went "from place to place, beating his breast, saying he would serve the county to the utmost of his powers, if he were chosen." Parsons tried to prevent the inspectors from qualifying, claiming they were not freeholders. He tried to prevent the Moravians from voting, claiming that they would not take an oath but only an affirmation and that, without the certificate required by an act of Parliament. He stated that Mr. Burnside had the assurance to declare that all who had taken the oath of allegiance were thus naturalized and could vote. One township in which there was not a single freeholder turned out en mass and voted.

Parsons appealed to the sheriff, who in turn called upon three freeholders: Mr. Brodhead, Mr. Dupui, and Mr. Jones. Mr. Parsons was overruled. I am not in a position to decide the merits of his claims. Whether he was right or wrong, it is apparent that politics in 1754 was no better than the brand with which we are familiar. Mr. Burnside was elected by a vote of 443 to 99. Mr. Parsons closed his letter with this remark: "If Sodom and Gomorra were spared for the sake of ten righteous persons, surely Northampton may have hopes of being spared for the sake of 99."

The first two years of the life of the infant city were just about what would be expected under the circumstances. The town grew slowly. A jail was built in 1753. Times were bad and work was hard to get. In these first few years the Indians gave no trouble. Moses Tunda Tatamy and his family as well as a few Indians who might have been traveling from place to place, were the only ones ever seen. In the county there were many fine settlers among the Scotch Irish. Also the Moravians were all that could be desired. Many worthless settlers, however, moved into the county. In the first three years, nine persons were convicted of horse stealing by the courts held in Easton.

Twenty thousand pounds had been raised in England and Holland for educational purposes in the colonies. Knowing of this the inhabitants of Easton and vicinity, in 1754, petitioned the trustees of this fund for the means to erect a school building and to pay for the services of a school master. The prolific letter writer, William Parsons, wrote to Richard Peters in connection with this school house. Of the petitioners, he says: "They are so perverse and quarrelsome in all their affairs that I am sometimes ready to query with myself whether it be man or beast that the generous benefactors are about to civilize." Here you have the opinion of the representative of the Proprietaries as to the character of the inhabitants of Easton in 1754. I quote again from Mr. Parsons letter: "I will not be negligent in whatever the Trustees may desire, though it seems to me like attempting to wash a Blackamoor white."

Virginia had sent Captain Trent to the Forks of the Ohio to construct a fort. Before this fort was half finished it was surrendered to a French force of 1,000 men, including Indians. The English force of forty men were allowed to return to Virginia. In the meantime, Virginia raised two companies to garrison the fort which they thought Trent was building. These troops were under the command of Colonel George Washington. He marched from Alexandria on April 2, 1754. On May 28th he met and defeated a small force of the French near the place where Uniontown, Pennsylvania, is now located. In this engagement the entire French force was lost. This was the first actual engagement of the French and Indian War. Washington proceeded toward Fort Duquesne, the name the French had given the fort which Captain Trent had surrendered. The French had advanced to meet Washington and found him entrenched in Fort Necessity (Fayette County) with 400 starving men, where on July 3rd, he was compelled to surrender. Washington was permitted to leave the fort with honors of war.

On July 6, 1754, the Iroquois, at a treaty held at Albany, sold to Pennsylvania a large tract of land west of the Susquehanna. At this same conference the Indians agreed not to sell the Wyoming lands, but the treaty was not completed before the Mohawks sold all the Wyoming lands to Connecticut.

The success of the French in western Pennsylvania and the action of the Six Nations in again selling land occupied by the Delawares and Shawnees had a most disquieting effect upon these Indians. Throughout the English colonies, Washington's defeat caused a feeling of alarm. In Easton this feeling existed, but the Forks of the Ohio were a long distance from the Forks of the Delaware and imminent personal danger was not thought of at this time.

About a year later, July 9, 1755, General Braddock was overwhelmingly defeated by the French and Indian allies. Bad news travels rapidly and the news of Braddock's defeat with his two royal regiments and troops from South Carolina, Maryland and Virginia, soon reached Easton and filled the hearts of the inhabitants with fear.

The Delaware and Shawnee Indians hesitating no longer, joined the French, threw off the shackles of subserviency to the Six Nations, and descended upon the frontier in all the glory of their war paint. They killed and scalped men, women, and children. The frontier was about to reap the harvest from the seeds of discontent sown by the Proprietaries and the Provincial authorities.

As word of the defeat of Braddock reached Easton, a subscription list was circulated and signed by those interested in the construction of the school. Twenty-four inhabitants subscribed thirty-one pounds and one shilling. William Parsons headed the list with a contribution of five pounds. This must have been a political gesture, for we know his views on the project. The trustees to whom the petition was addressed contributed thirty pounds, making a total of sixty-one pounds and one shilling. Eleven men agreed to work on the building a total of fifty-nine hours, six men pledged themselves to furnish material, and one citizen signed for three days of carting. Thus the first school house in Easton was constructed three years after the town was founded, and just as the French and Indian War broke out. The building was a one story log structure, with one large front room which was used as a school room and two rear rooms which were the living quarters of the schoolmaster. The building was erected just east of the present Third Street Reformed Church and was one of the first, if not the first building to be erected on North Pomfret Street. In the first few years after its construction, divine services were held in the school room, sometimes by the Lutheran, and at other times by the Reformed denomination.

On October 16, 1755, occurred the first violation by the Delaware Indians of the treaty of 1683 between William Penn and Chief Tamenend. On this date, fourteen Delaware Indians descended on Penns Creek, near Selinsgrove. Thirteen men, women and children were horribly murdered and scalped, and about twelve persons were carried off into captivity.

Nine days later, John Harris and a party of men, returning from a trip to bury the bodies of the unfortunate settlers, were attacked near the mouth of Penns Creek and three of the party killed. On October 26th, the Delawares crossed the Susquehanna to the east side and killed many settlers from Thomas McKees' property to Hunters Mill, practically from Sunbury to Harrisburg.

A week later (Oct. 31, 1755) about 100 Delaware and Shawnee Indians from the Ohio Valley descended on the Scotch Irish in the valleys of what are now Fulton and Franklin counties.[3] These raids lasted several days and it is impossible to describe the fury of the Indians or the horror of the massacres. In what is known as the Great Cove, forty-seven inhabitants out of a total of ninety-three were either killed or carried away captive. Little children had their brains dashed out against door posts or trees and this in the presence of their shrieking mothers. Women were tied to trees and compelled to watch the torture or burning alive of their husbands or children. One woman had both breasts cut off and a stake driven through her body pinning her to the ground. The torch was applied to dwelling and barns. All crops were destroyed and the cattle which did not perish in the flames were driven off by the infuriated savages. It was not long before the news of these atrocities reached the county seat of Northampton county.

In November of the same year (1755) the Indians descended on the settlements along the Swatara and Tulpehocken Creeks. The depredations were getting closer and closer to Easton, Bethlehem and Nazareth. Constant appeals were made to the authorities in Philadelphia for assistance in the way of guns, ammunition, provisions and also for troops.

As the Indian raids and massacres spread eastward and northeastward, the Delaware and Shawnee Indians from Wyoming and Tioga were increasingly taking part. It seemed that each day word of new outbreaks was brought to Easton.

Information as to a possible raid in Northampton county had been received in Bethlehem and Timothy Horsfield requested William Parsons to have Colonel John Anderson, then in New Jersey, come to his assistance. The very bad weather prevented Anderson from marching until noon of Sunday, November 23, 1755. In his company there were several Eastonians and fifty to sixty men from New Jersey. He encamped about six miles from Gnadenhuetten on the evening of Monday, November 24th, the day that the first blow fell upon the inhabitants of Northampton county. On that day, at the supper hour, a band of twelve Delaware Indians attacked the Moravians at Gnadenhuetten which was located on the west side of the Lehigh River, opposite the present town of Weissport, and on the Mahoning Creek. Eleven were killed or burned to death, being trapped in their dwellings, to which the Indians had applied the torch. As soon as William Parsons heard of the massacre he advised the Secretary of the Province, Richard Peters, and in his letter he said: "Pray Sir: Help us, for we are in great distress."

While the frontier was being drenched with blood and the smoke from the burning homes hung like a pall from the sky, what were the authorities doing to stop the carnage? They did what legislative bodies generally do, they wrangled over technicalities and trivial matters. While their disputes continued, so did the frontiersman and his family continue to die most horrible deaths at the hands of the naked painted savage whose fury knew no bounds.

The calm and seeming indifference of the Assembly, the nonresistance policy of the Quaker, and the Governor's insistence that the lands of the Proprietaries be not taxed, for purposes of defense, aroused the indignation of the inhabitants. Public meetings were held in nearly all the frontier counties. At these meetings it was resolved to proceed to Philadelphia and demand that laws be passed which would provide proper defense for the country and offense against the enemy. Many of these frontiersmen went to Philadelphia, taking with them the mutilated bodies of those who had been murdered.[4] These bodies were hauled about the streets of Philadelphia, placarded as victims of the dilatory methods of the authorities. Maddened by the dreadful spectacle, the enraged mob surrounded the Assembly building and placed the disfigured bodies in the doorway. Immediate relief for the settlers on the frontier was demanded.

All this must have had the desired effect, for on November 25, 1755, an act was passed providing for a militia. On the following day the Governor signed an act appropriating 55,000 pounds to the use of the king for purposes of defense. In addition to this amount the Proprietaries made a gift of 5,000 pounds on condition that their estates in the province be not taxed.

These two acts were very necessary steps. But apparently the authorities did not at once take the action called for by them. The settlers on the frontier were still unprotected and under the dreadful suspense of having the howling savages descend upon them at any time. On December 10, 1755, the Indians attacked the family of Frederick Hoeth on Big Creek and murdered the family except one son who escaped. The dwelling, barn, and mill were destroyed by fire. The next day about 200 Indians attacked the families of Hartman, Culver and McMichael and killed many. On the same day Brodheads, near Stroudsburg, was attacked. Terror spread in that section of the county and the families on the north side of the Blue Mountains, and many on the south side, fled to Nazareth and Easton for safety. Nazareth had been stockaded by the Moravians. I quote from the Colonial Records: "During all the month (December) the Indians have been burning and destroying all before them in Northampton County, and have already burnt fifty houses there; murdered about one hundred persons and are still continuing their ravages, murders and devastations . . . . A large body of Indians under the direction of French Officers, have fixed their headquarters within the borders of that county."[5]

On December 15, 1755, William Parsons wrote to James Hamilton and Benjamin Franklin as follows: "I make bold to trouble you once more, and it is not unlikely that it may be the last time . . . . We are now the frontier of this part of the country. . . . Pray do something or give some orders for our speedy relief, or the whole country will be entirely ruined."

The panic which had seized the people of Pennsylvania made it difficult for the authorities to secure definite information or to distinguish the true from the false. Therefore, a Commission consisting of Benjamin Franklin, James Hamilton and Joseph Fox made a trip to Easton in order to get at first hand accurate information and decide upon the proper method of defense.

In the meantime arms, ammunitions, blankets, and a hogshead of rum were sent to Easton for Captain Trump's Company. The Commissioners arrived in Easton on Saturday, December 23, 1755. On Christmas morning James Hamilton wrote to Governor Morris as follows: "The Commissioners came to this town on Saturday Evening where we found the Country under the greatest consternation, and everything that has been said of the distress of the inhabitants, more than verified upon our own view. The country along the river is absolutely deserted from this place to Brodhead's."

On December 29, 1755, Benjamin Franklin, while at Easton, appointed William Parsons to be major of the troops in Northampton County. On New Year's Day, 1756, Teedyuscung started a series of raids on the north side of the Blue Mountains, which eventually extended over the mountains, and overran the county from Lehigh Gap to Nazareth. Pennsylvania then began the construction of forts along the Kittatinny Range from the Delaware Water Gap to the Maryland line. On April 8, 1756, Governor Morris declared war against the Indians and offered a reward of 150 Spanish dollars or pieces of eight for an adult male Indian scalp and a lesser amount for scalps of women and children or for their capture alive.

The declaration of war against the Delawares was very distasteful to the Quaker members of the Assembly, and they with other prominent members of the Society of Friends, persuaded the Governor to make overtures of peace to the Indians. As a result the Indian, Canachquasy, or as he was called by the English, Captain Newcastle, was sent to Wyoming and Tioga to interview the Indians living in the Valley of the Susquehanna. Newcastle returned to Philadelphia early in June and reported that the Indians had agreed to bury the hatchet and to open negotiations for peace. A second trip was made by Newcastle to invite the Indians to a conference to be held at the Forks of the Delaware. On Monday, July 19th, he returned with five Indians and informed the Governor and Council that Teedyuscung, the Delaware king, with other Indians had returned with him as far as Bethlehem. Acting upon the advice of Newcastle, the Governor selected Easton at the Forks as the place of meeting and the date, July 24th (1756).

Governor Morris notified Major Parsons to prepare housing at Easton for the Indians and also to provide provisions for them. He was also to order an escort to proceed to Bethlehem to bring the Indians to Easton. After these instructions had been carried out, Major Parsons received another communication from the Governor, telling him that it had been found necessary to change the place of meeting from Easton to Bethlehem. Teedyuscung was not so easily moved. Upon being told of the change in plans he calmly remarked, that he had come 400 miles at their invitation to attend a council fire at Easton; that there he had come and that there he would stay; and demanded to know what they meant by sending him from place to place like a child. The treaty conference was held at Easton.

Fears that the Indians might prove troublesome were not unfounded. Major Parsons, who kept a diary, later reported to the Governor that Teedyuscung and his wild company were perpetually drunk and at times abusive to the inhabitants, for the Indians all spoke English well enough to be understood. Teedyuscung strutted about the town, bragging about himself and his ability. Major Parsons said that Teedyuscung could drink three quarts to a gallon of rum a day without becoming drunk. He also learned that the Delaware king and some other Indians had visited the French at Fort Niagara where he was made much of and that the French had presented Teedyuscung with a brown cloth coat, laced with gold.

The Governor left Philadelphia on Friday, July 23rd, and arrived in Easton the next day. With the Governor were four members of the Colonial Council. They were escorted by a Company of the Royal American Regiment and a Company of the Provincial Forces together with their officers.

An open shed had been constructed in the Great Square. Tables and benches were properly placed under the shed so that the Governor, the members of his party, the principal Indians, the secretaries and the scribes could all be under cover. The principal Indians sat in the front row. In addition to the Governor's party about thirty Quakers attended this conference, arriving in Easton the day after the Governor.

The Governor had his quarters at the Red Lion Inn. This Inn was conducted by Adam Yohe and was located at the northeast corner of Northampton and Hamilton (now 4th) Streets. There were but fifteen to twenty houses in Easton at the time of this conference.

Each time the Governor went to or returned from the place of meeting the order of march was as follows: First came the Color Bearer, with the flag of England fluttering in the breeze; then the drums and fifes playing the tunes of the day. Next a detachment of the Royal American Regiment, followed by the Governor who was guarded on each side by members of the same regiment.

Following the Governor were members of the Council, the Commissioners and the Secretary, with the Provincial troops bringing up the rear. After the Governor and his party had reached the scene of the conference the Indians left their encampment in single file. Practically all of these Indians had taken part in the frontier massacres.

Teedyuscung headed the file of Indians. He wore the brown cloth coat laced with gold which the French had given him, below the coat his bare bronze legs protruded. He wore moccasins decorated with procupine quills. On his head was the feathered bonnet indicative of his rank. The other Indians were dressed in similar manner, except that in place of the brown coat they wore more or less elaborate breech cloths. The heads of many of them were shaved, leaving only a tuft down the center like the comb of a chicken, which stood up in pompadour fashion. In this tuft of hair were fastened feathers. After the Indian chiefs and warriors came the women and children. It was noticed at this conference that some of the skirts which the Indian women wore were made from the table cloths taken from the German families that had been murdered. The children wore little or no clothing.

It is most interesting to visualize these treaty conferences which were held at Easton during this early period of the infant town. Easton with one school, a jail, several taverns and between fifteen and twenty dwellings, with poor roads for streets and most of the lots still covered with trees and underbrush, was a far different town from the one we know. In this setting, we find the Governor, the Council and the Secretary of the Province as well as about thirty of the most prominent Quakers from Philadelphia. Two encampments must be included, that of the Indians along the Lehigh and that of the troops, the location of which I do not know. These conferences presented most colorful and picturesque gatherings, full of great contrasts. The Governor and the foremost citizens of the province dressed in the height of fashion rubbed elbows with the frontiersmen and settlers in their shabby homespun. The Royal American Regiment was in bright uniforms and the Provincial Troops were a rabble in arms. The Indians with their naked copper colored bodies glistening in the sun, carried themselves with solemn dignity, except when drunk, belying the fact that practically all of them were murderers, the scalps of their victims not yet dry.

While at Easton the Governor received from New York, by express, a package containing letters from Mr. Fox, Lord Halifax, and Lord Loudoun. The letter from Lord Halifax informed the Governor of the appointment of Lord Loudoun as Captain General of His Majesty's forces in America. The letter from Lord Loudoun advised the Governor of his appointment and of his arrival in New York. The letter from Mr. Fox, His Majesty's Secretary of State, stated that the king had found it necessary to declare war against the French king and that he was enclosing the declaration which His Majesty had signed, saying: "I am commanded to signify to you the King's pleasure that you should cause the said Declaration of War to be proclaimed in the Province under your Government." On this Friday morning, July 30, 1756, the Governor marched to the place of meeting in the usual manner. The same audience, as on other mornings, had gathered. The Governor then arose and in a very solemn manner read His Majesty's Declaration of War. At the close of the publication of the Declaration the Royal American Regiment fired three volleys.

Thus in Easton, in Centre Square, Robert H. Morris, Governor of the Province of Pennsylvania, first read King George the Second's formal declaration of war, two years and four months after Colonel George Washington fired the first shot in what has become known as The French and Indian War.

---

[1]Snufftown, formerly called Williamstown, a part of South Easton.

[2]J. M. Levering, *History of Bethlehem* (Bethlehem, 1903), p. 202.

[3]C. H. Sipe, *Indian Wars of Pennsylvania* (Harrisburg, 1931), p. 217.

[4]John Churchman, *An Account of the Gospel Labors and Christian Experience of a Faithful Minister of Christ, John Churchman* (Philadelphia, 1781), p. 239.

[5]Pennsylvania Colonial Records, Vol. VI, p. 767.

David Martin and the
Easton Ferry

David Martin and The Easton Ferry

AS the counties in New Jersey increased in number and decreased in size, the territory now known as Warren county was successively in Hunterdon, Morris and Sussex counties.

Within the bounds of Warren county, there is a small stream of water which long ago was given the Indian name of Lopatcong. Its source is the Scott's mountains about one mile southeast of Roxburg on the Belvidere pike. It flows in a meandering course in a general southwesterly direction. Passing Lower Harmony, it flows through the Harkers Hollow golf course, crosses the Morris turnpike, runs a short distance north of Shimers Corners and then flows under Green's bridge and on westwardly to the Delaware river, a total distance of about ten miles. The mouth of the brook is about a mile and a half below the point where the Lehigh river joins the Delaware on the opposite shore line.

There is a tale of how this valley was settled by Baron von Brachlti[1] from Oberhessen, in Germany, a castle in the city of Giessen. He came with the Swedes in 1638 to settle on the shores of Delaware bay. However, soon tiring of the settlement and urged by the spirit of adventure, the Baron pushed on up the river until he came to Lopatcong. Here he built a manor house, overlooking this beautiful stream, about one half mile from the present Straw Church. Here Baron von Brachlti and his descendants, as the story goes, lived undisturbed, at peace and friendship with the Indians, for over one hundred years before our story starts. Fact, fiction, and buried treasure; folklore,

35

fables, and the black art, all mingled together to make a fascinating tale and throw a mantle of mysticism and romance over the valley of the Lopatcong. However, this interesting legend has no place in a narrative of authentic historical facts.

Some time before 1723, Joseph Kirkbride of Bucks County, Pennsylvania, secured a grant of twelve hundred and fifty acres of land in the province of New Jersey. This tract of land, including within its bounds the fertile valley of the Lopatcong creek, was about one mile wide and two miles in length, with a frontage on the Delaware river above and below the mouth of the creek.

In September of 1723, Kirkbride conveyed this tract to his son-in-law, John Hutchinson, who in turn sold the twelve hundred and fifty acres to John Pearce[3] (spelled Peairs in the deed), a "yeoman" of Solebury township, Bucks county. A large part of this acreage is included within the present limits of the town of Phillipsburg.

All of the transactions of John Pearce are not recorded, but from these deeds of record, it appears that in 1736 or earlier, he sold this property in about four tracts. Mathais Kirkendal (Kewkendael), William Scoley, and Johannis Hornbeck[4] (Hornbeick) were three of the purchasers.

The conveyances covering these tracts mention that they are located in Pearcetown, Hunterdon county, province of New Jersey. As each deed of record mentions houses, barns, stables, orchards, gardens, and improvements, the obvious conclusion is that in 1736 or earlier, there was a settlement along the Lopatcong creek partly within the present limits of the town of Phillipsburg. In fact several later conveyances continue to refer to this section of the present Warren county as Pearcetown.

Mathais Kirkendal, one of the purchasers, became involved in financial difficulties and the sheriff was directed to sell his property to satisfy a judgement for one hundred and forty-seven pounds and costs.

At this time David Martin was sheriff of Hunterdon county.[5] He had succeeded Bennet Bard who had been found guilty on September 24, 1736, of barratry and malversation of office. His appointment records him as "a gentleman of Trenton".

In the execution of the court order, Martin sold the property on October 26th, 1738, to Archibald Home[6] for the sum of one hundred and ten pounds.

About one month later, November 21, 1738, Home leased this plantation to David Martin[7] and on the following day executed a release[8] for the same amount which he had paid at sheriff's

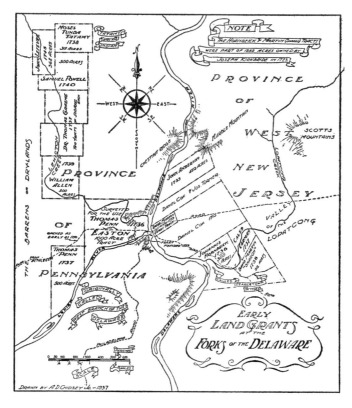

sale; namely one hundred and ten pounds. David Martin thus became the owner of three hundred and twelve acres located in Pearcetown, more than a year before he scured his Delaware river ferry rights.

It is a conjecture as to whether the acquisition by David Martin of this property in Pearcetown on the Lopatcong creek was the cause or the result of his application for exclusive ferry rights on the Delaware river.

However this may be, on February 12, 1739, he received a grant from King George II[9] covering the sole privilege of operating a ferry over the Delaware at the mouth of the Lopatcong creek or at any point, within limits, both up and down the stream. The northern limit of the grant was a point opposite the mouth of the Lehigh, then called the West Branch; the southern limit, the Musconetcong creek.

The charter from the King conveyed to Martin one hundred and five acres of land with a frontage on the east shore of the Delaware facing the Forks.

As early as 1733 David Cox of Trenton sold to John Anderson[10] four hundred and fifty acres of land in Hunterdon county located on the Delaware river, just above the Forks. As the conveyance specifically mentions buildings, we have a record of a settler on the Jersey shore of the Delaware opposite the future site of Easton nineteen years before the town was laid out.

On the Pennsylvania side of the river, the Indians still occupied the Forks. Some Scotch Irish had moved into the valley of the Monocacy, but the Moravians had not arrived, and the large tracts which had been sold by the Proprietaries in the Forks remained unoccupied. Some settlers had moved into Williams township. The construction of the iron furnace at Oxford, New Jersey, was not started until 1741. It is evident that the population centering about the Forks of the Delaware was very small and widely scattered.

In February of 1739, David Martin, gentleman and sheriff of Hunterdon county, province of New Jersey, and a resident of Trenton, was the owner of three hundred and twelve acres in Pearcetown, along the Lopatcong creek, and of another tract, just a short distance away, of one hundred and five acres. This second tract had a frontage of about fifteen hundred feet on the east shore of the Delaware river just opposite to the mouth of the Lehi. In addition to these two tracts he had secured the exclusive ferry rights in New Jersey for a distance of nine miles.

On December 22nd, 1741, the Proprietaries of Pennsylvania granted similar ferry rights to Martin covering the west side of the river from Marble Hill to Tinicum island, a distance of twenty miles. It is possible that before he secured the Pennsylvania rights, he had obtained an extension of his New Jersey grant; for the Penns stated that they were covering the same portion of the river as covered by David Martin's New Jersey grant.

When we consider Martin's activities, from the time he secured his ferry rights until his death, it becomes evident that he did not personally operate the ferry.

Just when Martin's term of office expired is not known, but on May 20th, 1740, he was again appointed sheriff of Hunterdon county,[11] and the records state that he was "a person well qualified and proper".

By this time, Morris county had been erected and the valley of the Lopatcong and Martin's ferry were within the limits of the new county and consequently beyond the shrievalty of Hunterdon county.

* * *

On May 14th, 1743, Benjamin Franklin printed a proposal to form a society. In this he said: "The first drudgery of settling new colonies, which confines the attention of people to mere necessaries, is now pretty well over; and there are many in every province in circumstances, that set them at ease, and afford leisure to cultivate the finer arts, and improve the common stock of knowledge. — — — — — But as from the extent of the country, such persons are widely separated, and seldom can see and converse, or be acquainted with each other, so that many useful particulars remain uncommunicated, die with the discoverers, and are lost to mankind; it is, to remedy this inconvenience for the future, proposed,

"That one society be formed of virtuosi or ingenious men, residing in the several colonies, to be called The American Philosophical Society, who are to maintain a constant correspondence." There is of course much more to the printed proposal.

In a letter which Mr. Franklin on April 5th, 1744, wrote to Cadwallader Colden of New York[12], he names the original members of the society, all of whom live in Philadelphia, and then adds: "— — — the following members have since been added, viz: Mr. Alexander, of New York; Mr. Morris, Chief Justice of the Jerseys; Mr. Home, Secretary of do.; Mr. John Coxe, of Trenton; and Mr. Martyn, of the same place."

This is our David Martin and the "ingenious men" of Philadelphia must have considered him sufficient of a virtuoso to select him as one of the first four members to be elected to the newly formed American Philosophical Society.

This honor and the personal qualities which prompted its bestowal did not prevent him from being an excellent sheriff. He was a man of force and character, fearless in the face of danger.

Great dissatisfaction existed in the province of New Jersey over the question of land titles. Disorders and riots occurred throughout the province. Many citizens, in defending their titles, were charged with high treason and placed in jail. Some time in December of 1747, a large number of men, in a riotous manner, armed with clubs and cudgels, advanced on the Trenton jail, bent on liberating David Brayley who had been charged with high treason. David Martin, deciding that a defense of the jail was impractical, went forward singlehanded and met the rioters in the street.[13] He told them that their action was criminal and attempted to arrest one of their number, Edward Bainbridge. The mob was not to be denied. They not only prevented Martin from arresting Bainbridge, but they broke open the jail and liberated Brayley. Martin wrote to the Governor and gave him a full account of this jail delivery.[14]

On September 6th, 1746, the Assembly of the province of New Jersey granted to Trenton a charter of incorporation as a "free borough town". David Martin, who still held the office of sheriff, was not only appointed one of the ten burgesses to govern the borough, but he was also selected as the town marshal.[15] In 1749 he was appointed a justice.[16] In May of 1750 he relinquished his position as sheriff,[17] for, as we shall see later, he was about to take up his residence in Pennsylvania. John Allen, Jr., was appointed in his place.

While David Martin was serving as a sheriff and justice in Hunterdon county, province of New Jersey, Benjamin Franklin, James Logan, William Allen, Richard Peters and others, a total of twenty-four of the most prominent citizens of Philadelphia were perfecting an organization for the establishment of an academy for the education of the youth of the province. Benjamin Franklin was elected president of the board. This was the inauspicious beginning of the University of Pennsylvania.

The Academy board took over the building which had been constructed in 1740-41 on the west side of Fourth street just below Arch, for the use of itinerant and unsectarian ministers and as a charity school where a plain English and Christian education was to be given to the children of the poor. It is interesting to note that Edmund Wooley, a carpenter, and brother-in-law of William Parsons, was one of the four artisans to underwrite this charity school project, and that they still held title to the ground when the Academy purchased it.

Before the solicitation of funds for the Academy was started, Benjamin Franklin published a pamphlet about the proposed school.[18] This pamphlet was distributed free to his newspaper subscribers. Franklin was particularly interested in securing the services of a first class man to be the head of the Academy, the rector as he was called.

In regard to the selection of the rector, he stated in his pamphlet "that the rector be a man of good standing, good morals, diligent and patient, learned in the languages and sciences, and correct pure speaker and writer of the English tongue."

At the meeting of the board to formulate rules and regulations for the operation of the Academy, Franklin's ideas were carried out and the chief requirements for the person to fulfill the position of head of the school were "polite speaking, writing and understanding the English tongue".

No sooner had the necessary alterations and repairs been started to their building than the board looked around for a head master or rector. To fill this important post they selected a member of the American Philosophical Society, the proprietor of the Easton ferry, a sheriff and justice of Hunterdon county, David Martin, Esquire, as the record modestly states, "a gentleman of the neighboring province."[19]   Under these conditions, his selection stamps him as one of the best educated men of the two provinces. Besides his duties as rector, he taught Latin, Greek, history, geography, chronology, and rhetoric. His appointment took effect on May 13th, 1750, and he received a salary of two hundred pounds per year.

Charles Thompson, a Friend, who after the Revolution became secretary of congress, was appointed a tutor to assist Rector Martin.[20] Thompson, who served as Teedyescung's secretary at one of Easton's Indian treaties, received the magnificent salary of sixty pounds for the entire year.

There were two other members of the teaching staff: David James Dove, who taught English "grammatically and as a language", and Theophilus Grew, whose subjects were writing, arithmetic, merchants' accounts, algebra, astronomy, navigation and all other branches of mathematics.

Benjamin Franklin was very much upset because the head of the Latin department received a larger salary than the head of the English department.[21] As a matter of fact, Franklin was opposed to the teaching of Latin and Greek. He felt that English was so important that it was a waste of time to study the dead languages. He states in some of his writings that he did not insist upon his views, as those who were contributing most of the money for the Academy were in favor of the old languages, and he did not think it advisable to cross those who held the purse strings.

David Martin's duties started on May 13th, 1750,[22] but the school did not open until the following January. In the interim he served as registrar and had his office in the Philadelphia Post Office, where he had hours from ten to twelve every morning, except Sunday.

The Academy during its first year had over one hundred scholars and the annual charge was about seventeen dollars and fifty cents. The Academy immediately became popular, and judging from its increasing enrollment, Rector Martin must have handled his duties in a highly satisfactory manner.

With all his other activities he retained his interest in the Episcopal church at Trenton. A lottery for raising three hundred and ninety-three pounds to be used in completing the construction of this church was undertaken in June of 1751. Martin was one of five men who agreed to sell tickets in Philadelphia.[23] He was also a contributor to a fund for erecting the steeple on Christ's Church, Philadelphia. [24] After his death, his administrator in Pennsylvania paid the church two pounds, the unpaid balance of his subscription.

From 1739 to 1752, there is no definite information in regard to the location of the ferry house or the name of the ferry man. When Martin secured his New Jersey ferry rights, he acquired one hundred and five acres of land in that province. His Pennsylvania rights conveyed no land. Martin had therefore selected the east bank of the Delaware for the home of the ferryman, the only ferry house required. It is possible that the men whom he employed or to whom he leased the ferry had other ideas and may have lived on the west side of the river.

In November of 1750, Dr. Thomas Graeme of Philadelphia, wrote quite a lengthy letter to Thomas Penn advocating the establishment of a town "on the point of the fforks".[25] In this communication, he mentions that the Moravians had recently opened a road starting at Bethlehem, running northeastwardly about a mile and one half, then passing through the Barrens and through Penn's one thousand acre tract "till they arrived at the fferry point of the same". The fact is thus established that as early as 1750 there was a road from Bethlehem to the Delaware river ferry which passed through Thomas Penn's tract of land, later the site of Easton. Consequently, the ferry in 1750 was located on the north side of the Lehigh river. This road was called by the Moravians the York Road, as it led to New York by way of Brunswick.

Dr. Graeme, a prominent physician of Philadelphia, and David Martin must have discussed the probability of the Proprietaries locating a town at the Forks of the Delaware. They were each in a position to profit greatly by such an event. Dr. Graeme owned one thousand acres on the Lehicton (Bushkill) creek just a short distance from Thomas Penn's thousand acre tract. A town built at the Forks would greatly increase the value of these acres and greatly multiply the use of the ferry. What increase in the income of the ferry was anticipated by David Martin depended somewhat on his imagination. Any one with an imagination vivid enough to foresee a profitable ferry at this location in 1739, must have had a feeling of great satisfaction, as he contemplated the increased revenue due to the building of a town on one, and perhaps both sides of the river. John Cox and David Martin, fellow citizens of Trenton for many years, were personal friends. Cox, who owned the land on the Jersey side of the Delaware at the Forks, no doubt confided in Martin his intention to establish a town at that place.

Just at the time when the rector of the Academy felt that at last he was to profit greatly through his ferry rights, he died. He did not live long enough to see even the first steps taken toward the establishment of these towns. Dr. Graeme lived to profit by their settlement.

*   *   *

In an action brought at Easton at the March 1753 term of court to recover twenty pounds, Joseph Parker,[26] prothonotary of Chester county, stated that Nathaniel Vernon was in Northampton county in 1746. Northampton county was not erected until 1752. Parker no doubt meant that Vernon was in that part of the province which, at the time he entered his suit, was in Northampton county. If Vernon was in the Forks as early as 1746 he was, more than likely, ferryman for David Martin. We know that Vernon operated the ferry across the Delaware and Lehigh rivers shortly after Easton was opened to settlers.

Condit, in his history of Easton, makes the statement that a traveler crossing the Delaware Ferry in 1795 told John Stewart, who was then ferryman, that fifty years previous when he crossed the river at the same point, the ferry was a bateau and his horse was obliged to swim. He also mentioned that the site of Easton at that time was entirely covered with trees except a small clearing at the point where the ferry house, a low log building, was located. This is rather vague circumstantial evidence, but fifty years previous to 1795 would be 1745, or two years before a flat boat was put in service. If any credence is to be given the statement recorded by Condit, the ferry house in 1745 was located at what is now Front and Ferry streets in the city of Easton.

Previous to 1747, the ferry consisted of a canoe or bateau; horses and cattle were compelled to swim. On February 28th of that year a freshet in the Lehigh river carried away the large flat boat which for nearly four years had been used as a ferry at Bethlehem.[27] The ferryman at the Forks caught this boat as it was being carried into the Delaware on the swollen waters of the Lehigh. David Martin then purchased the boat from the Moravians and at once put it into service. In June of the same year, he placed an order with the boat builders at Bethlehem for another flat. It therefore seems probable that as early as the latter part of 1747, there was a flat boat ferry across the Delaware and also across the Lehigh.

David Martin died intestate and was buried in Christ's Church burying ground in Philadelphia on December 13th, 1751. Theophilus Severns and Joseph Cleayton, both of Trenton, were appointed (March 12, 1752) administrators of his estate in New Jersey.[28]

John Allen and Joseph Higbee were appointed to appraise that part of the estate located in Trenton. William Schooley and John Anderson were selected to place a value on the property at Sharon.[29] Martin's Trenton property was valued at two pounds seven shillings, while the Sharon property was appraised at seventy-six pounds fourteen shillings. The values placed upon the estate were extremely low, for the final statement of the administrators shows that it amounted to over fifteen hundred pounds. Their accounts indicate that Sharon brought an annual rental of twenty pounds and that it was finally sold for five hundred and fifty-three pounds.[30]

Where and what was Sharon? Since it was sold, it must have been a property which Martin owned and not the name of a town. It must have been quite a distance from Trenton or a separate set of viewers would not have been appointed. This being the case, men living in the vicinity of the property would naturally have been selected. The only clue to the location of Sharon is in the names of the viewers. William Schooley, one of the viewers, owned and lived on property adjacent to Martin's property at Pearcetown, and John Anderson, the other viewer, owned a property a short distance from Schooley's. In the absence of proof to the contrary,[31] the conclusion is that the three hundred and twelve acre tract which Martin owned in Pearcetown on the Lopatcong creek was, in a manner, his country estate to which he had given the biblical name of Sharon, that fertile plain in northern Palestine where King David pastured his herds. Here Martin no doubt at times retired for rest and to overlook the operation of his ferry. This property proved a good investment, for it sold for five times the amount which he had paid for it.

David Martin died in Philadelphia where he had been living since May of 1750. John Jenkins was appointed administrator of his estate in Pennsylvania[32]. From his accounts, we learn that Rector Martin lodged with a Mrs. Gibbs, owned a bay horse, and had among his personal possessions a silver hilted sword and belt, two pairs of doctor's scales, a microscope, and a set of surgeon's instrumentts.

From the notes and papers found in his desk, the administrator prepared a list which showed that there was due the estate, from fifty-two individuals, over two hundred and sixty pounds. A footnote records the unfortunate fact that "the administrator never received any of all ye above, except Ralph Norton's". Norton was a doctor and his account was for ten pounds.

An interesting item in the administrator's account deals with Gisbert Bouger of Easton. In November of 1752, John Jenkins hearing that Bouger was about to run away to avoid paying twenty pounds, due the estate for rent of the ferry, threatened him with legal action and collected the debt. Bouger, therefore, becomes the first ferryman of record, and must have had charge of the ferry about the time Easton was laid out.

John Ford, high sheriff of Morris county, seized the ferry tract of land in New Jersey to satisfy a judgment which the administrators of the estate of Abraham Bennet, Jr., secured against the administrators of the estate of David Martin.[33] On August 1st, 1753, he sold the land and ferry rights to Richard Peters. William Parsons and John Jones became security for the payment of the purchase money amounting to four hundred and thirty-four pounds and executed a bond to this effect.[34] On August 10th, 1754, payment was made by Parsons and Jones, and a receipt in full was signed by Thomas Barnes, acting for the executors. This signature was witnessed by Richard Peters and William Main. At the foot of the receipt, Peters made a memorandum that the amount paid was to be charged against the Proprietaries' general account.[35] It is therefore evident that Peters purchased the ferry for the Proprietaries and with their money.

While the title to the ferry land and rights remained in Peters' name for a long time, he faithfully held it in trust for the Penns.

Some time before May of 1754, William Parsons made application to the Proprietaries, through Richard Peters, for the exclusive right to operate the ferry in Easton.[36] In his application, he points out that the point of land in Easton between the Delaware and Lehigh Rivers is the place best suited for the ferry and that a ferry had been located at that point for some time. On May 15th, 1754, Parsons received a lease for land at that point.[37] This lease has not been found and the amount of land which it included is not known. From other information available, it can be assumed that seven or more acres were included in the tract. As the lots in this part of Easton had not been sold at this early date, the lease may have included many lots and the adjacent streets, keeping open Ferry street, which led to the ferry.

On the same day on which Parsons received his lease, he also secured a grant from the Proprietaries covering the ferry privilege on both rivers within a limit of three miles from the Point.[38] The grant was for seven years and was confirmed to William Parsons, his executors, administrators and assigns. Parsons was to furnish all flat boats and maintain attendants at the ferry. The annual rent of five shillings would indicate that Parsons was being favored.

Nathaniel Vernon was in full possession of the ferry at the time Parsons leased it. Under whatever arrangements he may have operated the ferry, the agreement must have been made with the administrators of David Martin's estate.

The Proprietaries through their agent, Richard Peters, had purchased the New Jersey ferry rights from Martin's administrators[39] and at the same time had bought back the Pennsylvania rights which they had granted Martin.

When Parsons acquired the ferry rights, he found that he could not enjoy the full privileges of his grant. Vernon had secured a lease or concession for a period of years before Peters bought the ferry and these rights were not abrogated by this purchase. Parsons could do nothing until Vernon's lease expired but collect his rent and fret over the situation. He did bring suit to have Vernon's lease broken, but this he lost. Vernon collected his costs, in defending his rights, from the executors of William Parsons estate.[40]

With the settlement of Easton, the ferry and ferry house were both paying good profits. The Indian treaties were as profitable to the early taverns as conventions are to the hotels of today.

Parsons was somewhat embittered to see Vernon reap a large profit as a result of this business, when he, who held the ferry rights, received only a relatively small rental. In a vindictive frame of mind he wrote to Richard Peters. He complained that Vernon had been employed to buy all the skins which the Indians would bring to the treaties and that thus he would be in a fine position to sell liquor to the savages and reap a large profit. Vernon's opportunity for gain gave Parsons more concern than the debauching of the natives. Parsons asked if it would be amiss if his honour issued a proclamation against selling strong liquor to the Indians at the time of the treaty.

Parsons and Vernon were continually quarreling and became involved in several law suits. That Parsons was desirous of getting rid of Vernon can not be questioned. On April 10th, 1757, he wrote that Vernon had until November to stay at the ferry, for his lease expired at that time. When November came, Parsons was a very sick man and in his illness and suffering, the ferry was not a matter of importance. In December of that year Parsons died and Vernon continued to operate the ferry. Parsons' executors were busy men and had too much to do to continue the feud. To them a tenant was a tenant and Vernon remained the ferryman until he returned to Chester county in November of 1758.

After Nathaniel Vernon left Easton, there is no record of who leased or operated the ferry until the year 1762. It is true that immediately after Vernon returned to Chester county, John Rinker made application for a retail liquor license,[41] which was allowed. His application states that he was then located at the Ferry House in Easton. It is likely that he also operated the ferry for a short time.

In 1762 we find that Lewis Gordon had the ferry under lease and either sublet it to Daniel Brodhead or employed him to operate it.[42] The small log ferry house was by this time very much decayed and the wind whistling through it threatened at times to blow it down. The stable was in the same condition. Gordon, as an inducement to Brodhead, agreed to rebuild the house in the fall of the year. This promise was not fulfilled at that time. Daniel Brodhead writing to Mr. Peters said that the house was dangerous to live in and barely worth repairing. He further states that he had cleared about six acres of land which he had fenced-in. Mr. Gordon's refusal to make improvements was based on the uncertainty of having his lease renewed.

During the tenure of Vernon, the property was evidently allowed to run down and certainly between the years 1758 and 1762 it must have been sadly neglected. A well built log house should last a long time and this house could not have been more than twenty-one years old, assuming it was built in 1741, which is extremely doubtful. If poorly built and then neglected, the elements would have wrecked it in twenty-one years or less. The evidence at hand would indicate that the ferry house or tavern was rebuilt shortly after 1762.

During the period from 1762 to the Revolutionary War the ferry did an ever increasing business. As the ferry prospered, so did the ferry house or tavern. Here man and beast quenched their thirst while waiting for the ferry-boat or before continuing their journey to Bethlehem or further into the wilds of the province. As Lewis Gordon held the ferry lease for this period, he reaped the financial benefits which naturally accrued with the increase in business. With the exception of Daniel Brodhead, the records do not divulge the names of the ferrymen until the ferry assumed increasing prominence as the transportation of troops and supplies became of vital importance during the Revolution.

The title to the ferry and the ferry tract of land in New Jersey remained in Richard Peters' name until the 16th day of February, 1773, when he conveyed it to Richard Penn,[43] the grandson of William, and at that time Lieutenant Governor of the Province.

Lewis Gordon leased the ferry from 1761 to 1783. As he died in 1778, his executors operated it for about five years.

During the period of the Revolutionary War the ferry became of great military importance. Robert Levers kept a patriotic eye on its operation and from time to time wrote to the authorities in Philadelphia about the lax manner in which it was managed and its great inadequacy should it be necessary to move a large body of troops across the river.

From the fall of 1777 to the spring of 1778, Lewis Gordon, the lessee of the ferry, was under arrest, but under parole, had the freedom of the town and a restricted area beyond. In November of 1777, Gordon attempted to place his brother-in-law, Joseph Jenkins, in charge of the ferry.[44] This met with great opposition. Whether Jenkins ever took charge is not known, but in January of 1778 Gordon sublet the ferry to Jacob Abel and Peter Ealer.[45] They continued its operation until Gordon's lease expired some time in 1783.

Undoubtedly there were times during this period when the operation of the ferry was taken over by the Army. In 1775, Captain Abraham Miller, with his company of riflemen, ferried across the Delaware and started on their long march to Boston to join General Washington.

In December of 1776, two ferry flat boats from Bethlehem and one from the mouth of the Saucon Creek[46] were brought to Easton and placed in service to expedite the crossing of General Lee's division under command of General Sullivan. This division was then in retreat from New York and on its way to join General Washington on the west bank of the Delaware north of Trenton.

A few days before General Sullivan crossed, wagons filled with suffering humanity, the wounded, and the maimed from the New York campaign, were ferried across the river on their way to Bethlehem.

Beside General Sullivan, the following Generals used the the Easton ferry during the war :—Gates, Stirling, Arnold, Glover, de Fernoy, Schuyler, Greene, Knox, Steuben, Pulaski, Conway, Ethan Allen, Maxwell and Armstrong.[47] DeKalb's division of Washington's army crossed the Delaware at Easton some time in June of 1778.

On June 15th, 1777, Mr. William Whipple of New Hampshire and Mr. William Ellery of Rhode Island, both signers of the Declaration of Independence, crossed the ferry on their homeward journey from Philadelphia. They had spent the night at Theophilus Shannon's tavern[48] at the northeast corner of Northampton and Fermor (now Second) streets. Mrs. Shannon and Mr. Whipple renewed an acquaintance formed in the West Indies when Mr. Whipple was a sea captain. Other signers who used the ferry were John Adams and of course our own George Taylor.

Lady Washington, on June 14th, 1779, returning to Mt. Vernon from Morristown, where she had visited her husband, was ferried across the river with her servants and military escort.[49] General Washington, with two aides, used the Easton ferry on July 26th, 1782, en route to Newburg on the Hudson. John

Hancock and James Lowell were other notables who used the ferry at Easton.

* * *

Richard Penn executed a deed of trust on June 7, 1787, to Tench Francis, Thomas Willing, and Philip Livingston.[50] This deed conveyed the one hundred and five acres of land in New Jersey as well as the ferry rights in trust, with the right to any one or all of them to convey the property. The money thus secured was to be used as Richard Penn directed.

In September of 1788, Tench Francis conveyed the rights and land to John Penn, Jr.[51] About two years later Penn sold them to Jacob Arndt, Jr.[52]

Before the Revolutionary War, the ferry was of little more than local importance, carrying the products of Northampton County across the Lehigh to Philadelphia and across the Delaware to New York. Supplies for the county brought back from these marts of trade had to be ferried over the rivers.

During the Revolution the ferry was of great military importance in transporting troops and supplies.

After the war it became a national necessity and the demands then placed upon it soon wrote its doom.

With the opening of the Ohio valley the immigrants from New England to this new frontier became numerous. Easton was one of the main routes of travel and all the traffic had to be ferried across the river.

Even those travelling in Conestoga wagons drawn by oxen became impatient at the delay in crossing the ferry—a delay caused by the necessarily slow operation of a ferry, by the great numbers desiring to cross and, at times, by the ferry's inactivity, due to high water, ice and storms. At times the ferry would be idle for several days to a week. During these periods the traffic accumulated on both sides of the river. Then it would be several days before these early traffic jams could be adjusted and normal operations resumed.

The ferry now lay in the path of commerce and it became totally inadequate to handle the local traffic and the great lumbering wheeled vehicles, common carriers of civilization to the new lands in the middle west. To remedy this condition, a number of Easton's citizens applied for a charter to build and to operate a bridge. This was granted in 1795 and was the first charter granted for the construction of a bridge over the Delaware at any point. The account of the construction of this structure is another story. It was opened to the public October 1st, 1806, eight months after a bridge at Trenton had been put in use.

The opening of the Easton-Phillipsburg bridge was the death knell of Martin's ferry.

* * *

The title to the ferry changed hands seven times after the original grant to David Martin and each time the amount of the consideration increased. In 1753, it was sold by sheriff for four hundred and thirty-seven pounds. John Penn, Jr., purchased it in 1788 for one thousand pounds and sold it two years later to Jacob Arndt, Jr., for eleven hundred pounds. In 1794, Frederick Lewis Goch of Philadelphia paid sixteen hundred and thirty-seven pounds for the title,[53] and, in 1798, he conveyed it to Thomas Bullman for two thousand five hundred pounds.[54]

Paradoxically as it may seem, Thomas Bullman not only purchased the ferry at the time the briidge was building, but paid the highest price, a fifty per cent increase over the amount it brought only four years previous. In the face of these facts, it becomes evident that the increase in the value of the one hundred and five acres of land at the eastern terminus of the bridge more than offset the total loss in the value of the ferry rights. A ferry was of absolutely no value in competition with a bridge.

Thomas Bullman was not antagonistic toward the erection of the bridge. In fact he gave the bridge company a strip of land one hundred feet in width and extending back from the river a distance of two hundred and sixty-five feet. This land was part of the ferry tract and comprises practically all of the present Union Square in Phillipsburg.

* * *

What an epoch was spanned in the life of Martin's Ferry!

From a primeval wilderness under King George the Second of England in 1739 to a thriving borough in the United States of America in 1806!

For sixty-seven of the most important years of this nation, the old flat bottomed ferry boat was laboriously poled back and forth across the rivers at the Forks of the Delaware, each trip doing its bit toward the building of a mighty nation.

---

[1]"In the Time of Matthais Brakeley of Lapatcong," printed in 1888 for private distribution.

[2]Deed filed at Newton, N. J., Deed Book A.

[3]Deed filed in Secretary of State Office, Trenton, N. J., Deed Book A-N, p. 21.

[4]Ibid.

[5]New Jersey Archives, 1st Series, Vol. XIV, p. 535.

[6]Deed, Secretary of State Office, Trenton, N. J., Book E-F, p. 481.

[7]Ibid, p. 478.

[8]Ibid, p. 479.

[9]Deed, Tench Francis to John Penn, Jr., filed at Newton, N. J., Deed Book A, p. 271.

[10]Deed, Office of Secretary of State, Trenton, N. J., Book M, p. 368.

[11]New Jersey Archives, 1st Series, Vol. XV, p. 118.

[12]"Franklin Works," by Jared Sparks, Vol. VI, p. 28.

[13]New Jersey Archives, 1st Series.

[14]Ibid.

[15]Publications of the Genealogical Society of Pennsylvania, Vol. IX, p. 227 and 228.

[16]History of Hunterdon County (N. J.), p. 258.

[17]Publications of the Genealogical Society of Pennsylvania, Vol. X, p. 51.

[18]"Franklin's Works," by Jared Sparks, 1840, Vol. II, p. 134.

[19]"University of Pennsylvania," by General J. L. Chamberlain, 1901, Vol I, p. 58.

[20]Ibid, p. 59.

[21]"Franklin's Works," by Jared Sparks, 1840, Vol. II, p. 134.

[22]"University of Pennsylvania," by General J. L. Chamberlain, 1901, Vol I, p. 58.

[23]New Jersey Archives, First Series, Vol. XIX, p. 182.

[24]Account of Administrator of the Estate of David Martin, Register of Wills Office. Philadelphia, Penna. Original papers in vault in Envelope No. 52.

[25]The Pennsylvania Magazine of History, Vol. 39, p. 445.

[26]Original paper—Archives Room, Court House, Easton, Pa.

[27]Moravian Archives—Bethlehem, Pa.

[28]New Jersey Archives, 1st Series, Vol. XXXII, Abstract of Wills.

[29]Original papers re. Estate of David Martin, Office of the Secretary of State, Trenton, N. J.

[30]Ibid.

[31]Deed, Theophilus Severn to Philip Kearny, dated November 22, 1762, filed at Trenton, N. J., in the Office of the Secretary of State in Deed Book A-G, page 197, conveys the Martin tract of 312 acres on the Lopatcong creek and refers to it as a plantation called SHARON. The fact that Sharon was the tract of land acquired by David Martin in what is now Warren County is thus established. This information was not at hand when the paper was written.

[32]Register of Wills Office, Philadelphia, Pa., Administration Book F, page 428. See also envelope No. 52 as per item 24 above.

[33]Deed, John Ford, Sheriff, to Richard Peters, Filed at Newton, N. J., Deed Book A, p. 271.

[34]Pennsylvania Magazine of History, Vol. 38, p. 112.

[35]Ibid.

[36]Patent, Messrs. Penn to William Parsons, Land Office, Harrisburg, Pa., Patent Book A-17, p. 469.

[37]Ibid.

[38]Ibid.

[39]Recital in deed, Tench Francis to John Penn, Jr., filed at Newton, N. J., Deed Book A, p. 271.

[40]Itemized Statement which Nathaniel Vernon rendered Timothy Horsfield, Executor of the Estate of William Parsons. Original document in Historical Society of Pennsylvania.

[41]Application of John Rinker for liquor license at Ferry House. Original paper in Archives Room, Court House, Easton, Pa.

[42]Historical Society of Pa., Peters Manuscripts, 1752 to 1762, page 117. Letter of Daniel Brodhead to Richard Peters.

[43]Recital in deed, Tench Francis to John Penn, Jr., filed in Newton, N. J., Deed Book A, page 271.

[44]Pennsylvania Archives, 1st Series, Vol. VI, p. 6.

[45]Ibid, p. 342.

[46]Pennsylvania Archives, 2nd Series, Vol. XIV, pages 605, 648 and Pennsylvania Archives, 3rd Series, Vol. XIX, pages 19, 111, 196, 209, 216, 313.

[47]Pennsylvania Magazine of History, Vol. 38, p. 110.

[48] Ibid, Vol. 10, p. 368 and 369.

[49]Ibid, Vol. 38, p. 110.

[50]Recital in deed, Tench Francis to John Penn, Jr., filed at Newton, N. J., Deed Book A, p. 271.

[51]Ibid.

[52]Deed, John Penn, Jr., to Jacob Arndt, Jr., July 1, 1790, filed at Newton, N. J., Deed Book B, p. 15.

[53]Deed, Jacob Arndt, Jr., to F. L. Goch, September 4, 1794, filed Newton, N. J., Deed Book M, p. 326.

[54]Deed, F. L. Goch to Thomas Bullman, May 15, 1798, filed at Newton, N. J., Deed Book C, p. 288.

John Lefevre, Tavern Keeper

John Lefevre, Tavern Keeper

J OHN LEFEVRE was not an Eastonian. His tavern, near the present town of Stockertown, was the hostelry which entertained William Parsons and Nicholas Scull, when, on a day early in May, 1752, they dismounted after a long and hard ride from Gardenville, where, at "The Sign of the Plow", they had spent the previous night. Host Lefevre and the Surveyor General of the Province, Nicholas Scull, were old friends. Eight years earlier, Scull had surveyed the property in Worcester Township, Philadelphia County, which John had inherited from his father, Abraham.

There were no taverns closer to the Forks, and Parsons and Scull did not wish to stay with any of the residents of Williams Township or of New Jersey. Recollections of the good German cooking of Frau Lefevre, coupled with the assurance of a plentiful supply of "slings and punch", were the factors which decided these two town builders to board at least five miles from the scene of their labor.

So while John Lefevre was not one of the first citizens of Easton, he, nevertheless, lived in the neighborhood when Easton was but a dream and the site of the town but a beautiful grove in an untamed wilderness.

There can be no doubt that the ancestors of John Lefevre were French. John Lefevre would then have been Jean Lefevre, which in English is plain John Smith. The migration of this branch of the Lefevre family was typical. They were driven from France at the time of the persecution of the Protestants and settled in Holland. From Holland they came to America and settled in New York, from which place they moved into Pennsylvania, settling in a German community in Philadelphia County. It was from this location that John Lefevre moved into what was then Bucks, but shortly thereafter became Northampton County, and settled on his 368 acre tract on Tatamy's Creek.

During these migrations the name Lefevre changed but little; but the Jean in France became Jan in Holland, Johannes in Philadelphia County, and John in Northampton County. All the early and recent references to the subject of this short biography, as well as the official court records, spell the name L-e-f-e-v-r-e. John himself, as well as his sons, his father, and his grandfather, spelled the name L-e-f-e-b-e-r, using the letter B in place of the V. In the year 1752, especially in this part of the Province, spelling was a lost art, although picturesquely phonetic. No matter how poorly a person could spell, if he had the accomplishment at all, he should be able to spell his own name correctly. If I am correct, John Lefevre was in reality Johannes Lefeber. There is not the slightest doubt, in my mind, that the surname was originally Lefevre. In common with all records and previous writers, I shall continue the error, and henceforth call this Dutchman, who had a German wife, by his English given and French surname: — John Lefevre. For convenience, simplicity, and consistency, I will use the spelling L-e-f-e-v-r-e thruout.

* * *

Isaac Lefevre arrived in America in 1683 and settled either in, or close to, New York. In 1685, he married Janneken Boudounck at the Reformed Church of New York. It was at this church that their son Abraham was baptized on July 3rd, 1687. Isaac Lefevre took the oath of allegiance in Brooklyn in 1687. On June 23rd, 1689, he married for the second time, his bride being Wyntje, daughter of Myndert Korten of New Utrecht. Isaac's name appears as a witness on several wills, but, with the exception of the above, little is known about him.

Isaac's son, Abraham, evidently felt the call of the frontier. With many other Dutch pioneers from New York, he crossed New

Jersey and on into Pennsylvania. Perhaps he stopped for a short time in Bucks County before finally settling in Philadelphia County, in what was then known as New Bristol Township, but later Worcester Township (now in Montgomery County). Here on October 5th, 1710, he purchased 500 acres of land. By a deed from Abraham Lefevre to John Switzer dated June 6th, 1720, we learn that his wife's name was Mary. Nothing more is known of Abraham and Mary Lefevre, although it is quite certain that they had a son named Johannes, who was naturalized between January 9th, 1729 and 1730. Records show that Johannes or John was one of twenty-five taxpayers in Worcester Township in 1734, and that he paid quit rents previous to that time. He was probably born between 1708 and 1710.

At the death of his father, Abraham, John Lefevre requested a resurvey of the property of which, by several conveyances and descents, he was then possessed. The warrant for the survey was dated April 8th, 1743, and the survey was made by Nicholas Scull, who later became Surveyor General of the Province. Scull, in his return of the survey, stated that the tract, which was supposed to contain 500 acres, actually contained 567½ acres. John Lefevre disposed of most, if not all, of this tract. I believe, however, that he retained a small portion. In the survey which Scull made he mentions that Peter Wentz was one of the abutting property owners. This Peter may have been the father-in-law of John Lefevre, for the maiden name of John Lefevre's wife was Christina Wentz.

Early (April) in 1736 Augustus G. Spangenberg arrived in New York and soon entered upon his labors among the Schwenkfelders, in Worcester Township, Philadelphia County. He lived with Christopher Wiegner, whose residence was the home of the first Moravians in Pennsylvania. Here many of those who later were members of the Moravian settlements of Northampton County, gathered to worship God.

On the 3rd of May, 1740, George Whitefield agreed to purchase from William Allen, 5000 acres of land in the Forks of the Delaware. Two days later Whitefield preached at Skippack and in his journal he says:—"It was seemingly a very wilderness part of the country, but there were not less, I believe, than 2000 hearers." As this was a Dutch community most of his audience must have been Holland Dutch. John Lefevre, no doubt, was among those present for his home was but a few miles distant.

Peter Bohler, a Moravian minister, at the request of Whitefield, engaged the Moravian Brethren, many of whom were from Worcester Township, to do the carpenter work on the house which Whitefield intended to erect on his lands in the Forks, lands which he had named Nazareth. This tract was eventually purchased by the Moravians and settled by them. Many of these settlers were acquaintances and friends of John Lefevre, having been his neighbors in Worcester Township.

The child of a pioneer must feel the call of the frontier, and as the land about him becomes more thickly settled, he becomes restless, and eventually moves on to the very verge of civilization. This was the case with John Lefevre. When the Indians were driven out of the Forks of the Delaware, in 1742, John Lefevre decided to move into that part of the Province, especially since many of his erstwhile Moravian friends and neighbors were now living there.

It so happened that the beautiful meadows of the Lehicton Creek attracted his attention. Therefore, in August, 1743, he secured title from William Allen to 368 acres just north of the present town of Tatamy, and including part of the present borough of Stockertown. In consideration of the sum of 5 shillings and the annual quit rent of one shilling for each hundred acres, the Proprietaries issued a confirmatory patent which was dated June 5th, 1745. Some time between 1743 and 1745 he moved and built his new home, a log cabin, not far from the banks of the stream known as Tatamy's Creek, a short distance above the point where it joins the Lehicton Creek.

This creek was called Tatamy's Creek, after the Indian, Moses Tatamy. The Scotch-Irish gave it the name of Lefevre's Creek, soon after John Lefevre settled on its banks. The Van Bogarts, who with many Dutch came into Pennsylvania from Esopus, named the Lehicton Creek, Bushkill Creek, by which name the stream is now known. The East branch of this creek, now called Little Bushkill, is even today sometimes called Lefevre's Creek. Most of the Dutch who came into Pennsylvania from Esopus settled north of the Blue Mountains.

One of the neighbors of John Lefevre was Moses Tunda Tatamy, a Delaware Indian, who had been converted to Christianity by David Brainerd. History records the fact that he was a chief of his tribe and that he was born in New Jersey. As a reward for services to the Province, the Proprietaries in consideration of their love and affection, on April 28, 1738, made him a gift of 315 acres, which tract adjoined the land later patented to John Lefevre. Tatamy had married a white woman, and no doubt had a large family, although his son William is the only child of record.

With the exception of Tatamy, the Indian, Lefevre had no close neighbors for a number of years. From 1745 until 1750, he and his wife were busy raising a family and providing for their subsistence and maintenance. That he had a large family is evident from the fact that at the time of his death in 1778 or 1779 he had eleven living children. At the time he moved to the Bushkill Creek, some of his children were old enough to help with the farming, but the raising of a family under the circumstances which then existed was no easy task. It is true that the Moravians at Nazareth were not far distant, and the relations between the Lefevres and the Moravians were most cordial. His home was on the path or road which led between the Scotch-Irish settlements of Lower Mt. Bethel and Allen Townships. It was a most convenient stopping point for the traveler between these two settlements. If he early conducted a tavern, the lonely traveler must have invariably stopped to quench his thirst as well as that of his horse. These infrequent guests kept the Lefevre family fairly well posted on the news of the outside world.

William Allen owned the land to the north as well as to the west of the Lefevre farm, but on January 3rd, 1750, he sold 324 acres to Henry Antes, who, in 1752, sold the tract to the Moravian Trustees. Antes early in January, 1750, started the construction of a mill on this tract. The iron work for the mill was secured from the iron furnaces at Durham in Bucks County. The mill was first put into oeration on August 21st of the same year. This event was celebrated by a love feast held in the mill. The settlement which grew up about this mill in the tranquil valley of the Bushkill was given the very appropriate name of Friedensthal, meaning Vale of Peace. John Lefevre's meadows were but a short mile below the mill. The cordial relations which had hitherto existed between the Moravians and the Lefevre family now ripened into a closer friendship.

A warrant for a survey of 50 acres in Bucks County was granted to Patrick Deveny on March 21st, 1747. The title for this tract, which was located on Lefevre Creek, about two and one-half miles above the Lefevre tract, became vested in John Weidman, who, in 1752, started the construction of a mill. This was located at a point now called Werkheisers. Weidman did not have sufficient funds with which to complete the mill, so he borrowed about 46 pounds from John Lefevre and Dill Bower. To secure the payment of this obligation Weidman, on December 5th, 1752, gave a mortgage on his property, including the mill, to Lefevre and Bower. In this mortgage, it is stated that John Weidman was a millwright, Dill Bower a smith and John Lefevre an innholder, and that all three were residents of the "Forks of Delaware," the name by which Forks Township was then known.

On the 19th of June, 1753, John Lefevre petitioned the "Worshipful" the Justices of the Court of Quarter Sessions of Northampton County, to reccommend him to the Governor for a license to keep a Public House or Tavern at his dwelling house in Forks of Delaware. The petition states that he had "heretofore been licensed to keep a house of Public Entertainment." It therefore seems extremely probable that Lefevre had a licnse to operate a tavern at his residence on Lefevre Creek when Parsons and Scull made his house their headquarters in May of 1752, when they laid out Easton. The fact that he sold them drink is almost conclusive evidence that he had a license.

The tavern, which John Lefevre and his good wife Christina kept, must have been well above the average frontier tavern of its time. Most of these early taverns or public houses furnished food, drink and shelter for man and beast. With a clientele not overly particular, and accustomed only to the bare necessities of life, their accommodations were ample and they well served their purpose. But when we know that a man of culture and learning and the foremost citizen of the county seat of Northampton County — William Parsons — often repaired to John Lefevre's and there spent several days at a time, perhaps weekends, as a rest from his cares and duties, we must realize that this Inn was not only the best in the vicinity, but really quite good. Parsons may have been a fisherman. If so, the trout in the Bushkill Creek, and they must have been plentiful, were an added attraction. However that may be, we know that Mr. Parsons not only stayed with Host Lefevre at various times, but also that he took his servants with him, and there, at times, he entertained his friends. This fact is proved by a suit which Lewis Gordon, on behalf of John Lefevre, entered at the December term of Court, 1758, against Timothy Horsfield, Executor of the Estate of William Parsons. This suit was for eighty pounds, which William Parsons had contracted during his lifetime for "Meat, Drink, Washing, Lodging, and Hospitality for himself and Servants and divers other persons and for pasturage and fodder for his and their Horses and Geldings." The log cabin tavern was not our idea of a modern hotel, but it must have been clean and attractive, with an excellent and bountiful table and an amiable host and hostess, bent on the comfort of their guests.

In the evenings of the spring of 1752, after Parsons and Scull had returned to Lefevre's Tavern from their day's work of laying out the streets and lots of the new town, they naturally talked of their work. Between clouds of smoke and an occasional drink of punch, they outlined the bright future for the town which Thomas Penn had conceived and ordained should be the county seat. Believing the county would become more thickly populated, and the seat of justice of ever increasing importance, the original town planners of Easton became enthusiastic. They envisaged a real estate boom with the lots, which the Proprietaries were to sell at a low figure, doubling and trebling in value in but a few years.

John Lefevre must have absorbed some of the enthusiasm and optimism of his guests for he promptly decided to purchase a lot. This may have been pure speculation on his part, or he may have desired a lot where he could build a home, should he in the future wish to retire. What his motives were is uncertain. After discussing the matter with his son Isaac, who worked as a laborer helping Parsons and Scull in the development of the town, and therefore had first hand information, he selected lot Number 76. His request for this lot was granted. The lot was located at the northeast corner of Northampton Street and a 20' alley (now Sitgreaves Street). The agreement, of whatever nature it may have been, stated that he must build a house on the lot within three years from the date of purchase. The house was to be at least twenty feet square, with a good stone chimney. Lefevre never completed the transaction, and this lot was sold by the Proprietaries in 1765 to Adam Yohe, he having no doubt purchased whatever rights John Lefevre had in it.

In May or June of 1752, John Lefevre started another real estate transaction, which he failed to complete. There was issued to him, at his request, on June 5th of that year, a warrant for 100 acres of land. I have not determined the exact location of this land, but it was in what is now Plainfield Township and I believe somewhere between Rasleytown and Wind Gap. Lefevre never secured a patent for this tract. He either sold his rights or allowed them to lapse.

Through the friendship of William Parsons, Lefevre might have reached a position of some little prominence in the community, but he failed to grasp the opportunities which Parsons threw his way. He was content with his life as he then found it, or he was too tied down to engage in public work. He served on the grand jury at various times.

The first need of the new town was for roads leading to it. A road to Philadelphia was of first importance. As early as June 12th, 1752, there was read in Council at Philadelphia, a petition calling attention to the great want of High Roads and asking that a road be laid out from Easton to the great road leading from Saucon to the City of Philadelphia. The petition was granted.

The fine political hand of William Parsons is easily seen in the selection of the nine viewers. There were no Moravians, no Quakers and but two Germans. John Lefevre was one of the nine citizens named.

A trail had developed into a road and usage made it more or less passable. In order to give this road official standing, so that some little attention could be given it, it was necessary to legally lay it out. It was for this purpose that the nine viewers had been appointed. Any five of the nine named were sufficient to view the road and make the survey. John Lefevre's name was not one of the five signed to the report which was dated April 14th, 1753. He was not interested or too busy.

It was over two years after the county seat had been laid out that a school was seriously considered. A petition for aid was addressed to the Trustees for a fund which had been raised in England for the construction of schools in America. The petition was granted and, in addition to the help thus received, funds were solicited locally. As usual, William Parsons made recommendations as to the selection of the local trustees. His recommendation, which was dated November 23rd, 1754, included the name of John Lefevre. On July 31st, 1755, six trustees were appointed. In addition to John Lefevre, they were William Parsons, James Martin, Peter Kachline, Lewis Gordon and Peter Trexler.

John Lefevre must have been selected to represent the territory adjacent to Easton. That he was well thought of and enjoyed a good reputation is evident from his selection to serve on a committee or board of trustees of such representative citizens of the county. It would be interesting to know if John Lefevre took any interest or part in the work of this committee. The only record which I have found in connection with the building of this school is a list of contributors to the project in money, labor, or material. In this respect John Lefevre contributed nothing.

William Parsons must have given up the attempts to bestow local honors on the Tavern Keeper of Forks Township, for this is the last public position for which he was recommended or which he held.

Isaac Lefevre, John's son, was appointed constable of Forks Township. A return for 1755, which he made for the Township, shows that his father, John Lefevre, was the only person licensed to sell liquor for that year.

* * *

During the summer of 1755, word of the Indian uprisings reached Easton. These raids started along the Susquehanna and spread northeastwardly, until in the latter part of November they reached Northampton County. On the 23rd of that month, the Gnadenhuetten massacre occurred. The usual clear sky became darkened by clouds of massacre and rapine, and as the days of 1755 became fewer and fewer, the clouds became darker and darker. Friedensthal — the Vale of Peace — became a Valley of Fear and Depression. To the north and northwest the storm had broken. The peaceful Moravians and Lefevres were fearful that at any moment they might feel its fury.

Christmas was a gloomy day. In Easton, Benjamin Franklin and James Hamilton, commissioners, appointed by the Assembly to investigate conditions in the County, met with William Parsons. On that day, James Hamilton wrote to the Governor that the county was under the greatest "consternation" and that the conditions as reported were more than verified.

For some time, settlers from the frontier on their way to Easton, had been passing the Lefevre Tavern. Christmas day was no exception. The refugees were penniless, their clothes were in rags, and many had too few to cover their nakedness. Many a terror-stricken pioneer, retreating before the fury of the savages, stopped at the Tavern to rest. The hospitable Lefevres gave them food and drink, and it may well be assumed, clothing to cover their battered bodies. Many of the fl'eeing inhabitants turned off the Easton road, and found refuge with the Moravians at Friedensthal, where Captain Sol. Jennings, of "Walking Purchase" fame, was stationed with a company of eighteen Ulster-Scots.

John Lefevre and his family were in great fear and terribly worried over the situation. He and his sons had carefully checked their ammunition. Their guns were always in good condition.

There was some powder on hand, but hardly sufficient. During the previous summer, they had sold the greater part of their supply to William Parsons. He used it to construct a well in Northampton Street in front of the Red Lion Tavern, conducted by Adam Yohe. This powder would now be sorely missed. They may have had some little feeling of security when the Moravians stockaded the mill at Friedensthal. John Lefevre and his sons very likely helped in this work, for they were good neighbors and, in addition, must have realized that they were building an asylum for themselves as well as for others.

On December 13th, the first refugees arrived at Friedensthal, and by January 13th, 1756, there was a total of seventy-five. Of this number, 13 were women and 49 were children.

The Spring of 1756 passed. Great danger and constant fear of Indian raids and massacres remained with the inhabitants during this period.

On August 24th, 1756, sparks from the bake oven set fire to the shingle roof of the dwelling at Friedensthal. "The Lefevre People," as the Moravians referred to them, saw the fire and, hurrying to the scene, gave great assistance in extinguishing it. At the time, it was said that, without their help, the entire settlement might have been burned to the ground.

A chain of forts had been constructed along the Blue Mountains from the Delaware River to the Susquehanna River, and thence continuing to the Maryland line. In the course of duty, it often became necessary for the commanders of these forts to go to Easton to report and receive orders from William Parsons, who had been appointed Major in command of the forces of the county. Lefevre's Tavern was on the road leading from many of these forts to Easton and at a most convenient distance for those travelling to or from the County Seat. To be served by one of the six attractive daughters of the landlord made the food taste better, the drink more refreshing, and their rest a pleasure long to be remembered.

* * *

John Van Etten, of the Minisinks, was commissioned a Captain by Benjamin Franklin in January of 1756, and placed in charge of Fort Hyndshaw, located in what is now Monroe County, near the present town of Bushkill. He had not made many trips to Easton before the anticipation of again seeing Margaret Lefevre was a pleasure, the realization of which more than offset the hazards of the journey. This friendship soon ripened into love and eventually Margaret Lefevre became the wife of Captain John Van Etten.

At the time Benjamin Franklin granted the commission to John Van Etten, he also sent him a long letter of instructions. In this letter, the Captain was commanded to keep a diary or journal of each day's happenings. The diary which John Van Etten wrote is still preserved. It touches the romance of the Captain and Margaret Lefevre, provided you read between the lines. After a lapse of 178 years, this is now an easy matter. On June 3rd, 1757, Captain John Van Etten left Fort Hyndshaw for Philadelphia. The trip presented a fine opportunity to see his sweetheart; an opportunity which was not neglected. In his diary, under date of June 5th, he writes: "I lay sick by the way within five miles of Easton." Perhaps he was ill, but what a coincidence that he, a rugged frontiersman, should fall ill, figuratively speaking, at the very door of John LeFevre's Tavern. The next day he paid his respects to Major Parsons at Easton. It may be that his conscience troubled him a little, and for fear that his sudden case of indisposition might appear strange, he entered in his diary to allay suspicion and as a matter of confirmation or proof, the following, under date of June 7th: "Not withstanding the Ill Surcomstance of Body I was in I persued my Journey." On his return trip, he reached Easton on June 14th. His notes for that day end with the statement that he "left Easton about six o'clock (P.M.) and went about five miles." Due to a bashful and somewhat guilty feeling, he never mentioned Lefevre's Tavern, which was "about five miles" from Easton. It has taken almost two centuries to diagnose his illness.

* * *

The first treaty with the Indians was held at Easton in the summer of 1756, and the second one in October of the same year.

The inhabitants of the county were, naturally, more or less curious to see the conference, and many of them, overcoming their fear, went to Easton. John LeFevre and members of his family, no doubt, went "to town", and took in the sights. Between treaties, he and his friend and neighbor, Moses Tatamy, discussed the various questions which arose. Tatamy, an interpreter at the treaties, was certainly in a position to talk knowingly on the various subjects.

The Moravians had employed a number of Christian Indians to do scout duty during the summer of 1757. These Indians ranged the Moravian holdings as well as their outskirts, in order to protect and give warning of any impending danger to the people working in the fields. As the fields of John Lefevre joined those of the Moravians at Friedensthal, it is more than likely that he enjoyed their protection.

The Treaty of 1757 had hardly been brought to a close when John Lefevre's good friend and patron, William Parsons, passed away.

An enumeration of horses and wagons was taken in 1758. From this we learn that John Lefevre had one wagon and three draught horses. His son Abraham also had one wagon, but only two draught horses. His son Isaac had only a pack horse.

The years 1755, '56, '57 and '58, were strenuous ones for John Lefevre. The Indians were always threatening, and were frequently committing depredations on both sides of the Blue Mountains. There was no telling when they would attack Bethlehem, Nazareth, or Easton. No sooner were the treaties brought to a close and the announcement made of an agreement of peace with the Indians, than new outbreaks occurred.

At times a steady procession of settlers, fleeing from the frontier, passed Lefevre's Tavern. Lefevre realized that the frontier, which had been extended well beyond the Blue Mountains, was receding and that his home would again be on the very verge of civilization. Under these conditions and with the enthusiasm of youth now failing him, he looked with longing eyes toward the property which he still owned in Worcester Township (Philadelphia County). Eventually he joined the fleeing settlers and some time after 1761 he again became a resident of the home of his youth.

Some time before Nov. 12th, 1760, Lefevre sold a tract of about five acres to Peter Weigandt. On the date just mentioned, he sold the southern part of his tract in Forks Township, containing a little over 100 acres, to Cornelius Weigandt. On May 21st, 1764, he sold to his son-in-law, Captain John Van Etten, the remaining part of his 368 acre tract. In this deed, he mentions that he was "of the Township of Worcester in the County of Philadelphia." His wife Christina joined in the deed and the consideration of 500 pounds.

All of his daughters married. As I have before mentioned, Margaret married Captain John Van Etten, who in 1759, and 1760, was coroner of Northampton County. Susanna became the wife of Gabriel Frey, and Catherina married Jacob Best and settled in Moore Township. Anna Mary married Peter Mellig, while Christina married John, the brother of Peter Mellig. The sixth daughter, Elizabeth, married Leonard Greeseman (Creaseman?).

There were five sons, namely:—John, Isaac, Abraham, Nicholas, and Henry, who was the youngest. Abraham Lefevre served on the Northampton County Grand Jury in June of 1759. In 1761, he purchased a tract of two hundred acres in Norriton Township, Philadelphia County. In 1766 he and his wife Elizabeth sold about half of this tract.

In 1762, John Lefevre Sr. and his wife Christina gave an acre of ground, in Worcester Township, to the Wentz Reformed Church. Another acre was given by Jacob Wentz and his wife Elizabeth. On these two parcels of land a new church was built.

During the years previous to the Revolutionary War, the records of Worcester Township show that John Lefevre Sr. owned one hundred acres of land, and that Isaac owned a like amount but that John Lefevre Jun. owned no land. In some manner, John Lefevre Sr. secured a tract of land in Loudon County, Virginia. In his will, he gives to his son, John, 125 acres of this tract and to his son, Henry, 150 acres.

In the Revolutionary War there were enlisted from Worcester Township, privates by the names of John, Isaac, and Samuel Lefevre. I do not know what relation they bore to John Lefevre Sr., but most likely they were his sons or grandsons.

On October 20th, 1778, John Lefevre, yeoman, then of Hereford Township, Berks County, Pennsylvania, far advanced in years, weak in body, but of perfect mind, memory, and understanding, wrote his last will. The will was proved on February 3rd, 1779, and is filed in Philadelphia. His wife is not mentioned. So she must have preceded him in death.

John Lefevre inherited the religious zeal and perserverance of the Huguenots and the plodding honesty of the Dutch. He was a member of the Dutch Reformed Church and carefully kept and treasured the family Bible. In it he entered with his own hand the births, deaths, and marriages of his children. During the peaceful days he spent in the quiet valley of the Bushkill, he used it to bring up his children in his faith. During the dark days of trial and tribulation, it gave him comfort and hope. Then as his days grew fewer and fewer and his death approached, he bequeathed to his favorite son Isaac, that, which had been his strength and comfort, his Dutch Bible.

William Parsons,
Easton's First Citizen

William Parsons, Easton's First Citizen

THE Easton Public Library was built on land which was formerly the graveyard of the German Reformed Church. It was the oldest burial ground in Easton. With one exception, the remains of all those whose graves could be identified were removed. One grave was allowed to remain and over it the citizens of Easton erected a tomb. On its flat marble slab is this inscription:[1]

WILLIAM PARSONS, Esq.
Born, May 6, 1701.
Died, December 22, 1757.

"He rocked Easton in her cradle and watched of her infant footsteps with paternal solicitude."

A very pretty sentiment, but the expression "paternal solicitude" is subject to contradiction.

* * *

William Parsons was a native of England. There he served his apprenticeship and learned the trade of a shoemaker.[2] With his trade fully mastered, he sailed for America and settled in Philadelphia sometime before he reached his majority. He at once opened a shop of his own and soon established a paying business.

He was married in Philadelphia, in the year 1722, to Johanna Christiana Zeidig.[3] Her father was a gloomy pietist, who, in

common with others of that school of theology, shunned all worldly amusements.

Parsons was industrious and ambitious. He was fond of
reading and in his spare moments read all the books he could
secure. His greatest interest lay in mathematics and many vexing
problems were solved by him while bending over his last, fashion-
ing the dainty slipper for a daughter of one of his customers or
clogs for a servant in the same household.

On a certain Sunday morning, in October of 1723, William
Parsons, looking up from his reading, may have seen a boy of
seventeen, in dirty working clothes, whose stuffed pockets over-
flowed with wearing apparel, enter a bake shop on Second Street
not far from his home.

Now Parsons at this time was a firm believer in astrology.[4]
If the stars had been functioning properly for our amateur astrol-
ager, he would have observed with great intenseness this youth as
he emerged from the baker's and sauntered down the street,
munching one roll while he carried two others, one under each
arm. The celestial bodies could hardly have foretold that this
boy, in a few years, was to be his best friend.

This travel-weary youth, who had but that morning arrived
in Philadelphia, found shelter that night at the Crooked Billet
Tavern. The next morning he called upon Andrew Bradford and
told him that he was a printer looking for work and that his name
was Benjamin Franklin.

Whether Franklin became acquainted with Parsons at this
time is not known; for about a year after his arrival in Philadelphia he went to London where he remained for about eighteen
months, returning to Philadelphia in October of 1726.

Benjamin Franklin formed his friends into a club called the
Junto. This club for mutual improvement met every Friday evening. Franklin drew up the rules and regulations. These required
that each member, in his turn, should propound a question on
moral, political, or natural philosophy, which questions were to
be discussed by the members. Once every three months, each
member was to present an original essay on any subject whatsoever.

Among the members of this somewhat select organization of artisans was William Parsons. Franklin in his autobiography says:—"William Parsons, bred a shoemaker, but, loving reading, had acquired a considerable share of mathematics, which he first studied with a view of astrology, and afterwards laught at it."

Just how intellectual these Friday night discussions may have been we have no way of telling. The subjects selected indicate that no topic was too difficult or too complicated for the members to undertake. Most of the political and philosophical subjects could well be debated today, such as:—

"Is self interest the rudder that steers mankind, the universal monarch, to whom all are tributaries?"

"Can any one form of government suit all mankind?"

"Is it consistent with the principles of liberty in a free government to punish a man as a libeller when he speaks the truth?"

William Parsons took a most active interest in these proceedings and his remarks were intelligent and serious; for Parsons was neither witty nor frivolous.

The first volunteer fire company in Philadelphia was formed by the versatile Franklin in 1736.[5] It was called the Union Fire Company and William Parsons was one of its charter members. When a fire occurred it was not an uncommon sight to seen Benjamin Franklin and William Parsons running through the streets carrying a green leather bucket in each hand.

In 1730 Franklin suggested that the members of the Junto pool their books and thus make available a fair-sized library for the use of their organization. Franklin soon broadened this plan and proposed a subscription library. Accordingly on November 8, 1731, the directors, hand picked by Franklin, and including William Parsons, met and elected a treasurer and secretary.[6] The price of a share in the library was placed at forty shillings and ten shillings was established as the amount of the annual dues.

With the money thus raised, an order for books was placed in London. In October of 1732 the books arrived. There were about one hundred volumes in all.

William Parsons helped unpack the trunk with considerable satisfaction. He no doubt stopped to admire and thumb through Dechall's Euclid, L'Hospital's Conic Section, Ozanam's Course of Mathematics in five volumes, Hayes on Flexions, and Keil's Astronomical Lectures. As a director, Parsons may have had a hand in the selection of these mathematical works.

On March 14, 1734, William Parsons was elected librarian.[7] He was to attend the library on Saturday of each week from four o'clock in the afternoon until eight in the evening. His salary was set at six pounds per year.

William Parsons' Book-Plate

Rules for the duties of the librarian and the operation of the library were made as occasion required. Slumber in the reading room was considered a loud and objectionable noise and instructions were issued, that "if any person hath to be awakened twice he shall be requested to leave."

The proprietaries of the province granted a charter to the library and on May 3, 1742, fifty-three subscribing members, including Parsons, signed a document formally accepting the charter in the name of "The Library Company of Philadelphia", by which name the institution is still known.

There can be no doubt that Parsons' association with the library was of infinite value to him. His contact with the books and with the patrons of the library could not fail to increase his learning and culture as well as his position in the community.

In October of 1741, Parsons was elected a member of the Common Council of Philadelphia.[8]

In 1743 Benjamin Franklin organized the American Philosophical Society which was "formed of virtuosi or ingenious men, residing in the several colonies." William Parsons not only qualified for this exclusively intellectual organization but, at Franklin's solicitation, became a charter member.

During the period between the years 1730 and 1745, Parsons led a very active life. In addition to the time which he devoted to his literary, educational, and political organizations, he carried on his trade as a shoemaker, conducted a wholesale general merchandise business,[9] continued his studies, and became a practicing surveyor.

His first professional surveys were made in 1730 and by 1734 he was quite active in this line of work.[10] His ability as a surveyor attracted the attention of Richard Peters, who was in charge of the land office, with the result that in August of 1741 he was appointed Surveyor General of the province.[11]

* * *

The domestic life of William Parsons was not a happy one. By temperament he and his wife were entirely unfitted for each other. Mrs. Parsons inherited the gloomy outlook of the pietists.[12] Her restless, morbidly religious craving could not be satisfied. At times she became despondent. In her search for spiritual peace she joined each new sect with which she came in contact. First she joined the Tunkers, by whom she was immersed. Then she became affiliated with the French Prophets. Not finding peace with them she became a Separatist. George Whitefield's preaching caught her fancy for a time. Then came the Moravians and here at last she found that peace of mind and heart for which she had been yearning so long.

Parsons was a Lutheran,[13] but he was not an active church member. His industry, study, social life, and public activities were guided by his great ambition to succeed in a worldly way. He could not understand his wife's religious melancholy, and she was entirely unsympathetic with his desires.

Many rumors and false statements had been circulated about the Moravians. At that time they were not looked upon with favor by those men in the province whose friendship Parsons wished to cultivate. Fearful that his wife would join their church and that thus he might lose the friendship of persons of influence, he forbade her and his six children to attend their services. This order was accompanied by a threat that disobedience to his command would result in his leaving them.

In 1745, when he found that he could not control the religious activities of his family, he put his threat into effect and forsaking his wife took the two youngest children, Grace and Sarah, aged nine and seven, to his plantation on the Swatara Creek in the Blue Mountains, about thirty-five miles northwest of the present city of Reading. Parsons and his wife were never reunited.

This action made it necessary for him to resign the office of librarian, a position which he had held for twelve years.

*   *   *

Leading the sedentary life of a shoemaker during his early years, his constitution was not rugged enough to withstand the rigors and hardships connected with the office of surveyor general. His health failed. His troubles from this source were not helped by the fact that his official residence was in Philadelphia and his actual residence was now in the wilderness on the frontier eighty miles from his office. In poor health and away from his friends and the scenes of his triumphs and successes, he saw his plans and ambitions crumble before him, a hopeless wreck.

In his depressed state of mind, he blamed the Moravians for all his troubles and came to look upon them with intense bitter hatred.

What Parsons' feelings toward his wife may have been at this time is unknown, but he still had an affectionate feeling for his children. In 1746, his daughter Hannah and his son Robert died. Richard Hockley writing to Thomas Penn said:[14]—"William Parsons is so indisposed since the death of his son and daughter that Richard Peters must do his work."

In 1748, he was compelled to resign the office of surveyor general.[15] His weakened constitution could no longer withstand the strain of the work. So he now moved with his two children to Lancaster, where through his friendship with Benjamin Franklin, Richard Peters, and members of the proprietary party, he secured commissions as justice, prothonotary, register of wills, and recorder of deeds, for Lancaster county.[16]

Parsons, a native Englishman, had spent the best years of his life in Philadelphia, with English friends and acquaintances, and where there were relatively few Germans. He did not care for the characteristics of the predominantly German population of Lancaster county. Perhaps this feeling was intensified by the fact that his wife was a German. Whatever the cause, he came to despise the Germans. In a letter, written in a sarcastic vein, he says:[17]—"The world has ever been changing, even this new world has taken a great turn of late and now we must acknowledge that the earth with the fullness thereof belongs to the Dutch, at least they think so."

His fondness for surveying continued and, when his health permitted, he undertook work of this nature. As early as 1743, Parsons had some direct correspondence with Thomas Penn in regard to a proposed town on the Schuylkill.[18] This correspondence continued until 1748 when a final plan was accepted and Parsons laid out a town which was given the name of Reading.

Parsons continued his private work as a surveyor and now and then undertook work of a public nature. One of the most important surveys undertaken by him was the establishment of the southern boundary of the "three lower counties", now the State of Delaware. The story of the establishment of the division line between the grants to Lord Baltimore and to William Penn is a long and interesting tale of meetings and discussions, lawsuits and arguments, legislation and appeals. For over eighty years comedy and tragedy, ridicule and scandal, were interwoven in the various ramifications of this long drawn out contest.

Our interest in the establishment of the dividing line between the present states of Maryland and Delaware starts with the year 1750 when the province of Maryland and "the three lower counties" appointed commissioners to establish this boundary, and the Penn Commissioners selected William Parsons as their Chief Surveyor and Clerk.[19]

The commissioners, their surveyors and clerks, met at New Castle, where Parsons and his assistants surveyed the town to find its exact center. At night they established a true meridian by the use of a plumb line, a candle swung from the court house steeple and observations on the last star in the tail of the Little Bear.

The commissioners could not agree upon any of the points which necessarily arose and they adjourned. As a result of this disagreement, the surveyors decided to run the southern line of the lower counties. This was to be a due west line, starting from the extreme eastern point of Cape Henlopen. This work was started on December twentieth.

A cabin erected on the beach for their use caught fire one night, and its total destruction caused the surveying party to spend the balance of the night shivering and waiting for the dawn. Very much of the territory in the line of the survey was swampy and quite impassable. Writing of the difficult task, one of the assistant surveyors made this entry in his diary:[20] "William Parsons, as a person equal to the task imposed, was full of spirit and urged us on as much as he decently could." Due to the disagreeable weather, the work was temporarily stopped. In April of 1751 the survey was resumed, and completed on June the fifteenth of that year.

While the Maryland commissioners had their own engineers, William Parsons, the Chief Surveyor for the Penns, was the dominating head of the combined forces. Thus the southern line of the present State of Delaware was established by a former Philadelphia shoemaker.

* * *

On March 11th, 1752, the northern or wilderness part of Bucks was taken to form a new county which was named Northampton.[21] At the same time, Easton, a town which did not exist, except in the mind of Thomas Penn, was named the county seat.

It now became necessary to lay out the town, establish courts, and select the various county officials. Thomas Penn also required a representative in the new town and county. Richard Peters in looking over the possibilities decided that William Parsons was the one man who could satisfactorily fill all the positions.

Parsons was not enthusiastic over the prospect, but out of a sense of duty to the proprietaries and to please his friend Richard Peters, he reluctantly accepted. The appointment was a happy one for all concerned, with the possible exception of the appointee. His ability as a surveyor, coupled with his experience at Reading, eminently qualified him as a town planner. His services as justice, and in the various offices at Lancaster fitted him for the same positions in Northampton County. His seven years as surveyor general and the consequent contact with Richard Peters and the land office of the province made him an admirable representative of the Penns. Thomas Penn, in writing to Peters, said :[22] "You will please let William Parsons know the satisfaction we have in his appointment, on whose prudence we shall very much depend in the settlement and good government of the town."

On May 7, 1752, William Parsons and Nicholas Scull left Philadelphia for the Forks of the Delaware with instructions to lay out a town at the confluence of the Delaware and Lehigh rivers. William Parsons carried commissions issued by Governor Hamilton the day before, appointing him prothonotary, clerk of the orphans' court, and recorder of deeds for the new county.[23]

The following afternoon, they arrived at the Forks. Requesting the ferryman to secure laborers for the morrow, they continued five miles up the Lehicton Creek to the tavern of John Lefevre. This tavern was the headquarters of these two foremost surveyors of Pennsylvania while they labored in the development of the shiretown. Both Parsons and Scull had previously enjoyed the hospitality of the Lefevres[24] and well knew that the excellent table and scrupulous housekeeping of Mrs. Lefevre were more than ample compensation for the daily five mile ride to and from work.

It took two weeks to lay out the town, but Nicholas Scull returned to Philadelphia before the work was completed.[25]

It was under the direction of Parsons, who had been appointed a justice, that the first court was organized and held in June, 1752.

* * *

The ferry rights across the Delaware at Easton had been granted to David Martin. After his death, the title became vested in Richard Peters, who held it in trust for the Penns. Peters leased the ferry to Parsons at a very nominal rental.[26] Nathaniel Vernon held a lease from Martin and this lease was binding on Martin's heirs, successors, and assigns. So when Parsons tried to remove Vernon he found himself involved in a law suit. Much to his chagrin Parsons lost this court action and Vernon retained possession of the ferry. The animosity engendered resulted in many law suits with each party alternately taking the part of plaintiff and defendant.

* * *

The few scattered houses and taverns in Easton had hardly taken on the appearance of a village when the inhabitants realized that they were destitute of ministers and schoolmasters. No education facilities had been planned for the children, who were likely to grow up without the knowledge and benefit of the "blessed gospel."

A fund of twenty thousand pounds had been raised in Europe for educational purposes in the provinces. The poor Germans in and about Easton, in 1754, addressed a petition to the trustees of this fund, praying for the means to erect a school house and to secure the services of a schoolmaster.

The petition was given to William Parsons who in turn sent the paper to Richard Peters. His letter of transmittal was in general sympathetic, but he recommended that the petitioners be not permitted to contribute to the school fund, for he writes:—
"They are so perverse and quarrelsome in their affairs that I am sometimes ready to query with myself whether it be man or beast that the generous benefactors are about to civilize! — — — I will not be negligent in whatever the Trustees may desire,

though it seems to me like attempting to wash a blackamoor white."

The trustees granted the request of the "poor Germans" and donated the large sum of thirty pounds to the cause. William Parsons, with five others, was appointed to the local board to handle this contribution and manage the school. Either Parsons assumed the duties of the board, or their lack of interest thrust these duties upon him, for he became in every sense the superintendent of Easton's first school.

In the fall of 1755, when the war clouds hung heavy over the province and the fear of Indian depredations was ever present, the citizens of Easton, urged on by the German element, started the construction of the school house.

This school was in part a charity school. Not, however, as we understand the term, nor, to his credit, as William Parsons understood it.[27] It was the intention of those who could well afford to pay for the tuition of their children, and who had contributed to the construction of the building, that their children should receive free tuition, but that the poor Germans, who could ill afford any charge should pay for the privilege of having their children educated. Strange as it may seem, the Philadelphia Trustees held the same views. William Parsons, in defence of his principles was compelled to defend the position of the poor. The mere fact that the poor happened to be the despised Germans did not deter him from championing their cause. However the situation gave him some satisfaction, for his personal enemy, Nathaniel Vernon, had several children in the school for whose tuition he refused to pay. The very frank letter which Parsons wrote to the authorities in Philadelphia, on this subject, affords us an insight into his character which we otherwise could not have had. The following is taken from his letter:—"When I proposed to Mr. Vernon his paying something to the Master I acted from judgment and a principle of equality and justice. When Mr. Smith signified the minds of the Honorable Trustees to me I acted in obedience thereto in violation of principle and judgment for their will was a law to me. — — — If the original intention of the society was that the children of English parents should receive the benefits of the charity school freely and that the poor Germans should pay for it, then the school at Easton is upon a right establishment, otherwise it is not." He accuses Mr. Smith and the other trustees of partiality and says:—"I am very willing and desirous that the world may have the opportunity of judging which of us have acted with partiality." In this letter he also threatens to resign and states that if it had been a matter to do over again he would "do it in the very same manner as before."

How this first school rumpus turned out is not known, but let us hope that William Parsons was able to maintain his position.

* * *

Parsons undoubtedly considered his lot in Easton an unhappy one. He was living in the midst of the Germans and Moravians and his official duties threw him into personal contact with them. The causes of these contacts, lawsuits, legal matters, and elections brought out the worst side of the Palatinates.

From Parsons's own statement, we know that he did not get along well with the principal citizens of the town or county.[28] He complains to Richard Peters that he can have no idea of the wicked men with whom he is entangled. He calls Nathaniel Vernon a monster and a villain. He accuses Vernon and Gordon of planning to make his task in Easton an uneasy one. Jasper Scull, he says, is a rash indiscreet man, and he distrusts John Jones of Bethlehem. Chapman, Jennings, Gordon, Vernon, Scull, and Jones are all "wicked men", and he had no respect for James Burnside who defeated him for the Assembly.

In a letter to Peters he expresses the fear that he might have "incurred the imputation of being peevish and vindictive," which he states "truly can't justly be imputed to me."[29] A suspicion of its truth no doubt prompted the denial.

Parsons had his friends, but they were not numerous. Of three we are sure: Timothy Horsfield, Richard Peters, and Benjamin Franklin. In the course of his life at Easton, he became fond of Horsfield and named him one of the executors of his will. His friendship with Benjamin Franklin is herein fully shown.

Richard Peters in a letter to Parsons in November of 1754, says:[30]—"Pray let me know how you are and if possible I will come and pay you a visit, for no man loves you more or desired your welfare with a more sincere wish than I do."

The life of William Parsons in the first three years after the founding of Easton was filled with political squabbles, personal and religious animosities, business troubles, ill health, and bitter disappointment. However, his tribulations in this period were trivial when compared with the burden he carried for the next two years, the last two years of his life.

The defeat of Colonel Washington in the summer of 1754 and of General Braddock in the summer of 1755 by the French and Indians, caused the Delaware and Shawnee Indians to ally themselves with the French and to institute barbarous and relentless warfare on the frontier.

It is not necessary to draw upon our imagination to picture the dreadful conditions existing along the frontier in the year 1755. Richard Peters describes this in a letter to Thomas Penn: —"almost all the women and children, over the Susquehanna, have left their habitations and the roads are full of starved, naked, indigent multitudes, who but the other day lived with comfort and satisfaction."[31]

As the Indian raids spread toward the northeast, the same conditions became prevalent in Northampton county. With the Gnadenheutten massacre, the exodus from the Blue Mountains and their foothills received an impetus which Peters' description fails to do justice. Bethlehem, Nazareth, Friedenthal, and Easton became havens of refuge.

William Parsons realized he had been sent to Easton to help build and develop the town. He knew his responsibility to the proprietaries and, with intense loyalty and unassuming bravery, he stood like a rock and watched the human flood pass through Easton and on to safety. But his daughter Grace, whose well-being was of first importance to him, he sent to Philadelphia.

The authorities of Northampton county were without guns, powder, and lead. There was no food for the destitute and no funds with which to secure it, and the melancholy Parsons sank to the very depths of despair. His constant letters kept the authorities in Philadelphia in touch with the situation, but his appeals for aid remained unanswered. In this dreadful situation he wrote to his friend Benjamin Franklin.[32] His faith was not misplaced. In his reply Franklin told him "that an act is passed granting sixty thousand pounds chiefly for defence of the province — — —. Three hundred men are ordered to be immediately raised on pay, to range the frontier, and block houses — — — to be erected at proper distances and garrisoned. — — — I have - - - procured and sent up - - - a chest of arms, containing fifty and five loose, fifty-five guns in all, of which twenty-five are for Easton, and thirty to be disposed of to such persons nearest danger on the frontier, who are without arms and unable to pay. — — — By the same wagon we send twenty guns for Lehigh Township, and ten to Bethlehem to the Moravian Brethren."[33]

Ten days later, Franklin again writes Parsons and informs him that he and Mr. Hamilton were leaving Philadelphia on the following Thursday to visit him in Easton, in order to secure at first hand the true state of affairs in the hinterland. He ends this letter in the following manner:—"I enclose you twenty pounds toward buying meal and meat for the poor fugitives, that take refuge with you. Be of good courage, and God will guide you. Your friends will never desert you."[34]

Parsons had received some lead and powder and with Franklin's assurance of guns and militia he must have experienced a certain relief, although it is quite unlikely that he saw any silver lining in the clouds which hung so heavily over the Forks of the Delaware. True to his word, Franklin left Philadelphia December 18 (1755). Some time the following Saturday, he and his company rode over the crest of the hill at John Street in Easton and descended into the forlorn village.[35]

It must have been a comforting sight to the residents as the little cavalcade rode into town. The Moravian guide, William Edmonds, led the procession. Then came the rather portly Franklin, the fastidious Hamilton, the Quaker garbed Joseph Fox, and Franklin's son William dressed in the scarlet uniform of a grenadier. They were accompanied by a rather motley troop of cavalry led by Captain James McLaughlin.

The report had been circulated that the Indians intended to attack and burn Bethlehem on Christmas Eve. Added to the suffering of the refugees and the great fear of the citizens of Easton, the probabilities of the burning of Bethlehem cast additional terror among the people. It was in this atmosphere of gloom that Franklin, Hamilton, Fox, and Parsons gathered on Christmas Eve to discuss the situation. If there was any sign of cheer in this gathering, it must have come from Franklin, certainly not from Parsons. When the dawn of Christmas day found Bethlehem still safe and the rangers had made no report of Indian hostility, the citizens took on new courage.

Before Franklin and his party left Easton, he commissioned Parsons a major and placed him in charge of the troops in Northampton County.

* * *

In the summer of 1756, the first Indian treaty at Easton was held. As far as the official records are concerned, Parsons appears to have taken very little if any part. However, the demands made upon him, due to the unsettled condition of the county and the staging of treaties at Easton, were a burden which, coupled with his ill health, undoubtedly hastened his death.

It was a duty which fell upon him, as a representative of the proprietaries, to see that the settlers who had fled from their habitations and were temporarily living in Easton, or merely passing through, were fed, housed, and clothed. In a small community, struggling for its own existence, with poor accommodations and few houses, and with insufficient funds even to pay for the services of a messenger to carry their communications to Philadelphia, this was a hopeless task. The lean, haggard, and careworn women, who, with numerous ill clad, shivering children, dragged themselves into the village, were a pitiable sight. We must assume that Parsons handled this dreadful situation in a capable manner, for there are no records of any deaths from exposure or lack of sufficient food to keep body and soul together. Parsons drew on his own funds for this purpose and in one of his letters states that he had expended what little cash he had.

The caring for the refugees was not the only problem which was thrust upon the drooping shoulders of Easton's first citizen. He was instructed to provide living quarters for the Indians who attended the conference.[36] For this purpose he was provided with funds, but there was no material available with which to build the sheds.

The Indians who attended the conferences were troublesome and it was necessary to police the town. This too was Parsons' job. He was now Major of the local militia and had charge of the men stationed in Easton. It must have been a trying situation for any slight untoward incident would have caused the white men or the red men to attack the other with a resulting catastrophe which would have had an inconceivable effect upon the Indians and might have changed the final outcome of the French and Indian War.

The Indians, who were constantly drunk, were not the only cause of worry. Of the farmer, still living in the vicinity of the town, Parsons says:—"our rude neighboring farmers when they come to town seldom leave it sober. ——— and it will be necessary to have two sentries to keep off one of those headstrong drunken Dutchmen from the Indians." His opinion of the citizens of Easton was not much better. Of them he writes:—"Many of the town people are very ignorant and indiscrete and will with difficulty be brought to behave to the Indians as they should."[37]

With all the trouble due to the Indian uprising, and the holding of the treaties at Easton, Parsons still had his regular duties to look after. His office as justice, clerk of the orphans' court, prothonotary, and recorder of deeds made heavy demands upon his time. During part of this period he was also county treasurer. As major of the county militia he visited the frontier forts. All the troubles of a hastily organized militia, poorly drilled and equipped, and without discipline, were thrust upon him. He presided at court martials[38] and acted as quartermaster and commissary of the county troops. He carried on all of the official correspondence with Philadelphia and Bethlehem. With all this he found time to do some surveying and occasionally visited his plantation on the Swatara Creek.

There were times when, under the strain of his duties, his strength gave out and he visited his friend John Lefevre on the Lehicton Creek.[39] Here under the care of Mrs. Lefevre and a quiet rest in that "vale of peace", as the Moravians called it, he would regain some of his strength and return to Easton and to his arduous duties.

Parsons' interest in politics was due entirely to his desire to further the interest of the proprietaries. He actively supported all their candidates. At times he became quite worked up over the elections. Finally he overstepped the bounds of propriety and became involved in the first of Northampton county's many election contests.[40]

In 1756 William Allen was elected a representative to the Assembly from Northampton county. At the same time Lancaster county also selected him to represent them. As Allen preferred Lancaster, Northampton county held another election and elected William Plumstead. Before Plumstead took his seat, a petition was presented setting forth that the election was illegal and praying that Plumstead be not seated.

Most of Northampton's prominent citizens became involved in this contest. Among other illegal practices, it was claimed that Parsons failed to deliver to the sheriff the writ calling for the special election until so late that the sheriff could not notify the entire electorate of the county, and many of the citizens were thus prevented from voting. Parsons admitted his failure to deliver the writ to the sheriff promptly, but claimed it an "error of judgment" rather than due to "any party views or dishonest intentions." He was subpoenaed to appear at a later meeting of the Assembly, but when the time came for his appearance the clerk announced that he was not in the province, having gone to Amboy in the Jerseys for the recovery of his health. Apparently he never again appeared before the Assembly, which eventually declared the election illegal.

Parsons never regained his health. In almost every letter which he received from his old friends in Philadelphia they made inquiry as to his condition. There were no doctors in Easton, so Parsons was treated by his nephew, Stephen Wooley, who lived in Philadelphia and who was a doctor of sorts.[41] Now this 'practitioner of physic' at various times during the last few years of Parsons' life, prescribed treatment, which if it did not hasten death, certainly did not prolong life.

In the fall of 1757, Parsons returned to Easton from Amboy with no improvement in his health, but a much better outlook on life. His five years in Easton in close contact with the Moravians had changed his opinion of this denomination. He now realized why his wife and his children had embraced their faith. His prejudice disappeared and his contacts with them became more cordial.

With the establishment of friendly relations with the Moravians, the cause of his separation from his family was removed. "Time had cured the wounds which reason failed to heal." His health continued to fail and he realized that his end was near. Overtaken by remorse he sent a message, from his death bed, to his wife and children asking them to come to him. His pathetic appeal to his wife came too late for her to reach his bedside. However, his daughters, Grace and Molly, then living in Bethlehem, reached Easton in time to receive his blessing and to hear him acknowledge his error and pay tribute to the Moravian brethren.

On December 17, 1757, William Parsons died. At his request, Rev. Jacob Rogers of the Moravian Church, the husband of his daughter Molly, conducted the funeral services.[42] He was buried in Easton in the little grave yard on top of the hill. The remains of this pioneer, who served the Philadelphia library as librarian for twelve years, now rest in front of the Easton Library near the books which he loved so well.

Parsons in his will made numerous bequests. Among them was one of two hundred pounds to the Academy of Philadelphia for the benefit of needy scholars.[43] As this academy grew into the University of Pennsylvania, it is quite probable that this gift was the first bequest received by that institution. The residue of his estate was left to his wife and after her death to his children. Since his debts and his bequests absorbed his entire estate, his wife received nothing.

Hugh Roberts, a contemporary, in speaking of Parsons' gift to the academy, said that he had "bequeathed more than his estate — — — to raise a fame after death which he had the unhappiness to fail gaining in the conduct of his life."[44]

Three years after Parsons' death, Thomas Penn in a letter to Richard Peters says:—"I do not remember what you wrote about Mr. Parsons, am sorry he died poor. — — I do not remember he moved to Easton on our account — — — however what services you employed him in should be paid for and if you — — — — — think he ought to be allowed One Hundred Pounds, let it be paid him."[45]   Cold!   Austere!!

Benjamin Franklin was in London when he heard of Parsons' death. On February 16, 1758, he wrote to his wife:—"My dear Child: — — I regret the loss of my friend Parsons. Death begins to make breaches in the little junto of old friends, that he had long forborne, and now it must be expected he will soon pick us all off one after another."[46]

Franklin also wrote to Hugh Roberts:—"Dear Friend: — — Two of the former members of the Junto you tell me are departed this life. Potts and Parsons. Odd characters both of them. Parsons was a wise man, that often acted foolishly; Potts a wit, that seldom acted wisely. If enough were the means to make a man happy, one had always the means of happiness, without ever enjoying the thing; the other had always the thing without ever possessing the means. Parsons, even in his prosperity, always fretting; Potts in the midst of his poverty, ever laughing. It seems, then, that happiness in this life rather depends on internals than externals; and that, besides the natural effects of wisdom and virtue, vice and folly, there is such a thing as a happy or unhappy constitution. They were both our friends and loved us, so, peace to their shades. They had their virtues as well as their foibles; they were both honest men, and that alone, as the world goes, is one of the greatest of characters. They were old acquaintances in whose company I formerly enjoyed a great deal of pleasure, and I can not think of losing them without concern and regret.[47]

*   *   *

William Parsons did rock the swaddling clothed Easton in its cradle and he did guide its tottering infant footsteps, but he had no love for the new born village. For the successful accomplishment of this difficult and disagreeable task, the citizens of Easton honor his memory.

He was a faithful agent of the Penns. An acknowledgment of his loyal and unselfish devotion to the interest of the proprietaries is a tribute to his memory much greater than the words cut in the cold marble slab which marks his grave.

---

[1]The date of death given on Parsons' tomb is incorrect. The Moravian records give this date as December 17, 1757.

[2]Pennsylvania Magazine of History, Vol. 33, p. 340.

[3]Transactions of the Moravian Historical Society, Vol. VII, p. 41.

[4]Franklin's Autobiography.

[5]Pennsylvania Magazine of History, Vol. 56, p. 364.

[6]For most of the information in regard to Parsons' connection with the Library, see "Benjamin Franklin's Library," by Austin K. Gray, 1937.

[7]Pennsylvania Magazine of History, Vol. 39, p. 450.

[8]Ibid, Vol. 19, p. 65.

[9]Pennsylvania Historical Society. Manuscript. Receipt Book of William Parsons.

[10]Pennsylvania Historical Society. Manuscript. Original Index to William Parsons' Surveys.

[11]Pennsylvania Archives, 3rd Series: Vol. VIII, p. 41, etc.

[12]Transactions of the Moravian Historical Society, Vol. VII, p. 41, etc.

[13]Ibid.

[14]"The Foundation of Reading," by J. B. Nolan, p. 54.

[15]Pennsylvania Archives, 3rd Series: Vol. VIII, p. 605.

[16]Pennsylvania Magazine of History. Vol. 33: p. 340 to 344.

[17]Pennsylvania Historical Society. Northampton County Manuscripts—Vol. 1727-1758; p. 59. Original letter William Parsons to Samuel Rhoads, August 17, 1751.

[18]"The Foundation of Reading," by J. B. Nolan.

[19]"Resurvey of Mason and Dixon Line," published by Commonwealth of Pennsylvania.

[20]Pennsylvania Magazine of History, Vol. 38, p. 385.

[21]"The Statutes at Large of Pennsylvania," Vol. V: p. 140.

[22]Pennsylvania Historical Society, Peters Manuscript, Vol. III, p. 72.

[23]Pennsylvania Archives, 3rd Series: Vol. 8, p. 753.

[24]Pennsylvania Magazine of History, Vol. 38: p. 113. Expense account of William Parsons shows that he and Nicholas Scull stayed at Lefevre's tavern and that Scull remained only part of the time.

[25]Pennsylvania Historical Society. Letter William Parsons to Richard Peters, May 20, 1752.

[26]Lease mentioned in patent, Messrs. Penn to William Parsons, Filed in Land Office, Harrisburg, Pa., Patent Book A17: p. 469.

[27]Pennsylvania Historical Society. Northampton County Manuscripts, Vol. 1727-1758. Letter written by William Parsons, July 3, 1755, gives information in regard to school trouble.

[28]Pennsylvania Historical Society. Richard Peters Manuscripts, letter William Parsons to Richard Peters, April 10, 1757.

[29]Ibid.

[30]Pennsylvania Historical Society. Northampton County Manuscripts. Vol. 1727-1758. Letter Richard Peters to William Parsons, Nov. 7, 1754.

[31]Pennsylvania Historical Society. Richard Peters Manuscripts.

[32]Pennsylvania Colonial Records, Vol. VI: p. 761.

[33]"Franklin's Works," by Jared Sparks. Vol VII: p. 99.

[34]Ibid, page 101.

[35]"The Foundation of Reading" by J. B. Nolan.

[36]Pennsylvania Historical Society. Northampton County Manuscripts, Vol. 1727-1758, p. 209.

[37]Ibid.

[38]Ibid, pages 193, 233, and 249.

[39]Action of John Lefevre against Executors of William Parsons' will to collect for entertainment of William Parsons and his friends. Original document. Archives Room, Court House, Easton, Pa.

[40]Pennsylvania Archives, 8th Series, various pages between page 4422 and page 4635.

[41]Pennsylvania Historical Society. Northampton County Manuscripts, Vol. 1727-1758, Pages 215, 233, and 249.

[42]"A History of Bethlehem," by J. M. Levering, 1903, p. 265.

[43]Pennsylvania Historical Society. Northampton County Manuscripts, Vol. 1727-1758. Copy of Will of William Parsons.

[44]Pennsylvania Magazine of History. Vol. 38, p. 287.

[45]Pennsylvania Historical Society. Letter Thomas Penn to Richard Peters, November 15, 1760.

[46]"Franklin's Works" by Jared Sparks. Vol. VII: p. 163.

[47]Ibid, p. 181.

Grace Parsons

Grace Parsons

IN the introduction to his book, "The Wilderness Trail", Charles A. Hanna says:—"The Archaeologist in Europe has turned up the dirt of the Mediterranean countries, and has discovered that the history of ancient civilization will have to be in large part rewritten, and that it must begin before Adam. The antiquarian has searched the charter chests of families and the private and state archives of his own and neighboring nations, and found that the story of his institutions and governments and people has never been truthfully told." This is a broad statement. I should dislike to think that the story of the ride of Paul Revere, or the martyrdom of Nathan Hale, belongs in the same category as the story of Santa Claus or the Easter Rabbit.

That there is a great deal of truth in the statement of Hanna I am thoroughly convinced. In the little research work which I have done in connection with our local history, I have found a surprising number of inaccuracies and misstatements as well as stories built up on very slender foundations. These stories, no doubt, satisfy the historian's ego and meet the demand for a local hero or heroine. The story generally starts with a surmise, develops into a fact, and finally emerges with all the trimmings of heroism, patriotism, high ideals, romance, humor, pathos, and perhaps martrydom, with a glamorous setting which holds the eager reader's attention and tends to place the hero of the story on a pedestal, in a niche, in his own mental Hall of Fame. Such is the story of the ride of Grace Parsons.

In the latter part of November, 1755, the Indians murdered twelve Moravians at Gnadenhuetten. This was the first massacre within the County of Northampton and the citizens were naturally very much wrought up over the situation. The feeling in Easton was tense. There were practically no arms and ammunition, and very few men to aid in the defense of the town. Parsons immediately sent word of the massacres to the Governor and implored aid and assistance. At this stage, so the story goes, William Parsons sent his daughter to Philadelphia as the courier, bearing his message to the authorities pleading for arms, ammunition, and men. His daughter Grace was supposed to have heroically mounted her "favorite steed" and, through unbroken paths, and Indian trails, sped on her way, unmindful of personal danger, thinking only of the poor defenseless town and its terror stricken inhabitants. This, in brief, is the story of the ride of Grace Parsons.

I am going to read to you what the historians of the Lehigh Valley, of Northampton County, and of Easton, have to say of this incident in the early life of the county seat, then just three years old.

M. S. Henry in his history of Lehigh Valley, published in 1860, says, referring to Grace Parsons:—"she rode as express for her father to Philadelphia with a letter to the Governor in 1755, when the inhabitants were momentarily in expectation of being murdered by the Indians. Mr. Parsons tells us that he had not the money to pay any other express and therefore was obliged to send his daughter." Here is a direct misstatement. It may be on his "authority" that other historians have elaborated. In one of his letters, Mr. Parsons mentions that he did not have money with which to pay an express, so that he would be obliged to send his message by private hand. However, he makes no mention of his daughter.

In a manuscript history of Easton, this same author, says that William Parsons was a widower and had but one child, a daughter, named Grace. The fact is Mr. Parsons was not a widower, (his wife surviving him by sixteen years), and he was the father of six children.

In 1877, there was published a History of Northampton County by Capt. F. Ellis. The following is taken from this history:—"In the midst of all this terror and panic, Mr. Parsons wrote Lieutenant-Governor Robert H. Morris, under date of nineteenth of December, 1755, advising him of the general desperate state of affairs at Easton —— their lack of self protection, and of the universal flight of the inhabitants all along the river, and making an appeal for some measures to be taken to place them in a better condition for defense. This despairing letter he sent, with others, by a special messenger, and that courier was his own daughter Grace. In speaking of this Mr. Parsons said he sent his daughter as a matter of necessity, for he had no money to pay another messenger. - - - - - And lonely as was her two day ride to Philadelphia, she, herself, was no doubt lightened in heart, and accelerated in speed, by the thought that safety was before, while tomahawks were behind her. - - - - - We may imagine how proudly she stepped from the low door of her father's house, and how daintily she mounted, and how the bashful beaux stood at respectful distance, and gazed in rustic admiration on her aristocratic beauty, and how tenderly her father gave her his parting kiss - - the last he might ever give her - -as he bade her Godspeed."

"It is a matter of great regret, on behalf of the ladies of the present day, that no detailed account was preserved, enumerating and describing the articles of her attire on that occasion; but we may feel reasonably sure — and there is profound consolation in the belief — that Miss Grace was a young lady of correct and fastidious taste, and that her traveling dress, on that memorable ride, was of proper material, and irreproachably fashioned in the (then) prevailing mode."

William Parsons is again misquoted as saying that he sent his daughter Grace. As to her being an "aristocratic beauty", I question the artistocratic part, but freely admit she may have been a beauty. Knowing something of the town and its inhabitants, I can hardly imagine that her traveling dress was "of the proper material, and irreproachably fashioned."

After an interval of eight years, the Rev. Uzal W. Condit wrote a history of Easton. This was published in 1885. After telling of the Gnadenhuetten Massacre, which he says fell on the community "like a clap of thunder from a cloudless sky" he continues:—"Mr. Parsons wrote to Governor Morris, informing him of the desperate state of affairs at Easton. — — — — The letter implored aid in men, arms, and all necessary defense. But there were no mails to carry the letter, no money to pay a special messenger, and no man could be spared. There was no one who could be spared but his daughter Grace. If her father desired it, she would take the letter to the Governor, a distance of sixty-five miles, a two-day journey through unbroken forests, guided by Indian trails and bridle paths to Philadelphia. It may not be easy to tell the feelings of the father as his young daughter came from the house, somewhat pale from apprehension and excitement, mounted her favorite steed, and receiving what might be the last kiss from the lips of her fond father, started upon her mission. The brave father, and the braver daughter bore their mutual share of the dangers of those dark days in the history of our now beautiful town."

An historian should not permit his enthusiasm to get the better of his accuracy. Condit now cites a letter which Parsons wrote to Richard Peters under date of December 6th, 1756, advising him that he (Parsons) had supplied the various forts with powder, lead, etc., and stating how much he then had on hand in Easton. You will please note that Grace rode to Philadelphia the latter part of December, 1755 (that is according to Condit) and that the letter just quoted (and the date is correct) is dated December 6th, 1756, just about one year later.

I will continue quoting from Condit, who refers to the supplies just mentioned:—"This bountiful supply of ammunition came in answer to the message carried to Philadelphia by Miss Grace Parsons. The courageous girl succeeded in her mission, and brought relief to the terror stricken town, and the heart of her anxious father. She had braved the dangers of a long journey along which silent pathway the deadly missile might have been hurled at her trembling heart by lurking savages. She knew the danger, and dared meet it. — — — — This one deed has made her name honorable among the historic characters of the past history of our city. And the mothers of Easton may well feel proud of this noble daughter of those dark days."

Before proceeding further I will call your attention to two inaccuracies in Condit's narrative. First:—I feel quite sure that anyone who is familiar with the history of the first few years of Easton will readily agree that Mr. Parsons or his daughter Grace did not keep a paddock of horses from which she could pick her "favorite steed". Second:—If it was necessary for any one to dash to Philadelphia on horseback to secure help for the town, it is quite difficult to understand how the town could have waited patiently nearly twelve months for the aid sought. In 1892, the Rev. U. W. Condit published a book titled "Paxinosa and his Compeers". In this small volume of a little over a hundred pages, he again repeats the story of Grace Parsons. There had evidently been statements that the story was a "beautiful fiction" and Condit attempts to prove that the story was founded on facts. Again the author is carried away by his subject, repeats all his previous inaccuracies and inconsistencies, and plunges headlong into new difficulties. I shall give only the additional touch which he now adds.

Before doing this, I wish to tell you something about the married life of William Parsons. He was married in 1722. His wife of German descent was extremely pious. At times she was a religious fanatic and later, thru brooding over religious beliefs became morose. At various periods she became affiliated with most of the denominations and sects of the day. William Parsons was nominally a Lutheran. He was not actively religious and was by "temperament disqualified to appreciate the heart yearnings of his German wife". This led to separation and, sometime before Parsons came to Easton, he left his wife and never returned to her. Mrs. Parsons was never in Easton during the life of her husband. She lived for 16 years after her husband's death and, having finally embraced the Moravian faith, she moved to Bethlehem, where she died.

Now with the fact before you that Mrs. Parsons never lived in Easton, I will read what Condit writes:—"Early one December morning light was seen in the humble log dwelling of the Parsons family. The family was at breakfast long before dawn. If we could have looked into the humble room, through the little window, we might have seen Mrs. Parsons sitting before her daughter in tearful silence, thinking of the dangers in the long journey before her."

I found one writer who is more of a historian than a romancer. Rev. J. M. Levering has written an excellent history of Bethlehem, but it is from a paper written by him, on William Parsons and his family, and published in the Transactions of the Moravian Historical Society, that I wish to quote. He says:— "Grace Parsons — — — seems to have been his favorite daughter and remained with him in Easton until the danger from the hostile Indians in November, 1755, induced him to send her back to her mother." — — — "Her journey at that time enhanced by her being the bearer of one of his (Wm. Parsons) official messages to the Governor, was an episode amid the thrilling and pathetic experiences of the time, which successive modern writers, with a slim stock of facts, but aided by imagination, have developed more and more into a pretty picture with various embellishments."

While the inaccuracies and absurdities to which I have called your attention cast some doubt upon the authenticity of the story, I would have refrained from writing this paper if I did not have more definite and, in my opinion, absolute proof of my statements.

William Parsons did send his daughter Grace to Philadelphiia, as he did not consider Easton a safe place for her. She left at the first opportunity which presented itself after the Gnadenhuetten Massacre. She carried at least one letter from her father addressed to Richard Peters. However there is absolutely no evidence that she made the journey on horseback, alone, and in great haste, carrying an appeal to the authorities for help.

In substantiation of my statement, I must refer to and quote from letters which William Parsons wrote at that time. All these letters are printed in either the Colonial Records or the Pennsylvania Archives.

The Gnadenhuetten Massacre occurred on November 24th, 1755, and on Tuesday, November 25th, William Parsons wrote to Governor Morris and acquainted him with the calamity which had befallen the county. The following is taken from this letter :— "In this poor little town we are without men and arms to oppose the enemy, and if they gain possession either of this place or of Bethlehem or Nazareth, it will be impossible to remove them without a great and regular force. I thought it my duty to give your Honour this information by an express the very minute that I received Mr. Horsfield's letter, and to entreat your Honour, if it be possible, to order us a supply of arms and ammunition immediately or I am afraid it will be too late." The endorsement on this letter shows that the courier was John Weaver.

On the same day, Parsons wrote to Richard Peters, from which letter I have taken the following :—"By the letter herewith sent to his Honour the Governor, you will see that the enemy have attacked and burnt the Moravian Settlement at Mahoney, and killed all their white people except two who escaped. As soon as I received this account I dispatched John Weaver with it to the Governor, and as the enemy is near us, I shall be obliged to send continually Expresses, which will occasion an expense which neither myself nor the Town people will be able to bear. Pray Sir, help us, for we are in great distress. The powder and lead came to hand, but no letter, and I don't know what we shall do for want of arms. If I can get a wagon to bring my Daughter to Philadelphia, I will send her off immediately, by which wagon may be sent arms, etc., if any are to be had."

These two letters show the urgent need of arms and ammunition and the desire of Parsons to send his daughter to Philadelphia, where she would be safe. From this letter I understand that he hoped to engage a wagon to take her to Philadelphia and that on the return trip the wagon could bring back much needed supplies. He says nothing about her riding, nor does he say that he will send her at once as an express. He does say that he will send her just as soon as he can get a wagon. The fact that he intended to send her in a wagon shows that it was possible to get a wagon through and that the traveller did not have to depend upon bridle paths and Indian trails.

The next letter from Parsons was written the following Sunday, November 30th, and was addressed to Richard Peters. This letter is most important. The body of the letter is of no interest in connection with the matter we are considering. It deals with some Indians who were brought from New Jersey and put in the Easton jail. There is no appeal for aid in the body of the letter. After the letter was written, Parsons no doubt felt that he had omitted an opportunity of reminding the authorities that Easton was still sorely in need, for he adds the following after he had signed the letter. "P. S. If we are not furnished with supplies of men, arms, ammunition, and provisions, we shall not be able to hold our ground."

The important part of this letter is the endorsement on the back. As printed in the Pennsylvania Archives this endorsement reads as follows:—"Wm. Parsons, 30 Novr. 1755. Received Saturday Morning by Express, Grace Parsons." This letter was written on a Sunday and received in Philadelphia on the following Saturday, December 6th, six days later. This does not look as though any great haste was used in getting the letter to its destination. In the wording of the endorsement, I could not be certain whether Grace was the express, or whether she receipted for it when it was handed to her by the express messenger. Therefore, I secured from Harrisburg a photostatic copy of the original, as I wished to compare the signature of Grace Parsons with the name on the endorsement of the letter. Much to my surprise I found that the printed endorsement was incorrect, and it should have been "Rec'd Saturday Morn'g by Miss Grace Parsons." I have since inspected the original at Harrisburg in company with the State Archivist, Dr. Garrison, and he unhesitatingly agrees with me that the actual endorsement on the original is as I have just stated.

It is therefore evident that William Parsons wrote this letter on Sunday in November 1755 and that, being of minor importance, he held it until he found a means of sending it. In the mean time he either secured a wagon in which to send his daughter to the city, or made arrangements with some one making the trip; for, on the following Saturday, she personally delivers her father's letter to Richard Peters who marked on the back: "William Parsons, 30 Novr., 1755," Rec'd Saturday Morn'g by Miss Grace Parsons." We therefore know the leisurely circumstances under which she made the journey, the exact date of her arrival, and the contents of the letter she carried. Mr. Parsons considered the safety of his daughter of first importance. That she carried one of his letters, and this letter of but little account, was entirely incidental.

One more letter of Parsons is interesting because it is the letter on which Henry, Ellis, and Condit rely for the proof of their narrative. The letter was addressed to the Honorable James Hamilton and Benjamin Franklin. In the letter Parsons writes:— "Beside the losses which I have had reason to sustain in this general calamity, I have expended what little stock of cash I had, in public service, so that I am obliged to send this letter by a private hand, not being able to pay a person to go express with it." The error (?) of substituting the name of Grace Parsons for the phrase "a private hand" was made seventy-six years ago by the first historian of the Lehigh Valley. Succeeding writers have apparently accepted the statement without proper verificatfon and, with ever increasing embellishments, have handed it down to the present day. The date of the letter, Dec. 15th, 1755, nine days after Grace Parsons had arrived in Philadelphia, is proof that her distracted father did not have her in mind to serve as his messenger.

Settlers were passing through Easton continually, fleeing from the frontier to more thickly populated and protected parts of the Province. Almost any one of these refugees going to Philadelphia could have carried Parsons' letter, and they would have been considered a "private hand". His daughter Grace was safe with her mother and in this knowledge Parsons must have had a deep feeling of thankfulness.

Grace Parsons was born in Philadelphia on November 26th, 1736. When the separation took place between her parents, she and her younger sister Sarah went with their father and lived on a tract of land which he owned on the Swatara Creek. Grace, or Gracy, as she was called, was then nine years old, and her sister, seven. After William Parsons resigned the office of Surveyor General, he and his two daughters went to Lancaster, where they lived until Easton was named the county seat of the newly erected county of Northampton. This was in 1752, when Gracy was sixteen years old.

It was on December the 3rd, 1752, that Parsons said he had moved his family to Easton. His daughter Sarah was the third and only other member of the family who ever lived in Easton. Sarah must have left soon after her arrival, for, when the Indian uprising took place, Grace, who was then nineteen years of age, was the only one of Parsons' children with him. After she left Easton she remained in Philadelphia for nearly two years. Parsons must have missed her greatly.

The unsettled condition lasted for several years and in the spring of 1757 Grace would have returned to her father's side, but he had failed in health and had gone to the seaside to recuperate. On May 2nd, 1757, she went to Bethlehem and became a resident at the Sisters House. She was baptized at Bethlehem on May 29th, 1757, and given the additional name of Johanna, so that in the records of the Moravian Church she is known as Johanna Grace Parsons. She married July 29th, 1758, Nicholas Garrison, Jr.

During the time that Grace lived with her father, they occupied a log dwelling on the west side of Hamilton street (now North Fourth st.) between Northampton and Church streets. It was in April of 1757, that William Parsons moved to the new house he had erected at the northeast corner of Hamilton and Ferry streets. To this home he returned in the late fall of 1757 and, on December 17th of the same year, he passed on to his Maker.

Grace Parsons was only a girl when she moved to Easton and just budding into womanhood when she was compelled to seek a safe refuge in Philadelphia. During these few years she did her full part in the development of the town. She not only assisted in looking after her father's household, but at times helped him with his work. Her signature, as a witness, is often found on papers which her father had prepared. She was accustomed to live on the frontier and knew how to make the most of the situation. I cannot, however, think of her as either "fashionable" or "aristocratic."

Her father learned the shoemaker trade in England and followed it in Philadelphia until, through diligent study and work, he elevated himself to positions of trust and responsibility.

All credit and honor to him and his daughter; for it was under her care that he "Rocked Easton in her Cradle and watched her infant steps with paternal solicitude."

Nathaniel Vernon, Easton's First Ferryman

Nathaniel Vernon, Easton's First Ferryman

THE eleven families who braved the perils of the wilderness and spent the winter of 1752 and '53 at the Forks of the Delaware, under conditions far from ideal, were, without doubt, Easton's Pioneers. They laid the foundation on which Easton has been erected. They builded far better than they knew.

Of the first citizens, William Parsons was undoubtedly the most important. He had been appointed prothonotary and clerk of the court and represented the provincial administration.

Lewis Gordon was the best educated man of the group. He was a Scotchman and Easton's first lawyer. With the help of the Proprietaries he rose to a position of local prominence. But in the dark days of the Revolution he repudiated the cause of liberty, adhered to the Mother Country, and was placed under arrest.

Abraham Berlin was the village blacksmith, a solid citizen, who, in a quiet way, contributed much. Between the blows on his anvil he helped weld this community into a substantial town. When Lewis Gordon dropped from grace, Abraham Berlin let the burdens of the little community fall upon his strong shoulders and carried on.

"Toiling, — rejoicing, — sorrowing,
Onward through life he goes;
Each morning sees some task begun,
Each evening sees it close."

Another pioneer was Paul Miller, a tavern keeper, who at times served refreshments and drinks, and between times worked at his trade of stocking weaving.

Anthony Esser was the "vitualer", a term which seems inappropriate for such a small gathering of log houses on the outskirts of civilization.

Ernest Becker was a baker, who, 'tis said, walked to Bethlehem for his flour, and then carried it home on his back.

Henry Alshouse, the carpenter, and John Finley, the mason, helped in a mechanical way to build the town.

William Craig, originally of the Irish Settlement who presented the petition to the Assembly asking for the erection of Northampton County, is recorded as an innkeeper. He might be called the founder of what has become known as "The Court House Gang", being the county's first perpetual office holder.

The new town needed a merchant and Meyer Hart, a Hebrew, became Easton's first storekeeper.

The subject of this sketch, Nathaniel Vernon, is mentioned last. He was the ferryman and an innkeeper. Although not the most important from any point of view he was by far the most picturesque of Easton's pioneers. His contribution toward the foundation of the town may have been negligible, but his life is most interesting and gives a vivid picture of Easton in its infancy.

* * *

Thomas, Randall, and Robert Vernon, three brothers,[1] came to America some time before William Penn's first visit to his province. They were Quakers and had left England because of the persecutions to which, as followers of William Penn, they had been subjected. William Penn's prospectus appealed to them. His offer of free government and the right to worship in accordance with one's own belief far outweighed his warning "that some hardships would precede the advent of plenty". They settled in Chester County and acquired adjoining properties aggregating eleven hundred and eighty acres.[2] This land was in Nether Providence township, lying between Ridley Creek and the Great Providence Road. The northern corner of this property is now a part of Media. Thomas Vernon, who was the grandfather of Nathaniel, owned three hundred acres. Thomas and his wife, Elizabeth, had a son and a daughter. The son, who was named Thomas, was eleven years old when his father brought him to America.[3] He married Lydia Ralfe in October of 1702.[4] Of this union there were born nine children.[5] The seventh child born on February 5th, 1714, was a son whom they named Nathaniel. This was the Nathaniel Vernon, the subject of this sketch, who became Easton's ferryman.

* * *

Nathaniel grew to manhood on his father's farm in Chester County. He was brought up under the strict rules and regulations of the Society of Friends. While still a youth he fell in love with Mary Engle, who spurned his attention and married William Salkeld. After a few years of married life William died and Nathaniel then won the hand of his boyhood sweetheart. On July 30th, 1744, Nathaniel Vernon and Mary Salkeld stood up in the Chester Monthly Meeting and declared their intentions. John and Daniel Sharpless were appointed a committee to inquire into the fitness of Nathaniel for marriage, and Jane Hoskins and Mary Howell were to perform the same duty for Mary. On August 27th, Nathaniel and Mary stood before the meeting for the second time. The report of the committee must have been favorable, for on September 13th, 1744, they were married at meeting in the presence of eleven Vernons, two Salkelds, and sixty-five other witnesses.[6]

Two years later we find Nathaniel and his wife keeping a public house in Nether Providence township. In the same year, 1746, he leased the house of David Cowpland in the town of Chester and secured a license to conduct a tavern at that place. More than likely his Chester venture was a failure, for the following year he was granted a license in Upper Providence Township.[7]

Nathaniel Vernon now drops out of the records until, in June of 1752, he applies to the courts of Northampton county for a license to conduct a tavern. Later in the same year, he is listed as a resident of Easton and a ferryman.

* * *

What brought him to Easton? Did he come with the other pioneers or was he a ferryman for David Martin before Parsons

and Scull laid out the town? Of this we are sure: — his application for a license in June was refused, but granted in December,
and the ferryhouse late in 1752 became a house of public entertainment.

The ferry house was a one and one half story building. The
gray logs with which it had been constructed were chinked with
tawny clay, which gave it a striped appearance. It stood on the
northwest corner of Front and Ferry streets, facing but well
above the Lehigh River.

Vernon leased the ferry from the administrators of David
Martin's Estate. On August 1st, 1753, Richard Peters, the Secretary of the province, acting for the proprietaries, purchased the
ferry from the administrators.[8] This purchase did not abrogate
Vernon's lease which continued in full force for a period of about
seven years. Now William Parsons, with or without the knowledge of Vernon's lease, applied for and received from the Penns
a grant of the exclusive ferry rights. This grant was dated May
15th, 1754.[9] Vernon refused to surrender possession and Parsons
brought suit.[10] The local court decided in Vernon's favor and
he continued to operate the ferry. The unfriendly feeling thus
started soon grew into intense hatred.

Parsons was a prematurely old man, broken in health, irritable and fretful, and as Benjamin Franklin said, — "a wise man,
that often acted foolishly."[11] Vernon was in the full vigor of his
life, an arrogant Englishman, who considered himself the equal
of any man. He knew, or thought he knew, his rights and insisted upon them. William Parsons was also an Englishman.
Vernon, a Quaker, was opposed to the proprietary party; Parsons,
an office holder, was a strong supporter of the party. Parsons'
political activities irritated Vernon. Vernon's opposition to the
authorities, and consequently to the proprietaries, was offensive to
Parsons. Intense political feeling and differences in a small community are likely to cause personal ill feeling and animosity. This
was decidedly the case in this instance. The ferry and the ferry
tavern were the two most lucrative businesses in Easton, and William Parsons was very much put out to see one, whom he disliked
so violently, be successful in an undertaking which he considered

belonged to him. These two men were constantly quarreling, the monotony of which was only broken by periods or more or less intensity.

Nathaniel Vernon served on the first jury impaneled in Northampton county and according to his own statement he was twice called upon to serve on the grand jury.[12] He had four sons. There may have been other children of whom there is no record. Thomas was the eldest. Job was born in 1750. Frederick was likely born before that date. John was born after his father left Easton and returned to Chester county.[13]

In the fall of 1755, a small log school house was built on the east side of Pomfret (now Third) street, a few hundred feet north of the Great Square. Here the citizens cleared away the underbrush and the few obstructing trees and with contributions of money, material and labor, built what William Parsons called, "the free school". This was the first building north of Church street and east of North Pomfret street. All that section of the town was still covered with undergrowth and trees. The ranker vegetation had already made considerable progress in obliterating the streets which, three years before, had been cut through the virgin growth. These streets were now hardly more than a pair of ruts and in some instances merely a foot or bridlepath, which, keeping within the legal limits of the street, wandered in and out between the stumps and the ringed dead trees.

At least two, and possibly more, of Nathaniel Vernon's children attended this school. The path from the ferry house to the school led across lots, around the few scattered gardens, littered with stumps, and through the original underbrush which only here and there had been removed.

Although the school was presumably managed by a board of trustees, William Parsons was actually the real manager. The new free school was free only to a few. The poor Germans were compelled to pay for the education of their children, while the children of the more opulent English received their education free. While William Parsons had no love for the Germans, he took a courageous and just stand in this matter.[14] So, with malice of forethought, he selected Nathaniel Vernon as a test case and insisted upon his paying something to the school master. Vernon refused. He argued that he had personally contributed three pounds toward the cost of erecting the school and the Englisn Society had contributed thirty pounds. The poor Germans had contributed nothing. If they wished their children to have the benefits of an education, let them pay for it and not depend upon the English. Mr. Parsons' arguments as expressed in a letter to Mr. Peters were sound. He insisted that his character was "very much aspersed". Not one inch did he recede from his position that Vernon must pay. No records have been found which indicate the outcome of this agreement. It would seem that Parsons' views must have prevailed. A righteous cause, thus successfully championed, added fuel to the fires of hatred.

* * *

Thomas Vernon, the father of Nathaniel, died on the 4th of November, 1754, at his home in Chester county. He was eighty-four years of age.[15] Nathaniel was evidently his favorite son, for, by his father's will he inherited, after the death of his mother, the homestead in Nether Providence township.[16] This property consisted of a brick dwelling, barns, etc., and ninety-five acres of land.

In one of his quarrels with William Parsons, Vernon claimed that Parsons was unlawfully holding some of his furniture and household goods. He must have been correct in his charge, for at the March term of court, 1755, he secured a court order directing the sheriff to seize the goods and return them to him.[17] This order has but recently been found. It lists a gun, twenty-one pieces of furniture, and seventy other household articles. Enumerated in detail these consisted of walnut tables, chests, cupboards, bedsteads, chairs, andirons, tongs, glassware, pewter plates, dishes, spoons, a spinning wheel, a dough trough, and a looking glass, — quite enough to arouse the interest of any antique collector. All these household furnishings were taken from Parsons and returned to Vernon. It would be interesting to know why Parsons had originally seized them.

Three years later the situation was reversed. Nathaniel Vernon had secured a bateau belonging to Parsons and refused to surrender possession. Justice Timothy Horsfield thereupon issued a writ of replevin and the sheriff seized the boat and returned it to its rightful owner.[18]

It is quite evident that Vernon and Parsons, although on unfriendly terms, continued business relations. In August of 1756, Parsons sent a letter to the Secretary of the Province which was directed as follows:—"Richard Peters, Esquire, in Philadelphia. By favor of Mr. Vernon." The "Mr." is very indicative of a cold, distant formality.[19]

From an account which Nathaniel Vernon rendered to Timothy Horsfield as Executor of the Estate of William Parsons, it appears that from 1753 until the time of Parsons' death, many items were charged to Parsons' account, for which, according to Vernon, he never paid. These items cover lumber, gamon, tongue, pasturage, flour, ferriage, cheese, wine, "min", punch, mutton, and fowls. In addition to these items there were certain legal expenses in connection with the law suit over the ferry, which Parsons had agreed or was compelled to pay. Mr. Horsfield paid all of these claims.[20]

Mr. Parsons had a house warming in April of 1757, when he moved into his new home at the northeast corner of Hamilton and Ferry streets. Nathaniel Vernon supplied three bowls of punch for this festive occasion. For these he charged four shillings and six pence.[21]

Some time during this same month, William Parsons, for what reason is unknown, had in his possession the ferry flat boat and Vernon charged him two pounds and ten shillings for five days loss of the ferry. In a footnote in his account he adds "Mr. Parsons having it in his possession too long." It is evident that Vernon considered the ferry worth ten shillings a day or fifteen pounds per month.[22]

On July 4, 1754, Lieutenant Colonel George Washington was defeated by the French and Indians at Fort Necessity in Western Pennsylvania, and the inhabitants of the frontier became uneasy. A year later, July 9th, 1755, General Braddock was overwhelmingly defeated at Fort Duquesne. The citizens of Easton, in common with those in other parts of the province became thoroughly alarmed. In October of the same year, the Indians started their raids and massacres. These increased in number and intensity and were gradually getting closer and closer to Easton.

In the latter part of November, 1755, word of a possible raid on the Moravian settlement on the Lehigh, about twenty-five miles northwest of Bethlehem, reached that town. Timothy Horsfield immediately sent a letter by express to William Parsons asking for aid.[23] Colonel John Anderson of New Jersey was then in that province near the Forks of the Delaware, and Parsons prevailed upon him to march to the scene of the threatened attack. Colonel Anderson and his company of about fifty men left Easton at noon on Sunday, November 23rd (1755).[24] Very heavy rains prevented an earlier departure. Nathaniel Vernon and Lewis Gordon accompanied this force.[25] They encamped about six miles from Gnadenhuetten on the evening of the following day. On this very evening the Indians fell upon and massacred the white settlers. Colonel Anderson and his company were too late to be of any assistance. Did Vernon and Gordon accompany this force from a sense of duty or from their desire for adventure? With a wife and several children and a lucrative business, it would seem that protection of his family and his interests prompted Vernon, the Quaker, to take up arms against the marauding savages. Lewis Gordon was a personal friend of Vernon and the same incentive likely prompted him to accompany the expedition.

During court week, and particularly at the time of the Indian conferences, the drab log ferry house did a rushing business. Where only an occasional traveller stopped to bait his horse and to quench his own thirst, the influx of strangers, on these occasions, broke the usual quiet of the village and fairly swamped the taverns. At the sessions of court, it was the pioneer litigants, the Philadelphia attorneys, the county officers, the politicians, and the curious who composed the crowds. At the time of the Indian treaties, the character of the patrons of the hostelries changed. The litigants, attorneys, and politicians, were replaced by governors, councilmen, assembleymen, commissioners, Quakers, soldiers, interpreters, and Indians — men, women and children. The ferry house had its full share of the trade. In the evenings the members of the Royal American Regiment and of the provincial troops filled the tap room, drank to the King, and sang only as carefree soldiers can sing.

"Here's to the drink that makes us wink,
Rum Puncheon!
A tinker's damn for any dram
But Puncheon!
Oporto, Claret, Sangaree,
Let maids and striplings sip the three,
But rum's the liquor, so say we,
Rum Puncheon!"

The Indians gathered around the tavern in small groups, waiting for a drink to be surreptitiously passed out to them. It was against the law to serve the Indians liquor during the time of the treaty. Finally the last of the soldiers in their bright red coats and once white leggings, with unsteady step, left the ferry house and the last of the Indians faded into the night. As Nathaniel Vernon and his wife, Mary, did the necessary final chores and locked up for the night, they could hear, faintly in the distance, the last of the inebriated troopers chant the chorus:—

"We'll buss the bottle while we sup,
We'll troll the bowl and fill the cup,
A toast, my hearties, bottoms up,
Rum Puncheon."

Thoroughly tired out but satisfied with the day's business, the ferryman and his wife retired to a much needed but all too short rest. The rising sun found them up and about their duties for the coming day. During the Indian conferences one day was much like another, with the exception that on one night (Friday, September 29th, 1758) a number of Mohican Indians broke into Vernon's cellar and stole a quantity of rum and wine.[26]

The first of the Indian treaties was held in the summer of 1756. In the fall of the same year the second treaty was held, and in 1757 and 1758, the third and fourth conferences took place. Vernon had been appointed commissary to feed the Indians and several of the principal Indians, notably Teedyuscung, lodged at his tavern.

These were busy days for Vernon. He had the ferry and the tavern to manage. The great number of people who attended these conferences kept the ferry boat almost constantly in operation. The business at his tavern increased by leaps and bounds. His wife, Mary, capably handled the tavern and at the same time kept an eye on the children. Vernon was not without help. He had purchased, from Adam Moley, a redemptioner by the name of Henry Smith.[27]　Smith was a general servant and helped to operate the ferry and do other chores about the place.

We must not lose sight of the fact that many Quakers attended these treaties and that they were not in sympathy with the methods used by the Governor and his party in handling the Indians. Vernon, a member of the Society of Friends, a local resident, the ferryman, a tavern keeper, and commissary for the Indians, was of much help to the Quakers in contacting the Indians, in securing information from them, and in giving advice. His sympathy was all with the Quakers and he no doubt did all he could, consistent with his position, to further their plans. The Friends were of the opinion that the Indians had been wronged and that the solution of the situation was to correct past mistakes and to render just treatment to them in the future. While not condoning the past conduct of the Indian, they felt that the action of the Proprietaries was directly responsible for the Indian outrages and that a kind and friendly feeling toward the natives would accomplish more than the mailed fist, deceit, or false promises.

The Governor and party became greatly incensed at the Quakers, and their unfriendly feeling toward them was extended to include Vernon who was undoubtedly their local supporter. Parsons' hostility to Vernon made the situation more acute. In addition to the personal quarrels and law suits between Parsons and Vernon, we now have the setting where Parsons acting for the Proprietary party could persecute Vernon to his heart's content. That he lost no opportunity is evident.

All the taverns and private houses obtainable were pressed into service at the time of the treaties. Vernon's services as commissary must have been satisfactory, otherwise he would not have been called upon to serve in the same capacity for each succeeding conference. His efficiency and the location of the tavern must have more than offset the animosity which the authorities felt toward him.

Vernon might have been disposed of by a refusal to renew his liquor license. However, no one would consent to conduct the ferry house unless he also operated the ferry. Through his lease, Vernon had indisputable control of the ferry, and consequently the ferry tavern. It therefore became necessary to renew his license each year.

The Indian treaty of 1757 caused bitter feeling between the Proprietary party and the Society of Friends. The Governor and council felt that the Quakers were responsible for their failure to satisfy the Indians and to secure peace. There was very little the authorities could do in the way of retaliation. Nathaniel Vernon, operating on the very threshold of the community, ferrying Philadelphia and New Jersey travellers across the rivers, appeared as a constant reminder that here was one member of the Society of Friends who could be taught a lesson with impunity.

It was decided to prosecute Vernon on several rather flimsy charges. William Parsons was interested in the action and with others employed D. A. Henderson, an attorney from Philadelphia, to take charge of the case. Parsons died in December, 1757, before the case came to trial. In January of 1758, Henderson wrote to Timothy Horsfield about the case and referring to Vernon says:—"I hear the dog has been breathing out threatings and vengeance against me. I epected nothing else, tho I never did any act to serve so at his hand. I think I am able to wrestle with him, if he casts me down, it will be my own fault, as I am sufficiently forewarned."

The case was called at the March (1758) term of court, Justices Swaine, Martin, Klotz, and Horsfield sitting. The notes taken at the trial have been preserved and the conversation here given is exactly as it was recorded in 1758.[28]

On Saturday, March 18th, 1758, Nathaniel Vernon was summoned to appear before Justices James Martin and Charles Swaine, charged with selling liquor by small measure without a license. Vernon appeared and requested to be informed as to who furnished the evidence on which the charge was based. He was told that the informer was Yost Fullert. Fullert was the school teacher to whose salary Vernon had refused to contribute.

The justices then called the following witnesses for the Crown:—Balzer Hess, Jacob Best, Frederick Nungessor, Nicholas Scull, and Yost Fullert. When the Justices started to examine the witnesses, Vernon interrupted, saying:—

"You need proceed no further in the examination, I acknowledge I have sold liquor by small measure without license, and I have paid my fine for so doing to a proper officer before this prosecution."

"Who is that proper officer?" asked Justice Swaine.

"A Justice of the Peace for this county."

"He is not a proper officer, the fine belongs to the tax collector and not the Governor. Have you the Collector's receipt?"

"I have no receipt," said Vernon. "I apprehend the fine belongs to the Governor."

Whereupon Justice Swaine observed:—

"Then the case is quite clear; we will pronounce judgment immediately against you for the fine of five pounds with costs of suit and execution or attachment will be issued against your goods unless these five pounds be paid within the span of five days."

The judgment was then entered and signed.

Vernon then arose and said:—

"I appeal from your judgment; and desire my appeal may be entered."

Justice Martin who had taken a rather inactive part in the examination, then spoke up.

"The appeal must be entered in a certain form, you must enter it in form."

"I am not a lawyer," shouted the enraged Vernon. "I am an Englishman and think myself entitled to the benefits of the law. If the law grants an appeal the Justices are to enter it."

"There are lawyers present whose business it is, why don't you employ them?" said Justice Swaine. "The money ought to be lodged and deposited in a proper manner agreeable to an Act of Parliament before you can have an appeal. I tell you this as a lawyer."

"I will deposit or lodge the money or give security," agreed Vernon, "but I expect you will enter it in form as the law directs."

"No we ought not," replied the Justice, "for if we enter your appeal we are against you, not for you."

Vernon now perceiving that nothing was to be gained by further argument started to leave.

"Stay! Stay!" said the Justice. "We have something further to say to you before you go."

They then called the constable and placing him under oath examined him concerning words which he had previously stated he heard Nathaniel Vernon utter.

"I heard Mr. Vernon express these words: 'that he (Vernon) would sell liquor for all,' " testified the constable. This was not the answer which the Justices desired, so they addressed the constable rather sharply.

"You informed us Mr. Vernon said 'in spite of all'. If you have given us information before that you will not now abide by, you ought to be severely punished."

To this the constable replied in a hesitating manner, "Well then I believe it was 'in spite of all'."

For making this statement, Vernon was bound over to the next term of court and was compelled to furnish two sufficient securities for his good behavior and appearance.

On the following Monday, Vernon with witnesses appeared before Justice Swaine and demanded a copy of the judgment against him. This the Justice refused to give. Vernon thereupon made a second demand calling attention to his witnesses. At the time this seemed to have no effect upon the Justice, but shortly afterwards Mr. Swaine sent Vernon the following abstract:—

18 March 1758, Northampton.

"Nathaniel Vernon is convicted on the evidence of Balzer Hess, Jacob Best, Frederick Nungesser, Nicholas Scull, and Henry Fullert, of having retailed rum and wine without being duly licensed thereto and in breach of an act of General Assembly of this Province."

James Martin
Charles Swaine

The persecution of Vernon was not yet complete.

On Tuesday (March 21st, 1758) Justice Klotz issed a special warrant demanding his immediate presence. When Vernon was taken before the Justice he was confronted with John Jennings who, when examined under oath, stated that Vernon, about a year and a half before had assisted in enlisting into his Majesty's service, and against his will, a man by the name of Simpson. Upon this affidavit alone Justice Klotz charged Vernon with being a cheat and placed him under eighty pounds bail.

Nathaniel Vernon was thoroughly aroused and very angry. He expressed himself in no uncertain terms, not only about the Justices but in regard to his own future action. All of this was soon reported to the Justices who again demanded that he appear before them.

On the following day, Wednesday (March 22nd, 1758), John Jones, of Bethlehem, declared that Mr. Vernon appeared angry with the Justices and that he, Vernon, said, "What do they think I am, a fool? I have not served on two grand juries for nothing. The Grand Jury ought to keep the King's Council as well as their own. I defy them." Jones also testified that Vernon said, "I have another advantage over them, there is no fixed price on the ferry so I can charge under ferriage for what liquor is drank".

When Mr. Jones was about to be cross-examined by Vernon's attorney, Justice Horsfield called out:—"Don't interrupt Mr. Jones, let him proceed, he has something farther to say."

Whereupon Mr. Jones affirmed that Vernon added:—"Mr. Horsfield is a damned mean spirited rascal."

On this information Vernon was again bound over to the next term of court and compelled to again furnish two sufficient sureties for his good behavior and appearance.

The inquisition was not over.

Failing to find any new charges they fell back on one of the old ones. On Thursday, a bill of indictment was referred to the grand jury against Vernon on the charge of selling liquor by retail without a license. The indictment was brought notwithstanding the fact that judgment, on this charge, had been entered against him by Justices Swaine and Martin.

The grand jury was inclined to be lenient. They sent for Vernon, who produced his receipt for the fine which he had paid. This procedure was brought to the attention of the court, which immediately passed a resolution, which, had it been put into execution, would have committed the entire grand jury to jail. Vernon's attorney dissuaded them from such an unprecedented action and recommended milder measures. The jury was thereupon condemned in open court for "a manifest breach of their oath and duty". All this evidently had its effect on the jury, for they brought in a true bill against Vernon. The Court then dismissed the jury with a severe reprimand, delivered by the King's attorney, which was somewhat mollified by the thanks of the court for their services. The trial was put off until the next term. Balzer Hess and John Wagle became the bondsmen and sureties for Nathaniel Vernon.

The testimony against Vernon in regard to the enlistment charge was that he had slipped a piece-of-eight into the pocket of John Simpson and then affirmed that he saw Simpson accept the money from a recruiting officer, thus forcing Simpson into the King's service against his will. John Santee and William Shackleton testified that they were present at the enlistment, which took place in the summer of 1756, and that it was a proper transaction and perfectly satisfactory to Simpson.

In one of the other trials, Vernon testified, and presented evidence to prove, that John Jones approached him in a sneaking abject manner under pretence of great friendship to him, though they had not, for some time, been on any such terms. That he, Jones, told Vernon to humble himself to Mr. Horsfield, who, as executor of the Estate of William Parsons, would favor him in his account of that estate.. Vernon in a violent passion said:— "I want no favors of Mr. Horsfield, if he offers me any he is a damned mean spirited rascal, for as executor he is obliged to do justice to the estate and if he favors me he must injure it." The final disposition of these two cases is not known.

When the case against Vernon for retailing liquor without a license was called, at the June 1758 term of court, Jacob Best, John Jones, Nicholas Scull, Henry Vollert, and Frederick Nungesser were on hand to testify against him. Benjamin Chew, Attorney General of the Province, addressed the court stating that the King did not wish to prosecute the case. It was accordingly dropped. Just when Vernon had his license renewed is unknown but at the Indian treaty in the fall of 1758, his tavern was in full operation. The apparent failure to convict Vernon of any serious charge, and the death of William Parsons, rather discouraged this vindictive group of citizens and for the time being he was left in peace.

Notwithstanding the comparative large number of taverns in Easton, the accommodations during the Indian conferences were very inadequate. Vernon, although his standing with the authorities was not of the best, was, nevertheless, pressed into service. Again he was appointed to take charge of the feeding of the Indians and to entertain some of them at his tavern. The Quakers depended upon him to secure accommodations for them. It appears that Anthony Esser, the butcher, lived in a house owned by Vernon. At Vernon's request, Esser had ordered a large quantity of meat for the coming treaty.[29] Vernon wished Esser to move out of his house so that it could be used by the Quakers. Esser refused, whereupon Vernon cancelled his meat order. Esser was placed in the embarrassing dilemma of either moving or facing a staggering loss. Like many other records, this one fails to carry through to completion. Anthony Esser's decision and the final outcome is not known.

In some manner Jacob Arndt became possessed of a ninety gallon hogshead of rum, which Nathaniel Vernon claimed and by a court order had returned to him. He needed this rum at his tavern for the Indian treaty was just about to start.[30]

Just before the treaty of 1758, George Croghan, Deputy in Charge of Indian Affairs in the Province, and a strong sympathizer and supporter of the Proprietary party, wrote a letter to the authorities at Philadelphia.[31] In this letter he advised that the distribution of liquor be taken out of the hands of Vernon whom he calls an "infamous villain." In this same communication he practically convicts himself of the indiscretion with which he charged Vernon. Croghan apologizes for the appearance of his letter which he said was written in the midst of twenty drunken Indians and states that he will be ruined unless the "taps are stopped" as it costs him not less than three pounds a day to buy liquor for the Indians.

The lease for the ferry, which Vernon held, expired in November of 1758.[32] Notice that the lease would not be renewed may not have been served on Vernon, but the handwriting on the wall could easily be seen and read by all.

The belligerent ferryman evidently planned to hold the ferry and ferry tavern as long as possible and then return to Chester County. The homestead, which would be his after the death of his mother, was still occupied by her. When, in November of 1757, the sheriff of Chester County sold the property of his cousin, Joseph Vernon, to satisfy a judgment, Nathaniel Vernon purchased the one hundred and one acre farm on Ridley Creek, Nether Providence township, for the sum of two hundred and three pounds, three shillings, and one pence.[33] He thus secured, in his native county, a home for himself and family when they should be compelled to leave Easton.

The Indian treaty was concluded on Thursday, October 26th, 1758, and the last recorded act of Vernon, while at Easton, was, by order of the authorities, to serve wine and punch to the Indians as a farewell token of good will.

In November of 1758, Nathaniel Vernon, after six eventful and exciting years at the Forks of the Delaware, returned to Chester County, the land of his nativity.[34]

He had hardly returned to Chester County when he was called upon to furnish (in 1759) a wagon for the Forbes Expedition. The wagon which he furnished made two trips to Bedford, carrying provisions each time.[35]

After Vernon returned to Chester county, and until 1770, he operated a sawmill on Vernon's Run.[36] The lumber business was not as lucrative as the tavern and ferry and it was not long before Nathaniel found himself in financial troubles. The Chester Monthly Meeting, in January of 1770, and again in August of 1774, took him to account for neglecting to pay his debts.[37]

In 1774, he was elected sheriff of Chester county, which office paid one hundred pounds a year.[38] The tax lists show that Vernon owned farm land varying from two hundred to four hundred acres, together with horses, cattle, and sheep. He did not own any slaves.

Life in Chester county was peaceful compared with the turbulent days at Easton. This calm was broken by the advent of the Revolutionary War.

In the pre-war days, Vernon felt that the cause of the Colonies was just. Debts and taxes were the concern and problem of England, not America. If England had paid for the French and Indian war in gold, America had paid for it in blood and tears. England could well afford to pay for the war. They were rich with a vast accumulation of capital. America should not be compelled to pay both in suffering and in gold. It was tyranny to tax the Colonies for that which had so greatly benefitted England, especially when the colonies had no voice in the matter.

Nathaniel Vernon, with many others, joined a company of local militia and drilled in military tactics. In his just indignation did he forget his religious training, or had his frequent chastisements at the hands of the Monthly Meetings made him indifferent? His conduct in this respect was not long overlooked. In September of 1775, he and his nephew, Nathaniel Vernon, Jr., were complained of in Meeting for "being concerned in military preparations", and in the latter part of December they were read out of meeting because they would not "desist from practicing in the military service."[39]

When on June 7th, 1776, Richard Henry Lee, a member of Congress, moved that "these United Colonies are, and of a right should be, Free and Independent States," Nathaniel Vernon drew up with a start. He was willing to fight against tyranny, but treason, that was another matter. No longer a Quaker, he was still an Englishman. Why should the Colonies not help pay for their own security and happiness? Were not the acts of Parliament the supreme law of the entire Empire of which America was a part?

When, on July 4th, 1776, the great bell in Philadelphia, on which had been inscribed the prophetic quotation, "Proclaim liberty throughout all the land unto the inhabitants thereof," rang out the glad tidings of the adoption of the Declaration of Independence, Nathaniel Vernon became a Loyalist. He was now an ardent advocate of the crown and outspoken in its interests. In addressing a group of erstwhile friends and acquaintances, he said:— "You have blustered and bellowed, and swaggered and bragged, that no British Parliament should dispose of your money without your leave, and now you suffer yourselves to be bullied by a congress and cowed by a committee."[50]

The authorities soon took notice of Vernon's conduct and he and his nephew, Nathaniel Jr., were promptly declared traitors and commanded to appear for trial.[40] They were never apprehended, but their property was seized by the Commonwealth and sold. The nephew joined the Tory Light Horse Troop, later called Chester County Dragoons and served with the British.[41]

A large number of sheep which Nathaniel owned were driven into the woods in an unsuccessful attempt to hide them. They were seized and sold for three hundred and thirty-three pounds.[42] His personal property was sold for two hundred and forty-nine pounds, most of it being purchased by his son, Thomas.[43] His house and lands were not sold at this time. And so it happened that Easton's first ferryman, Nathaniel Vernon, a native-born

American, a Quaker, a tavern keeper, a friend of the Indian, a lumberman, a sheriff, and a Loyalist, with a price on his head, fled to the protection of the British, then in possession of Philadelphia.

* * *

We must return to the primitive schoolhouse on North Pomfret Street. William Parsons' endeavor to force Nathaniel Vernon to pay for the education of his children is sufficient proof that some of his children were among the very first pupils to enter the little log school house when it was completed in the fall of 1755.

The success of a school is measured by the success of its pupils in after life. It is interesting to know that at least two and possibly three of those enrolled in the years 1755, 56, 57, and 58, became patriots and helped in the cause of liberty and independence. They were Thomas, Frederick and Job Vernon, sons of the ferryman.

Job Vernon joined the revolutionary forces at the commencement of the war and served faithfully without intermission until the army was disbanded. He was commissioned Ensign in Captain Thomas Church's company of the Pennsylvania Battalion commanded by Colonel Anthony Wayne. He was promoted to Second Lieutenant in Captain Robinson's company on January 5th, 1776. On January 1st, 1777, he was advanced to First Lieutenant in the 5th Pennsylvania Regiment. He was again advanced, and on January 23rd, 1778, he was made a Captain Lieutenant and, in June of 1779, he was commissioned a Captain. His regiment was attached to the Army of the North and he participated in all its engagements up to the storming of Stony Point. In 1780, he was paymaster of the 5th Pennsylvania Regiment. He was a brave and judicious officer, and an intimate friend of General "Mad Anthony" Wayne [44]

Frederick Vernon also entered the army at the very start of the war. He was a Captain in the 4th and 5th Pennsylvania Regiments until June 7th, 1777, when he was promoted to the rank of Major and assigned to the 8th Pennsylvania. On January

17th, 1781, he was transferred to the 4th Pennsylvania and later to the 1st Pennsylvania. He was made a Brevet Lieutenant Colonel on September 30th, 1783.[45]

By an act of Congress there was printed a list of officers of the Revolutionary War who served to the end of the war and thereby acquired the right to half pay and bounty lands. In this list appears the names of Job and Frederick Vernon.

On October 6th, 1779, Pennsylvania passed an act vesting the estate of Nathaniel Vernon in his four sons.[46] The act states that Nathaniel Vernon was attainted of high treason by the laws of the Commonwealth but that it has been shown that however guilty he may have been of a crime to occasion the forfeiture of his estate, his four sons have ever demeaned themselves as good citizens and have manifested their attachment to the state, Job and Frederick by engaging in actual service as officers of the continental army, and Thomas by commanding a company of militia of the state, and that John was under the age of eighteen. The title was vested in the four brothers, subject to the payment of their father's debts.

The Revolutionary War was over. In the spring or 1783, most of the American army was encamped on the west bank of the river Hudson near Newburgh. Sir Guy Carleton, Commander of the British forces, occupied New York City. All were waiting for the signing of the terms of peace. The members of the American army were about to return to their homes. Swords were about to be forged into pruning hooks and cannon into plows. Eight years of privation and suffering had been crowned with victory. From the battlefield and strife all eyes were turned to home and peace. To keep alive their friendship and the bonds formed during the days of the war, the American officers formed an organization. Realizing that they were following in the footsteps of the old Roman, Lucius Quintius Cincinnatus, who four hundred and fifty years before Christ was called from his plow to save Rome, triumphed, dropped the implements of war and returned to his home and plow, they named their organization The Society of Cincinnati.

Now Job and Frederick Vernon, two of Easton's barefooted pioneer children, who watched with interest the Indians at the treaties and who more than likely played hookey from school to fish in the waters of the Lehicton Creek, became with General Washington, General Knox, General Wayne and others, founders of this patriotic society.[47]

During the period when the American Army was rejoicing in the prospect of disbanding and returning home, what of Nathaniel Vernon? He was in New York City frantically addressing memorials or petitions to Sir Guy Carleton, telling him how, from pure principles of loyalty and attachment to His Majesty's person and government, he had left his home and loved ones to serve as guide to the Royal Army while they were in the Province of Pennsylvania; how his knowledge of the country brought them success far beyond the expectation of those in command. He informed Sir Carleton that Sir William Howe had on many occasions thanked him for his services and had finally rewarded him with a Lieutenant's commission in the Corps of Guides and Pioneers. He regretted the absence of General Abercrombie, Colonel Balfour, and Colonel Simcoe, who knew of his work and would have testified in his behalf. He gave the names of Mr. Shoemaker and Mr. Potts of Philadelphia as references. He stated that he was not at the time attached to the corps but prayed that he might be given a portion of the land which was to be distributed among its members.[48] His prayers must have been answered. Sir Guy Carleton, with forty thousand men, women, and children, evacuated New York City in November of 1783. Many of these refugees were landed at Shelburne, Nova Scotia, which had sprung up like the magic city in the Arabian Nights. In the early part of 1783 the site of the city was nothing but a "stern and rockbound coast." In the latter part of the same year there was a mushroom city of twelve thousand inhabitants, of whom Nathaniel was one.

Was it hope and faith, or fear and despondency, which drove this multitude out of the newly formed American Republic into the wilderness? There was no hope or faith left in Nathaniel Vernon.

He had left his home, his wife, and his children and had staked all on the success of the British arms. He was disappointed; he was lonely; he was poverty stricken; and he was old. In his youth he had his adventure with pioneer towns at Easton. Shelburne did not appeal to him. The twelve thousand inhabitants soon started to find other more fertile fields and the village dwindled. For three years Nathaniel Vernon lived on the dole. His strength was sapped, his ambition was gone, and his morale was at a low level. The province of Pennsylvania, his wife, his sons, and his friends faded into the distance. There was more than the six hundred miles which separated them. He had suffered much. The past he could not recall. He lived for the present only. Had his wife died? He did not know, nor did he care. Under these circumstances he married a young woman of the only kind who would marry an old man in his condition. Today, his descendants, fruits of this marriage, eke out a worthless existence in that barren land.[49]

No monument marks the grave of Nathaniel Vernon, but the bones of Easton's pioneer ferryman are buried somewhere along that Acadian coast where "still stands the forest primeval" and where

". . . from its rocky cavern the deep voiced, neighboring ocean
Speaks, and in accents disconsolate answers the wail of the forest."

---

[1]History of Delaware County, by H. G. Ashmead, 1864, p. 653.
[2]Ibid, also Land Office, Harrisburg, Pa., Survey Books D44-48, B69-236, B69-224.
[3]History of Chester County, by J. S. Futhey & G. Cope, 1881, p. 754.
[4]Historical Society of Pennsylvania, Record of Chester Meeting, 1681-1870, p. 17.
[5]Ibid, pages 189, 197, and 209.
[6]Historical Society of Pennsylvania; Abstract of Minutes of Chester Monthly Meeting at Providence, 5 mo.-30 da.-1774; 6 mo.-27 da.-1744. Record of Concord Meeting 1684 to 1870, p. 61.
[7]History of Delaware County, by H. G. Ashmead, 1884, p. 663.
[8]The Pennsylvania Magazine of History, Vol, 38, p. 112.
[9]Land Office, Harrisburg, Pa., Patent Book A17, p. 469.
[10]Historical Society of Pennsylvania, Manuscript, Itemized bill from Nathaniel Vernon to Timothy Horsfield, Executor Estate of William Parsons.

[11]Franklin's Works, by Jared Sparks, Vol. VI, page 181.

[12]Historical Society of Pennsylvania, Manuscript copy of "The Tryal of Nathaniel Vernon before James Martin, Charles Swine, Esq., Justices at Easton, the 18th March, 1758."

[13]Statutes at Large of Pennsylvania. Vol. IX, pages 409, 410.

[14]Pennsylvania Historical Society, Northampton County Manuscripts, Vol. 1727-1758. Letter from William Parsons, July 3, 1755.

[15]Historical Society of Pennsylvania, Record of Chester Monthly Meeting, 1681 to 1870, page 319.

[16]Will, Register of Wills Office, West Chester, Pa., Will-book 3, p. 519.

[17]Court House, Easton, Pa. Among old papers, Replevin, Nathaniel Vernon vs. William Parsons, returned June, 1755.

[18]Historical Society of Pennsylvania, Mss. Northampton County, Vol. 1727-1758, p. 245.

[19]Pennsylvania Archives, 1st Series, Vol. II, page 747—"By favour of Wm. Vernon." This is a typographical error, original papers in Archivists Office at Harrisburg, Pa., plainly shown "By favour of *Mr.* Vernon."

[20] Historical Society of Pennsylvania, Manuscript, Itemized bill from Nathaniel Vernon to Timothy Horsfield, Executor, Estate of William Parsons.

[21]Ibid.

[22]Ibid.

[23]Pennsylvania Archives, 1st Series, Vol. II, page 515.

[24]Ibid.

[25]Pennsylvania Archives, 1st Series, Vol. II, page 521.

[26]Historical Society of Pennsylvania, Diary of Richard Peters.

[27]Original document found among old papers in the Archives Room, Easton, Pa., court house. "Chester County ss:—

[28]Pennsylvania Historical Society, Northampton County Manuscripts.

[29] Pennsylvania Archives, 1st Series, Vol. III, page 517.

[30]Original document—Archives Room, Court House, Easton, Pa.

[31]Pennsylvania Archives, 1st Series, Vol. III, page 545.

[32]Historical Society of Pennsylvania, Philadelphia, Pa. Richard Peters Manuscripts, Letter William Parsons to Richard Peters, April 10, 1757.

[33]Recorder of Deeds Office, West Chester, Pa., Deed-book L, page 37.

[34]Original document found among old papers at Easton, Pa., Court House. "Chester County ss:—The Deposition of Nathaniel Vernon of Nether Providence taken before me etc., - - - - and the sd. Nathaniel Vernon left sd. Easton in the year 1758 (he thinks in the month of November) Nath'el Vernon. Affirmed and Subscribed before me the 16th day of June 1773. Wm. Swaffer."

[35]History of Chester County, by J. S. Futhey & G. Coue, 1881, p. 57.

[36]History of Delaware County, by H. G. Ashmead, 1884, page 661.

[37]Historical Society of Pennsylvania, Philadelphia, Pa. Abstract of Minutes of Chester Monthly Meeting at Providence, Jan. 29, 1770, and Aug. 29, 1774.

[38]Pennsylvania Archives, 2nd Series, Vol. IX, page 691.

[39]Historical Society of Pennsylvania, Abstract of Minutes of Chester Monthly Meeting at Providence, Sept. 22, 1775. "The Smedley Family," by Gilbert Cope, 1901, page 221.

[40]Pennsylvania Archives, 4th Series, Vol. III, page 937.

Pennsylvania Archives, 6th Seriees, Vol. XII, page 221.

[41]History of Delaware County by H. G. Ashmead, 1884, page 653. (Nathaniel Vernon, Jr., was the nephew and not the son of Nathaniel Vernon.)

[42]Pennsylvania Archives, 6th Series, Vol. XII, page 230.

[43]Ibid, pages 220, 226.

[44]History of Chester County, by J. S. Futhey & G. Coue, 1881, page 755.

[45]Historical Register of Officers of the Continental Army, April, 1775, to December, 1783," by F. B. Heitman, pages 560, 632.

[46]Statutes at Large of Pennsylvania, Vol. IX, page 409.

[47]See records of the Society of Cincinnati.

[48]A Memorial signed by Nathaniel Vernon is among the "Transcripts of the Commission of Enquiry into the Losses and Services of the American Loyalists." On file in the New York Public Library.

[49]Office of the Register of Probate, Shelburne, Nova Scotia. Administration of the Estate of Nathaniel Vernon granted to Margaret Vernon, his widow, in 1808. From inquiry at Shelburne it was learned that the descendants of Nathaniel Vernon were "of little value to the neighborhood."

[50]Taken from an anonymous pamphlet of the period, and here attributed to Nathaniel Vernon as it expresses his views as understood by the author.

Lewis Gordon, Northampton County's First Lawyer

Lewis Gordon, Northampton County's First Lawyer

L EWIS GORDON, one of Easton's Pioneers, was a lawyer
and the first member of the Northampton County Bar.
Nothing is known of his ancestors. The date and place of
his birth are unknown. Where he spent his boyhood days and
the extent and character of his education is information much
desired but unfortunately lacking from the records.

One or two writers tell us that he was a native of Scotland
and that "tradition" says he was out with the Pretender, Bonnie
Prince Charlie, in 1745; that he thus became involved in political
troubles and fled to America.[1] They further state that his crest
shows that he was of the Gordons of Earlston. A good biographer
would do wonders with a glamorous background of this nature
and no biographer would overlook the possibilities of this "tradition." Unfortunately, I am denied even the privilege of making
the attempt. My research has brought out facts which convince
me that the "tradition" given was only the fruits of an imagination
spurred on by a vain desire to build up a glorious set of ancestors.

Charles Edward Stuart, Pretender to the throne of Scotland
and England, affectionately called Bonnie Prince Charlie, sailed
from France on July 13th, 1745, to seize his heritage. He landed
on the island of Eriska, one of the Hebrides, off the west coast
of Scotland. After rallying some of the Scotch clans about him,
he raised his standard on the mainland of Scotland at Glenfinnan.

To the pibroch and the clatter of claymores, clan after clan
joined the Bonnie Prince as he successfully marched eastwardly
taking Edinburgh, and defeating the Royal Forces at Prestonpans.

He then started southwardly for London and crossed the Eske river into England. He pushed as far south as Derby, where, in the early part of December, he turned back. His reverses now began and, in September of 1746, he sailed for France, a disappointed and discouraged Prince.

While Prince Charles Edward Stuart was meeting with signal success in Scotland and at the time when he and his supporters were riding the crest of the wave of success, our Lewis Gordon was in the province of Pennsylvania securing a warrant for a survey of land.

Lewis Gordon may have been of the Scotch nobility, but he certainly did not flee to America an account of the Jacobite uprising in 1745, as he was in America at the time.

Either the call of the frontier or the lure of land speculation prompted Lewis Gordon to secure warrants for three tracts of land in the northern part of Bucks county. All of these tracts were in that part of Bucks which later became Northampton county. The warrants were dated November 1st, 1745. In the patent given to Gordon for these tracts, he is referred to as a merchant of Philadelphia. The patent covering 527 acres was dated July 3rd, 1749.[2]

There is some doubt as to Gordon's being a merchant. In the year in which the patent was issued, he gave a receipt for fees which he had received in payment for legal services rendered.[3]

Proof that Lewis Gordon was a Scotchman is found in the formation of the St. Andrew's Society of Philadelphia, a beneficial organization formed in 1749 to aid needy Scotch immigrants. The first by-laws of the society stipulate that members must be native born or sons of native born Scotchmen. Lewis Gordon was one of the twenty-five charter members of this society which is still in existence.[4]

The organization was successful from its start and the foremost Scotchmen living in Philadelphia were and still are members. Its first president in 1749 was Dr. Thomas Graeme, an associate justice of the supreme court of the province. From 1750 to 1753, the Honorable James Hamilton, Governor of the province of Pennsylvania, was president. He was succeeded in 1754 by another governor of the province, the Honorable Robert Hunter Morris. On down the years the presidents have been men prominent in the affairs of the province, the commonwealth and the city of Philadelphia.

The St. Andrew's Society was not without its social features. Quarterly meetings were held at which a "plain and neat" supper was served. At first these meetings were held in the various taverns of the city, but greater privacy being desired, the place of meeting was changed to the assembly room of Mr. Hamilton's wharf. From the bills for food still in the archives of the society, it is evident that the Scotch idea of a "plain and neat" supper was more extravagant than the popular idea of Scotch thrift would suggest. The cost of these repasts must have become excessive, for in 1753 a resolution was passed limiting the cost of the suppers to five shillings per man "for eating." Not a small item in the 1750s. The cost of beverages was extra.

Early in 1752 it became necessary to elect a new secretary. At a special meeting of the society held on February the 7th, four members were fined forty shillings each for refusing to serve in this capacity. Finally Lewis Gordon was elected to the office and, either from a desire to serve or through fear of a forty shilling fine, he accepted.[5] He served until the quarterly meeting in May of 1752, when he resigned his office.[6] He had decided to move his family to Easton, the town to be built at the Forks of the Delaware. In 1770, the St. Andrew Society conferred honorary membership upon him.[7]

Several years before Lewis Gordon moved to Easton, he married Mary Jenkins, the daughter of Aaron Jenkins, a merchant of Philadelphia. The marriage took place on January 4th, 1749, at Christ Church in Philadelphia.[8] The first child of this union, a daughter, was born August 28th, 1750, and was named Elizabeth. On October 24th, both Elizabeth and her mother were baptized at Christ Church and the ceremony was performed by the Rev. Mr. Gordon.[9] Elizabeth Gordon married James Taylor, a son of George Taylor, Easton's signer of the Declaration of Independence.

Bucks County has always claimed George Taylor as their signer. There is some evidence to prove that he lived in Bucks county at the time of the adoption of this immortal document, but inasmuch as he resided at Easton both before and after July the 4th, 1776, Easton also has some claim to the honor.

On July 16th, 1752, the first court was held at Easton. It was a most primitive and informal affair. William Parsons, with the help of a few residents of Williams township and some adventurers who had followed him into the wilderness, had laid out the streets, and had to some extent cleared them of undergrowth and small timber. The streets were thus visible to the eye, due to the swath cut through the verdure rather than to the wear and tear of vehicles and beasts of burden.

At this time there may have been some sheds and shacks constructed, but certainly not any building which could house even this small and primitive court. We can but assume that the justices, pioneers without any experience in legal or judicial matters, and with but little education, met under the blue canopy of heaven, perhaps in the shade of a large tree, which Parsons and his axemen had left standing in the great square, an improvised temple of justice for the county.

The Governor had appointed nine justices of the peace for the new county. How many sat at this first session is not known. William Parsons, one of the justices appointed, had been prothonotary and clerk of the court at Lancaster, and was able to direct the other justices in their maiden effort.

One of the first matters before the court was the petition of Lewis Gordon praying that he be permitted to practice as an attorney-at-law before the courts of the newly formed county. Having produced evidence that he was an active practitioner in the counties of Philadelphia and Bucks, the worthy justices granted his petition and Lewis Gordon thus became the first member of the Northampton County Bar.

What a picturesque and solemn scene this first court must have presented; the justices sitting under a large tree at a rough slab table, dignified, but nervous; William Parsons, bustling around, a veritable master of ceremonies, telling the justices what to do and how to conduct the court; and Parsons axemen, with bared heads, standing around, leaning against the trees or sitting on the stumps, a group of curious and interested spectators!

Besides organizing, the court transacted but little business at this initial session. Lewis Gordon's petition was granted, but the petition of Nathaniel Vernon to sell liquor at retail was denied.

* * *

The period of the French and Indian War was a trying one for the frontier settler. In 1754, Colonel George Washington was defeated in western Pennsylvania, and in the following year General Braddock and his Royal regiments were almost wiped out by the French and Indians on the banks of the Monongahela river.

These reverses, together with the fancied and real grievances against the English, caused the Delaware Indians to take the warpath in support of the French. Indian raids and massacres occurred first along the Susquehanna and in Bedford county, and then along the Kittatinny mountains, extending northeastwardly through the province. The scene of each atrocity was drawing closer and closer to Easton.

In November of 1755, word reached Easton of a possible raid at Gnadenhuetten. On Sunday, the 23rd of that month, Colonel John Anderson of New Jersey and his company of about fifty men marched from Easton to protect the settlement on the Lehigh, some twenty-five miles northwest of Bethlehem. With this company went Lewis Gordon and his friend, Nathaniel Vernon.[10] On Monday evening, while the company was preparing its evening meal about six miles from its destination, some Delaware Indians in full war paint, as fierce and terrifying as savage art directed by unbridled passion could make it, fell upon the little Moravian settlement. While Colonel Anderson and Lewis Gordon sat in front of the camp fire discussing the object of their march, the Indians were burning the cabins of the white settlers and the catastrophe which the militia had set out to prevent was being consummated. Eleven of the settlers were either murdered or burned to death in their dwellings.

By the time Lewis Gordon and his companions reached the site of the massacre, the Indians had fled and the mountains which but a short time before had echoed to the blood-curdling cry of the savages looked down in dread silence upon the scene of the holocaust.

As Gordon gazed upon the scalped and charred bodies laid out by tender hands, he must have closed his eyes to shut out the dreadful sight. It is not difficult to assume that his wife and three small children were uppermost in his thoughts and that a similar fate might be their portion unless the raids of the Indians were stopped.

On the return march, Gordon could not shake off the effects of this tragedy. What had happened at Gnaddenhuetten could easily happen at Easton. With the authorities of the province doing little to stop the raids of the redskins, there appeared no likelihood of a cessation of hostilities. By the time he reached Easton he had made up his mind. He would move his family to a safer community. No doubt he talked this matter over with his wife. At any rate he decided to move to Bordentown on the Delaware, in the province of New Jersey. In the previous month of May he had been admitted to practice at the New Jersey bar and as Bordentown was near Burlington, the county seat, he could easily follow his chosen profession at that place, and at Philadelphia, Easton and Newtown, the county seat of Bucks County.[11]

Just when Gordon moved is not known, but the April 1st, 1756, issue of the Pennsylvania Gazette carries his announcement that he was then located at Bordentown, where he would be happy to handle any legal business which the public might have.

During the year 1758, William Bradford, of Philadelphia, published "The American Magazine or Monthly Chronicle for the British Colonies." This magazine was issued "by a Society of Gentlemen." It is quite likely that Lewis Gordon was a member of this group. At least he represented the publication in New Jersey at Bordentown, where subscriptions could be secured at the rate of one shilling a month.[12]

Gordon attended the Indian conferences held at Easton, but not in an official capacity, for his name is not mentioned in the various records of the proceedings.

He continued his law practice in the courts of Northampton county, and his name is frequently found in the old records of the court sessions of the period.

Eventually Gordon and his family returned to Easton. At the time he moved to Bordentown his daughters, Elizabeth and Isabella, were respectively five and three years of age, while his son, John, was an infant of seven or eight months. Two children were born to Lewis and Mary Gordon during their stay in Bordentown: Aaron, born January 31st, 1757, and William, born April 23rd, 1760. One other child, whom they named Alexander, arrived on January 17th, 1762, after their return to Easton. From these dates, it is evident that they returned to their former home some time in 1760 or 1761.

In the summer of 1763 Easton experienced a severe small-pox epidemic. During this period Lewis Gordon sent his children to Phillipsburg, where they stayed until all danger had passed.

* * *

On September 16th, 1755, Lewis Gordon purchased at sheriff's sale lots numbered 88 and 89, at the southeast corner of Northampton street and the "Great Square."[13] The price paid was fifty-one pounds, which indicates that a dwelling of some kind had been erected thereon.

On October 7th, 1773, he purchased for two hundred and fifty pounds lot number 171 on the south side of Northampton street, just east of Hamilton street, where the Embassy Theater now stands. On this lot was a "good stone dwelling, two stories high," which had been constructed previous to 1756.[14]

It is quite likely that the Gordon family, when in Easton, lived on the "Great Square" from 1755 until 1773, when they moved to the Northampton street property. In 1776, Gordon purchased the lot (No. 172) at the southeast corner of Hamilton and Northampton streets, now occupied by the Lafayette Trust Company. At the time of the purchase, the property was a vacant lot.[15]

Lewis Gordon was living in the stone house on Northampton street in 1776 and at the time of his death in the summer of 1778. Just before he died, he sold the property on the Square, which included a stone dwelling, to Michael Hart for four hundred pounds, continental money. At the time of this sale, the dwelling was occupied by John Murphy, clockmaker.

In 1759 Lewis Gordon was appointed Prothonotary and Clerk of the Quarter Sessions and in 1764 he was made one of the Justices for the County.[16] These offices he held until 1776.

*   *   *

For a period of ten years after the erection of the county, the county officers and the public had more or less patiently put up with the great inconvenience of carrying on the business of the public from the residences of the various office holders. The growth in the population of the county, as the frontier was extended into the hinterland, brought many additional cases before the courts, and the constantly increasing number of litigants, witnesses, and jurors, could no longer be accommodated in the large rooms of the taverns.

In September of 1762, the Proprietors conveyed to Thomas Armstrong, John Jones, James Martin, John Rinker and Henry Allshouse, a plot of land in the center of the "Great Square." This conveyance was in trust, the land to be used exclusively for the erection and occupancy of a court house. The annual quit rent was to be one red rose.[17] Some time in 1765, ground was broken for the court house, but it was not until March of 1766 that the first session of court was held in the new building.

The records do not state what part Lewis Gordon took in the planning and erection of the building. As a lawyer and the prothonotary, he must have been intensely interested and more than likely helped in its planning.

The very attractive substantial stone building in the center of the town not only added charm and dignity to the village but gave great satisfaction to those who had legal matters or official business to transact. To all it must have given a feeling of civic pride.

Some time in the early 1750s, two land companies were organized in Connecticut. The grant for this province extended to the Pacific ocean. The object of these organizations was the colonization of that part of their grant lying in the valleys of the Delaware and Susquehanna rivers and consequently within the limits of the grant of King Charles the Second to William Penn. These companies, taking their names from the rivers, were called "The Delaware Company" and "The Susquehanna Company." At Albany, in 1754, they secured a rather irregular deed from the Indians, a deed which the Delaware Indians and the authorities of the province of Pennsylvania did not recognize. For about twenty years, the settlers from Connecticut found difficulty in gaining a foothold in this territory. During this period, the Proprietaries and the province of Pennsylvania were put to great inconvenience and expense in their endeavor to repel these unwanted Connecticut immigrants. A little blood was shed in this struggle which became known as "The Pennamite War."

From 1755 to 1761, during the French and Indian War, the Susquehanna Company made no effort to place settlers on their Wyoming claim. Some time in 1760, the governor received word of settlements being made by the Delaware Company of Connecticut at Cushitunk, on the upper Delaware river, thirty miles above the present town of Port Jervis.

In September of 1760, Richard Peters wrote to Lewis Gordon ordering him, in the name of the governor, to visit these settlements and render a full report.[18] Gordon was to take with him at least two of his Majesty's justices. They were to serve notice of trespass on the settlers and order them to leave or to suffer punishment at the hands of the authorities of the province of Pennsylvania.

Gordon desired Lewis Klotz and Timothy Horsfield to accompany him on this journey.[19] Horsfield declined to go. Klotz was objected to by the governor.[20]   But as he had been requested to make the journey and had accepted before the governor's objections were received, the original arrangement was carried out. John Moor and Aaron Depui completed the party.[21]

Friends tried to dissuade Gordon from making the trip. They claimed that the territory fifty or sixty miles north of Easton was encumbered with laurel, cedar, and spruce swamps, which could not be penetrated and were so dark that the path through them could not be seen. However Lewis Gordon wrote, "I will attempt it, and please God, perform the journey."[22]

It was decided that the justices were to assume the mien and dress of farmers in quest of land upon which to settle.[23] Accordingly on Wednesday, the 8th of October, Lewis Gordon, with the three justices, servants, and horses, left the home of Aaron Depui, north of the Water Gap, and in the guise of farmers arrived at Cushitunk on the following Saturday.[24] Their reception was entirely friendly and they secured a complete statement from the New Englanders. There were twenty men, besides women and children, in the settlement. A like number had returned to Connecticut on account of the shortage of provisions. These settlers expected to return in the spring with at least one hundred families.[25]

The settlers based their title on the Connecticut grant from the King and the Indian Purchase of 1754, and stated that they would not remove until the highest authority decided in whom the title was vested.

Lewis Gordon and his associates sent a full report to the Honorable James Hamilton, lieutenant governor and commander in chief of the province of Pennsylvania. The report was dated October 15th, 1760. This report was forwarded to Thomas Penn in England, who lost no time in laying it before Lord Halifax. In January of 1761, both the attorney general and solicitor general of England advised Thomas Penn to petition the King in council for the settlement of the dispute. However, legal opinion in England had no effect in stopping the influx of Connecticut families into the province of Pennsylvania.

In February of 1761, the Susquehanna Company decided to follow the example of the Delaware Company and open their claim on the Susquehanna river. In the spring of 1762, about seventy armed men arrived from Connecticut, but the Indians drove them back. From 1762 to 1768 the Susquehanna Company was inactive. In 1768 the Indian treaty at Fort Stanwix in New York State settled the boundary line between the lands of the white settlers and the land of the Indians. This left the Wyoming lands in the hands of the English.

Immediately the Pennsylvania land office sold thousands upon thousands of acres in tracts of from one thousand to five thousand acres. These sales were to friends of the Proprietors, officials of the province, and wealthy land speculators. After most of the fertile valley land was sold in this manner, the land was opened to settlers, who were permitted to buy tracts not larger than three hundred acres at the rate of five pounds per hundred acres.

The Pennsylvania authorities placed Amos Ogden, Charles Stewart, and John Jennings,[26] at Wyoming to operate a trading post at that place. They also received certain land concessions with the understanding that they were to defend the land against all intrusions. Both Ogden and Stewart were from the province of New Jersey and in their land dealing favored the citizens of that province.

In February, 1769, forty men from Connecticut arrived at Wyoming. John Jennings and Lewis Gordon kept the authorities of the province advised as to the movements of the settlers toward Wyoming. The appeals to the governor of Connecticut and to the authorities in England brought no relief from the immigrants. Neither did the presence of Amos Ogden and his associates have a restraining effect upon these settlers.

The officials of Northampton County, led by Lewis Gordon, were more effective. Lewis Gordon went to Wyoming in March of 1769, and served warrants on thirty-one settlers from Connecticut.[27] These men surrendered to prevent bloodshed. They were placed under arrest and brought to Easton. Eleven escaped during the journey and the remaining twenty were placed in the Easton jail until they were liberated on bail and bound over to the June term of court. They immediately returned to Wyoming. Two attorneys from Connecticut attended the June court (1769) only to learn that the bonds had been increased and the case continued until the next session. However, the Susquehanna Company continued to send settlers to Wyoming and the year 1769 marked the first stage of the permanent settlement by this company.

In August of 1769, Lewis Gordon wrote to Edmund Physick and complained bitterly of the land monopolies for private profit and the practical exclusion of the Northampton county pioneers from the Susquehanna territory.

Thomas Penn complained of Lewis Gordon's charges for his services in connection with the attempts to prevent the immigrants from Connecticut securing a hold in the valleys of the Susquehanna and Delaware rivers. Penn felt that Gordon, who held a lucrative office, should not charge for every hour he spent in service of the Proprietaries.

* * *

Lewis Gordon had become one of the wealthiest men in the county. In addition to his various salaried positions, he was constantly engaged on other duties for the province or the Proprietaries for which he was amply compensated. His law practice paid him well and he operated, under lease, the ferry across the Delaware and Lehigh rivers. The ferry was the best paying business in Easton.

The building of the court house, the influx of Connecticut settlers, the duties of prothonotary and justice of the peace, the operation of the ferry, and a large law practice made the life of Lewis Gordon a very busy one.

Shortly after he returned from Bordentown, he entered that period in the history of the country which might well be called The Eve of the Revolution. The publications of the day kept him fully informed of events and his friends and relatives in Philadelphia and his contact with the provincial officials supplemented the printed news. He was well posted in the eventful happenings of the period.

The cost of the French and Indian War had been a great drain upon the mother country. The passage by parliament in 1765 of the Sugar and Stamp Act to increase the revenue from the colonies was not received in America in a friendly manner. By these acts, asked Samuel Adams, "are we not reduced from the character of free subjects to the miserable state of tributary slaves?"

In the evening, by his fireside, Lewis Gordon, reading the New York Mercury and the Pennsylvanai Gazette, kept himself informed as to the events of the times and the inflammatory speeches of patriotic firebrands. In the Virginia House of Burgesses, Patrick Henry in an impassioned burst of oratory thundered, amid cries of "Treason": "Caesar had his Brutus; Charles the First his Cromwell; and George the Third . . . may profit by their example. If this be treason, make the most of it." It was not long before the citizens of Easton learned of this and that, in spite of the protests, the Virginia house passed resolutions declared by many to be most treasonable.

The Stamp Act required that stamped paper printed in England, and sold by officers appointed for that purpose, be used for all legal documents, for all customs paper, for appointments, for grants of privilege and franchise, for liquor license, and for many other purposes. The colonies refused to use the stamped paper, which in most cases was destroyed by mobs. In some of the colonies, the courts were ordered closed, for without the stamped paper which had been destroyed, any court proceeding or action would be illegal. The courts of Northampton county, however, held regular sessions.[28]

The merchants in the large seaport towns refused to move their ships, and trade with Great Britain fell off. As a result, parliament repealed the Stamp Act to the great rejoicing of the colonies. In New York, the celebration was climaxed by the assembly erecting on Bowling Green a lead equestrian statue of "His Majesty, King George the Third, of ever glorious memory, the Restorer of Liberty." Lewis Gordon must have applauded this gracious gesture on the part of a neighboring province. He had no reason to think that in a few years this statue, in the form of bullets, would be directed against the forces of this same king.

Parliament now passed an act levying a small tax on a few articles, among which were tea and Madeira wine.

Events of great importance were of more frequent occurrence, and the small town of Easton, in common with other parts of the province, began to discuss the pros and cons of the rights and privileges of the mother country and of the colonies.

A Board of Customs Commissioners was sent to Boston to collect the import taxes. The battleship "Romney" floating in the harbor enforced the authority of the commission.

The Boston massacre occurred on March 5th, 1770.

About this time, the New York Assembly was suspended by an act of parliament.

In 1771 and 1772, the differences between England and her colonies in America seemed to have blown over.

On December 16th, 1773, a cargo of tea, consigned by the East India Company to the unpopular governor of Massachusetts (Thomas Hutchinson) and valued at fourteen thousand pounds, was thrown into Boston Harbor, because the consignees refused to return it to its port of shipment. At New York and Philadelphia, the company's tea ships returned to England without attempting to land their cargo. Consequently, parliament remodeled the Massachusetts charter, removed the governor, and made General Gage, commander of the American forces, governor of that province.

King George the Third, he of the leaden statue, now the destroyer of liberty, declared: "The die is now cast, the colonies must either submit or triumph."

* * *

In the fall of 1774, the first meeting of the Continental Congress was held in Philadelphia. This congress adopted a series of resolutions known as The Association, by which the signers bound themselves and recommended to the people that certain retaliatory measures be put in force. There was no doubt a period when Lewis Gordon and his household patriotically denied themselves the pleasure of a cup of tea.

One of the recommendations of the congress was that each city, town and county organize a committee, whose business it would be to observe the conduct of all persons, those who refused to sign the Association as well as those who signed it.

Just a few days before Christmas of 1774, there gathered at the court house in Easton a considerable number of representative freeholders of the county. This meeting was called as the result of the resolution of the Association of the Continental Congress, and on the recommendation of the assembly of the pro-

vince of Pennsylvania to select a Committee of Observation and Inspection. George Taylor, Peter Kachlein, and Henry Kooken were chosen as Judges of Election. As a result of this meeting, thirty citizens representing all the townships of the county were the members selected. Lewis Gordon, Peter Kachein, and George Taylor were the members selected from Easton. The committee immediately met and selected from their number the three Easton members, and Jacob Arndt, John Okely, and Henry Kooken, to be a standing committee of correspondence.[29]

Lewis Gordon was elected to serve as treasurer and Robert Traill, who was not a member of the committee, was chosen clerk, a position for which he received remuneration.[30]

George Taylor was chairman of the committee up until July 1st, 1775, after which date his name does not appear in the minutes. Lewis Gordon was then chosen chairman and served in that capacity as well as treasurer until he voluntarily withdrew from the committee.

The membership of the committee changed from time to time, but Robert Traill continued as clerk throughout its entire existence.

The duties of the Committee of Observation and Inspection were varied, numerous, and trying, and carried great responsibility. During this period some of the work of the courts fell upon the committees. In addition to this work, it was their duty to see that the county quota of men for the militia was raised, equipped, and officered. The granting of commissions was part of their duty. Persons of tory tendencies, whose actions and speech were objectionable, were summoned before the committee and unless they publicly admitted their error, paid the costs and gave security for their good behavior, they were invariably sentenced to jail. A few weeks in the jail soon convinced the culprit that an outward compliance with the demands of the committee was preferable to a prolonged stay in the Easton jail, caused by a bragging manner and a sharp tongue.

Lewis Gordon, as chairman, carried his responsibility with dignity and ability. He attended to the numerous details with fidelity and accuracy. While at times his decisions and actions may seem harsh, it must be remembered that the colonies were at war with the mother country.

On July the 8th, 1776, he stood on the court house steps and with bared head listened to Robert Levers read the Declaration of Independence. The citizens of the town and the surrounding country had gathered to hear what was destined to become an immortal document. With serious faces they quietly listened and a solemn silence held them for a time after Levers had finished the reading with these final words: "with a firm reliance on the protection of Divine Providence we mutually pledge to each other our lives, our fortune, and our sacred honor." The First Battalion was then drawn up at attention, the drum and fife corps struck up, and the Moravian bell in the cupola pealed forth the birth of a nation.

As the cheers of the crowd mingled with the music and the ringing of the bell, Lewis Gordon walked slowly home. He had worked hard in an endeavor to make England alter her attitude toward the colonies, but not for liberty or independence. The situation was now changed and he was greatly disturbed. However he continued as chairman until December 2nd, 1776, when he sent word to the committee that he would no longer attend their meetings.[31]

With the refusal of Lewis Gordon to continue on the Committee of Observation, the natural question arises: was he a patriot, a tory, or a traitor?

It will be necessary to understand the status of the conflict between England and America in the early part of December 1776 in order to determine the effect it may have had on the decision of Lewis Gordon to withdraw from active participation in the cause of the new republic. In April of 1775, the attempt to arrest Samuel Adams and John Hancock was followed by the defeat of the English forces at Concord and Lexington. The following month, Ethan Allen and Benedict Arnold captured Ticonderoga. In July of that year, General Washington took charge of the army before Boston and, on March 17th, 1776, General Howe with eleven thousand British troops and one thousand loyalists evacuated that town and sailed for Halifax. In the meantime, General Arnold led an expedition through the wilderness of Maine in an unsuccessful, though gallant, attempt to capture Quebec.

Early in 1776 George Washington, who had left Boston with his army, started preparations for the defense of New York City, which the British were planning to attack. Now began a series of defeats, and the future of the colonies became most uncertain. In June of that year, the American forces were defeated at Three Rivers in Canada, and were compelled to retreat up the Richelieu river, across Lake Champlain to Crown Point.

On July the 4th, 1776, the Declaration of Independence was adopted.

In August, the American troops were defeated at the Battle of Long Island. In September, the Americans were driven from lower New York and retreated to Harlem. In the same month, Washington won a small skirmish called the Battle of Harlem

Heights. The Battle of White Plains was fought with a slight advantage in favor of the English. However, a few days later, reinforcements for General Howe caused Washington to withdraw.

In November, Fort Washington on the upper end of Manhattan surrendered to the British. Two days later, Fort Lee, on the New Jersey side of the Hudson, was abandoned and the American forces put to rout. The American losses were three thousand men. The loss in ammunition was appalling and more than the Continental treasury and the limited resources of the colonies could well stand.

It was at this particular moment, with the American army in full retreat, that Lewis Gordon sent word to the Committee of Observation that he would no longer attend their meetings. As chairman of this committee, he knew all the facts in regard to the successes and failures of the Continental army. He understood the difficulty of raising men, arms, ammunition, and equipment. He was aware that the men composing the army were without military training or discipline, and that their enlistment was for a very short period. He had seen the men from Northampton county march away to join the army of General Washington. Many of these men were personal acquaintances and friends, untrained and poorly equipped, but inspired with a belief in the righteousness of their cause, and steeled in a determination to win at any sacrifice. As a background to this picture, he saw the British army and their mercenaries, the Hessians, well trained and fully equipped, with the vast resources of a wealthy nation behind them and at that moment victoriously pursuing the Continental army and militia across New Jersey, perhaps in the direction of Easton.

Early in December of this year (1776) General Washington wrote to congress that "the situation of our affairs is truly critical." Under these conditions, many who had before espoused the cause of the new republic now openly declared for the crown. Lewis Gordon, who in 1755, fled from Easton through fear of the Indians, no doubt now feared for the safety and well-being of himself and his family. He did not declare in favor of the king, nor did he take the oath of allegiance to the United States of America.

Hardly had Lewis Gordon resigned, when the horrors of war were forcibly brought home. On December 3rd, Abraham Berlin, who had taken Gordon's place as chairman of the Committee of Observation, notified the Moravians that Bethlehem had been selected as the place for the general hospital.

For the next few days the wounded, the maimed, and the dying, crossed the ferry at Easton and continued on through to Bethlehem. Wagons of every description fiilled with suffering humanity were snagged down the Jersey bank of the Delaware, onto the ferry and tediously poled across the river. The groans of anguish from the pain-racked human freight, mingled with the cursing of the drivers, as the horses tugged to get the wagons up the river bank and then up Ferry street hill, brought to Easton the awful horror of war. Many of the injured had only their ragged clothes to cover them and these were unwashed and caked with blood and filth. The extreme cold added to the hardships of their journey. Nearly five hundred of these moaning, half dead men, were hauled up from the ferry and through the rutted, frozen streets of Easton and on to Bethlehem. Some of these unfortunates remained in Easton to be cared for. Several days later, wagons followed with the hospital supplies.

* * *

As Lewis Gordon stood on the river bank and watched this heart-rending scene, he likewise stood at the crossroads of life. Which road should he travel? On the one, the new Republic moved forward to martial music and flying flags and then retreated, crest-fallen, discouraged, and wounded. On the other, were the forces of the British government. They too surged forward and backward. What passed through the mind of Lewis Gordon will never be known. It is probable that he never got beyond the crossroads and that he was still standing there undecided when the grim reaper called him two years later.

A few days of normal activity and again the ferry was busy to the point of inadequacy. On December 17th (1776), General

John Sullivan with several thousand troops, the remnants of General Lee's division, passed through Easton. The dilatory tactics of General Lee, resulting in his own capture, made it necessary for his troops to detour around Morristown (N.J.) and join General Washington on the west bank of the Delaware north of Trenton, via Easton and Bethlehem.

These troops had tasted bitter defeat; their ranks had been decimated; and they were tired, haggard, tattered, and slovenly. The gun and the accoutrement of the soldier seemed a staggering load which he could hardly bear. The fife and drum hung idle at the side of the musician as he stolidly trudged along.

* * *

The last years of the life of Lewis Gordon were very unhappy ones. As prothonotary, an officer of the county appointed by the Provincial Council with the approval of the Proprietaries, he had enjoyed the respect and admiration of the citizens. As chairman of the local Committee of Observation, he was considered the foremost patriot of the county. His activities in raising troops and supplies and in punishing those whose tory activities brought them within his jurisdiction stamped him as an ardent advocate of the American cause. His sudden refusal to attend the committee meeting as a member stunned the community. His continued contempt of the order of the committee to appear before them and explain his actions led to but one conclusion. His defiance in telling the committee that if they wished to see him, they could call upon him, brought down upon him the contempt of the majority and the retaliation of those in office.

One month after his withdrawal (January 2nd, 1777) from all activities in support of the new government, the Supreme Executive Council ordered the committee of Northampton county to immediately take over the ferry, which was operated by Lewis Gordon, and operate it under their own control and regulation.[32] It is difficult to tell from the records if this order was put into effect. On several occasions, Robert Levers, who had succeeded Lewis Gordon as prothonotary, wrote to the council, Secretary Matlack, and to the governor, and complained of the lax manner in which the ferry was operated and the lack of guards at the ferry. A vast number of wagons, officers, soldiers and travellers, were constantly passing over the river. The ferry thus became a source of great profit and as this ferriage was paid to Lewis Gordon or one of his family, the opportunity to gather items of interest to the enemy and then pass them on was unlimited.

Some time early in November (1777), Joseph Jenkins, Lewis Gordon's brother-in-law, came from Philadelphia to take charge of the ferry for Mr. Gordon.[33] As the political preferences of Joseph Jenkins were unknown in Easton, his holding the important post as ferryman caused much criticism.

If Joseph Jenkins ever operated the ferry, it was for a very short time. In January or February of 1778, Lewis Gordon sublet the ferry to Jacob Abel, and Peter Ealer. Gordon had no sooner sublet the ferry than Levers wrote to Timothy Matlack, secretary of the commonwealth, as follows:—[34] "– – – Mr. Gordon has lately leased the ferry to one Jacob Abel and one Peter Ealer; I have nothing against the men, they have both taken the oath of allegiance, but yet, in Justice to my Country, I must add, that I have my Fears." It would seem that the fact that they leased the ferry from Mr. Gordon was their greatest crime.

*   *   *

Robert Levers today is looked upon as possibly *the* leading patriot of Northampton County during these troubled times. Still in reading his many letters written to the authorities, you cannot help but feel that he had an excellent opinion of himself, that he tried very hard to ingratiate himself into the good graces of those in authority, and that, for some reason, he felt a great animosity toward Lewis Gordon.

*   *   *

In August of 1777, John Jennings, the sheriff, acting under instructions received from the Executive Council, called upon Mr. Gordon and placed him under arrest.[35] The letter accompanying the order of arrest stated that since all of the officers of the king of Great Britain located in Philadelphia had been arrested and held as prisoners of war, it was but right that the same proceeding should extend to all parts of the province and that they were therefore enclosing the warrant for the arrest of Lewis Gordon. There was no other charge against him. Mr. Gordon was immediately placed on parole, which permitted his freedom within six miles of his residence, with the one exception that he was not to cross to the east side of the Delaware river. He felt the restriction of being unable to cross the river in his own ferry, but otherwise his parole was liberal and he was not inconvenienced in the least. He was not surprised at his arrest nor did the fact that he was virtually a prisoner affect him to any great extent. He had become more or less accustomed, although not reconciled, to the snubs and insults of the public. He spent most of the time within his dwelling. This was due in part to the fact that his health was failing.

The activities of the citizens annoyed him. The "Great Square" had become a drill ground where the ununiformed recruits were taught the rudiments of drill and the manual of arms, often a sapling cut to length substituting for a gun. The shrill notes of the fife and the rattle of the drum furnished the time for the awkward squad whose members, enthused with patriotism, were eager to acquire the technique of a soldier.

The court house, where Lewis Gordon spent a great part of his time as a lawyer, prothonotary, magistrate, and lately as chairman of the Committee of Observation, was the center of the town's activities. The many meetings of the committee, the increased activity of the county, civil, criminal, and military, focused on this attractive stone building in the center of the square.

A large quantity of stores were daily passing through Easton from the north and northwest on their way to the front. At times quantities of ammunition and other supplies for the army were stored in Easton. For a time there were no regular troops stationed in the town to guard the inhabitants or the stores. A few decrepit individuals who are reported "as dying by inches for want of cloathing" formed the only guard for the supplies and these were insufficient to prevent a certain amount of pillage which was constantly taking place.

Men about to depart for the front, those whose terms of service had expired, as well as the convalescent wounded, were constantly on the streets or celebrating in the taverns.

The women of the town, when their household duties were completed, helped nurse the sick and injured in the church on North Pomfret street.

Strange to say that in the midst of all these activities pertaining to the birth struggles of the republic, there mingled officers of the English army. These men were prisoners of war who had been sent to Easton and placed on parole, giving them the freedom of the town. Several of these officers lodged with Lewis Gordon, where in the most friendly manner they whiled away the hours playing backgammon with the erstwhile chairman of the Committee of Observation.[37] Lewis Gordon was now living in a community of which he was no longer a part, a man without a country.

*   *   *

John Gordon, the eldest son of Lewis Gordon, was 22 years old during the winter of 1777-78. He spent considerable time in Philadelphia, where he stayed with his sister Isabella. Isabella's husband, Thomas Affleck, had been suspected of tory tendencies and, in the fall of 1777, had been placed under arrest and, with a number of other citizens of Philadelphia sent to Virginia.[38] In April of 1778, he was returned to Pennsylvania and given his freedom. John Gordon was in Philadelphia at the time the British entered the city. He remained there for some time during the British occupation and returned to Easton on February 18th. Robert Levers immediately sent for him and plainly told him that he had become a suspicious character, due to his long and voluntary stay in the enemy occupied city of Philadelphia. Levers not only insisted that John take the oath of allegiance, but that he sign a parole and give security. John agreed to take the oath, but asked until the next day in order to consider the matter. The afternoon of the same day he rode up the Bushkill to John Arndt's and before Arndt he voluntarily swore allegiance to the United States of America.[39] John Arndt, knowing nothing of Robert

Levers' plan, never mentioned the matter of parole or security. The next morning John Gordon called on Robert Levers and much to that gentleman's discomfort frankly stated what he had done. Mr. Levers, who on every occasion tried to influence the authorities against the father, now considered it his duty to carefully watch the son. He soon learned that young Gordon visited Philadelphia after he had taken the oath. On March the 8th, when John Gordon returned from Philadelphia, Levers sent him a note demanding that he call upon him immediately.[40] (Levers lived on South Pomfret street; the site of his residence is now occupied by the Pomfret building.) Young Gordon could see no reason for his obeying a demand from Robert Levers and ignored the note. Levers then issued a warrant and in fear that the serving of the warrant by the constable might be resisted, he requested Colonel Sidman of the local militia to furnish some assistance.[41] Much to Mr. Levers' chagrin, Colonel Sidman secured a young lieutenant of a Massachusetts regiment, who, with four soldiers armed with fixed bayonets called upon Mr. Levers and offered him their assistance. The fact that the soldiers were Continentals and from another state infuriated him, for he considered that the situation was one which could easily be handled by the local militia. He dismissed the lieutenant and his squad and sent the constable single handed to bring in young Gordon.

The meeting between Mr. Levers and John Gordon was rather heated. John Gordon was so furious over the treatment which both he and his father had received at the hands of Mr. Levers that he lost all respect for the older man and for the position which he held in the community. He frankly told Mr. Levers that he did not intend to dance after him. If he wanted to see him, he knew where he lived. If he wished to go to Philadelphia to visit his sister, it was nobody's business. Mr. Levers told the young man that he was impertinent, that his many trips to Philadelphia cast suspicion upon him and that he had taken the oath of allegiance under conditions which were a direct insult to him. He demanded and secured his parole, which he immediately, and from the tone of his letter of transmittal I might add gleefully, sent to the Supreme Executive Council, then meeting at Lancaster.

On July 27th (1778), William the second son of Lewis Gordon, took the oath of allegiance. He also went to John Arndt for this purpose. William Gordon was at that time 18 years of age. A younger brother, Alexander George Gordon, was 16 years old.

* * *

On March 7th, 1778, Robert Levers wrote to council and informed them that he was persuaded that Lewis Gordon was a "fixed, determined enemy of the American States" — — and — — "is capable of being a dangerous man."[42] The part of this letter dealing with Lewis Gordon, as well as subsequent ones, was apparently ignored by the Supreme Executive Council until April 23rd (1778). On that date, council determined to discharge Lewis Gordon from his parole and liberate him from all restraint whatsoever.[43] A communication was therefore sent to Mr. Levers, instructing him to wait upon Mr. Gordon and inform him of the act of council and return to him his signed parole. What a bitter pill this must have been for Mr. Levers!

Mr. Gordon was now in ill health and as he appeared in no hurry to be released, Mr. Levers did not formally liberate him until his parole, which had not been forwarded by council, could be returned to him. On May 20th, Mr. Levers wrote that both Lewis Gordon, Esquire. and his son, John Gordon, had been discharged and that Lewis Gordon had taken the oath of allegiance a few days before the date of his letter.[44]

Some time in January or February of 1778, Mary Jenkins Gordon, the wife of Lewis Gordon, died.[45] This was the climax of all the trouble which had steadily been piling upon the late prothonotary, since that memorable day in December of 1776, when he withdrew from the Committee of Observation. His failing health took a turn for the worse and on February 22nd (1778), he wrote his will.[46] He lived to be released from his arrest and parole and long enough to somewhat reestablish himself in the opinion of the local citizens, when, on that day in

May, he took the oath of allegiance to the United States of America.

Some time during the summer of 1778, he died. It is quite possible that with good health and a slightly longer life, he might have regained his former position. The funeral services were held at his residence, and the Rev. Ingold, pastor of the German Reformed church on North Pomfret street, preached the sermon.[47]

After the services, the funeral procession started for the burial plot on Juliana street, now the grounds of the Easton Public Library. A peculiar stillness fell on the small groups of citizens who had gathered and, with mingled feelings, watched all that was mortal of Lewis Gordon pass on its last westward journey. As the rays of the afternoon sun came over the hill at Northampton and John streets, the little funeral cortege turned into Juliana street and was lost to view.

There, on the hill overlooking the village which he, more than any other man, had helped to build, they buried Easton's first attorney, "unwept, unhonored, and unsung."

---

[1]"Gordons of Virginia"—1918, by A. C. Gordon.

[2]Land Office—Harrisburg, Pa.—Patent Book A-14, p. 519.

[3]Pennsylvania Historical Society — Autograph Collection — Original receipt signed by Lewis Gordon.

[4]Pennsylvania Historical Society—Historical Catalogue the St. Andrew's Society of Philadelphia, Page 23, etc.

[5]Ibid; also "Pennsylvania Gazette," issues of Nov. 28, 1751, May 28, 1752, August 13, 1752.

[6]Ibid.

[7]Pennsylvania Historical Society—Historical Catalogue the St. Andrew's Society of Philadelphia.

[8]Pennsylvania Archives—2nd Series, Vol. I, p. 112.

[9]Pennsylvania Magazine of History—Vol. 16, p. 116.

[10]Pennsylvania Archives, 1st Series, Vol. II, p. 521.

[11]New Jersey Colonial Documents, Vol. XX, p. 14.

[12]Ibid, p. 148.

[13]Recorder of Deeds Office, Court House, Easton, Pa., Deed Book C, Vol. 1, p. 472.

[14]Ibid, p. 50.

[15]Land Office, Harrisburg, Pa., Patent Book AA-9, p. 220.

[16]Pennsylvania Archives, 2nd Series, Vol. 9, pages 811, 812.

[17]Land Office, Harrisburg, Pa., Patent Book AA-6: p. 115.
[18]Pennsylvania Archives, 1st Series, Vol. III: p. 754.
[19]Ibid, p. 775.
[20]Lbid, p. 777.
[21]Ibid.
[22]Ibid.
[23]Pennsylvania Colonial Records, Vol. VIII, p. 564.
[24]Ibid.
[25]Ibid, p. 565.
[26]Pennsylvania Archives, 1st Series, Vol. IV: p. 350.
[27]Pennsylvania Historical Society, Autograph Collection, original letter Lewis Gordon to John Penn, March 18, 1769.
[28]The various court and county records still in existence at Easton indicate that court sessions were held regularly.
[29]Pennsylvania Archives, 2nd Series, Vol. XV: p. 605.
[30]Ibid, p. 606.
[31]Ibid, 631.
[32]Pennsylvania Colonial Recoords, Vol. XI: p. 73.
[33]Pennsylvania Archives, 1st Series, Vol. VI, p. 6.
[34]Ibid, p. 342.
[35]Penncylvania Archives, 1st Series, Vol. V: p. 489, 490.
[36]Ibid, p. 651.
[37]Register of Wills,' Office, Court House, Easton, Pa., Sale of Personal property of Lewis Gordon lists a backgammon table.
[38]Pennsylvania Colonial Records, Vol. XI, pages 284, 309, 460, and 473.
[39]Pennsylvania Archives, 1st Series, Vol. VI: p. 345.
[40]Ibid, p. 344.
[41]Ibid, p. 346.
[42]Ibid, p. 342.
[43]Ibid, p. 435.
[44]Ibid, p. 534.
[45]Ibid, p. 342.
[46]Register of Wills' Office, Court House, Easton, Pa. Will of Lewis Gordon.
[47]Register of Wills Office, Court House, Easton, Pa. Account of John Gordon, Executor and last will and testament of Lewis Gordon lists payment to Rev. Ingold for funeral sermon and to John Dingler for digging grave. Ingold and Dingler were members of the German Reformed Church, so Lewis Gordon must have been buried in their burying ground.

The Indian Treaty
of 1758

The Indian Treaty of 1758

AS a result of the European Seven Years' War (1756-1763) a maritime and colonial conflict broke out between England and France. That part of the conflict which was fought in North America became known as the French and Indian War. This was due to the fact that large numbers of the American Indians joined the French.

The reason for the alienation of the Pennsylvania Indians was a debatable question in 1758. Today, one hundred and eighty-two years later, it has not been definitely determined. It is too involved to attempt an explanation in connection with this paper.

It must, however, be understood that at the time of the French and Indian War the Indians in Pennsylvania had been driven to the north and west of the Blue Mountains. The Delawares and a few Shawnees occupied the valley of the North Branch of the Susquehanna River. These natives were quite embittered against the English. The Shawnees and some Delawares lived in the extreme western part of the province. These western Indians were close neighbors of the French who then held the Ohio Valley and who had cultivated their friendship.

There were very few Shawnee and Delaware Indians among those who aided the French in defeating General Braddock on the banks of the Monongahela River in July (9th) of 1755. This defeat of the English was the final and deciding factor which caused the western Indians to enter the conflict on the side of the French.

By October of 1755 the frontier west of the Susquehanna was stained with the blood of the massacred settlers. At the mouth of Penn's Creek, fourteen men and women were murdered and in the valleys of what are now Fulton and Franklin counties forty-three were massacred in one day.

What were happy homes became funeral pyres lighting the sky with a red glow which spread terror throughout the frontier. Like the first taste of blood to the savage beast, the fury and frenzy of the Indians, after their first taste of rapine and murder, knew no bounds. Many settlers were carried into captivity and the atrocities committed on the living and the dead defy description.

While the western Indians were committing these depredations, an Iroquois Indian named Scarouady, a chief of the Oneidas, who had fought with Braddock, visited the Delaware and Shawnee Indians living in the valley of the North Branch of the Susquehanna. He secured their promise to fight with the English, provided Pennsylvania would take up arms against the French.

In November (1755) Scarouady went to Philadelphia and demanded an audience with the Governor, the "wise-men", and the people of the province.[1]

The Governor, the Council, the Assembly, and a large number of citizens gathered in the State House to hear what this proud warrior had to say. In what "was the most dramatic spectacle that the State House saw prior to the Revolution" this aboriginal forest diplomat mounted the rostrum, squared his shoulders, and without supplication or mincing of words told the Governor and the entire province what they must do to retain the friendship of the Delawares.

He demanded that the province of Pennsylvania supply the Indians with arms and ammunition and raise troops to fight the French.

The peace-loving Quaker-controlled assembly was not sympathetic, whereupon Scarouady, turning to them, concluded:—
"We do, therefore, once more invite and request you to act like men, and be no longer women, pursuing weak measures, that render your names despicable."[2]

The Quaker Assembly refused to approve the raising of funds unless the Proprietaries' lands were taxed. The proprietorial Council refused to tax these lands. Under these conditions the demands of the Indians could not be granted. No funds were available.

Scarouady received the message of refusal from the Governor with amazement, saying that it would occasion the absolute defection of the Delawares.

The alienation of the Delaware and Shawnee Indians was now complete.

The Indian depredations now rolled back the frontier and the wave of retreating terror stricken settlers, reduced to abject poverty, filled to overflowing the little villages of Nazareth, Bethlehem, and Easton. On top of this situation, Easton, without an opportunity to say 'yea' or 'nay', had the questionable privilege and honor of being selected as the place for holding the conferences with the Indians.

The Treaties held at Easton were an effort to regain the friendship of the natives. Their success was an important factor in the triumph of the forces of Great Britain.

The trails from the lands of the Iroquois, the Delawares and the Shawnees, whether by way of Wyoming or Minisink, passed through Bethlehem on their way to Philadelphia. When Teedyuscung, chief of the Delawares, decided to accept the invitation of the Governor of Pennsylvania to hold a peace treaty, he, accompanied by a small number of Delaware Indians, came to Bethlehem. There he stopped and instructed New Castle, the Governor's Indian messenger, to tell the Governor that he had come to the Forks of the Delaware, where he would await the lighting of the council fire.[3]

The Moravians made such a strong protest[4] against the holding of the treaty at Bethlehem that Governor Morris instructed William Parsons to conduct the Indians to Easton and there to make proper provision to care for them.[5] This order had hardly been carried out when the Governor changed his mind, and issued a second set of instructions to Parsons.[6] These demanded that the Indians be returned to Bethlehem. However, these orders were given without considering the chief of the Delawares. Teedyuscung refused to return to Bethlehem. He sent word to the Governor that, at his invitation he had come to Easton "a distance of four hundred miles" and that there he would stay, and if the Governor wished to see him he should come to Easton. He demanded to know what they meant by sending him from place to place like a child.[7] So the first Indian treaty was held at Easton.

It was a custom of the Indians, based on superstition, that the location of a council fire should not be changed until the work for which the council was called had been completed. As the subsequent meetings were continuations of the first treaty, they also were held at Easton. So, with one exception, Easton became the seat of all the Indian treaties held in Pennsylvania during the French and Indian War.

* * *

Our story opens in the fall of 1758. General Forbes was cutting a road through the mountains in the southwestern part of the province in order to attack the French at Fort Duquesne. At Easton, three treaties had been held, two in 1756 and one in 1757. This infant village, only six years old, with not over twenty-five houses and a population of about one hundred and fifty souls, was about to pass through the throes of another Indian treaty.

All roads now led to Easton and all manner of men traveled these roads.

The forests were a blaze of autumnal foliage. Against the dark green of the pines and hemlocks, the vivid yellows, browns, and reds of the maples and oaks, stood out in a brilliant display of color, while the scarlet of the sumach ran like a ribbon of fire along the edge of the clearings.

Out of the forests of the north came the Six Nations, the Mohawks, Oneidas, Onondagas, Cayugas, Senecas, and Tuscaroras. From the valley of the Susquehanna came the Delawares and the Shawnees, led by their chief, Teedyuscung.

From the west bank of the Hudson River and the upper Delaware valley came the Munsies, the Mohicans, and the Wapings.

The Nanticokes, the Tutelos, and the Chugnuts accompanied the Delawares to Easton.

The records state there were five hundred and ten Indians who attended this treaty,[8] composed of thirteen principal chiefs, ten lesser chiefs, about two hundred warriors, and nearly three hundred women and children.

There was no equal suffrage among the Indians. The squaws did not journey from the finger-lake country to Easton to participate in the council fire, to advise the Indian braves in matters of diplomacy, or to see the world and civilization. On a trip of this kind there were blankets and provisions to be carried and on the homeward journey there was the additional luggage caused by the presents given to the Indians. These women furnished the transportation. They were the pack animals who, footsore, weary, and bent, carried this material over the wilderness trail, while the men, as proud warriors, walked in the van with a gun in the crook of their elbow and a tomahawk in their belt.

Governor Denny, by virtue of his position as head of the provincial government, led the English delegates from Philadelphia through the rolling farm lands of lower Bucks County and over the wooded hills of Williams Township down into the little hamlet of Easton.

The provincial Assembly, always at loggerheads with the Governor, sent a committee of eight,[9] all of whom were Quakers.

The Council, at the request of the Governor of the Province were always of the Proprietary party and worked in close harmony, but this ill-tempered Governor had succeeded in losing the sympathy and cordial cooperation of his own Council.

Governor Denny had invited the Governors of New Jersey, New York, Maryland, and Virginia to attend the treaty.[10] All the Governor's declined except Governor Bernard of New Jersey. His acceptance was due entirely to the fact that the Minisink

Indians had requested his presence. Sir William Johnson, who two years previous, had been appointed sole Superintendent of the Affairs of the Six Nations and "other northern Indians", found it inconvenient to accept the Governor's invitation and delegated his deputy, George Croghan, to represent him.[11]

The treaty was originally scheduled for the middle of September and some of the Indians arrived at that time. Conrad Weiser, of Berks County, Indian Agent and Official Interpreter for the province, came to Easton early to look after them. As they were constantly drunk and very disorderly, he feared ill consequences and applied to the Governor for help.[12]

At the request of the Governor, Richard Peters agreed to aid Weiser in his difficult task.[13] Peters had been the very efficient Secretary of the province under a number of Governors, and was Secretary at this time, although a short time before, he had been dropped from office during an unusually bad fit of gubernatorial temper.[14]

Without doubt, the Hon. William Denny, Governor of the province, and George Croghan, Deputy Agent of Indian Affairs, should have been the two men to direct the destinies of this important conference. However, as far as their contribution to the success of the treaty was concerned, they might just as well have remained away. Richard Peters, with the able assistance of Conrad Weiser, was the impressario who staged this drama of the frontier with a heterogeneous cast selected from irreconcilable groups. Out of a hopeless chaos he wrought a peace which materially helped in the success of the Forbes Expedition and in the winning of the French and Indian War.

In addition to the officials and the legislative bodies of the province there was another group of citizens from Philadelphia who were intensely interested in the Indians and who attended all the treaties. The Society of Friends had formed an organization called the Friendly Association, the object of which was to befriend the Indian to an extent consistent with their profession of "fearing God, honouring the King, and promoting Peace among men."[15]

The Indians were very friendly with the Quakers whom they looked upon as the children of William Penn, whose memory they held in great reverence. The Quakers not only advised the Indians at the various conferences, but they raised large sums of money and gave them presents which in some instances overshadowed the gifts of the province. They also held private conferences with the Indians. Very often their advice was contrary to the desires of the Proprietors and soon the Penns, the Governor, and the entire Proprietary party became incensed at this interference. In their opinion this religious organization was obstructing the early establishment of peace, by giving the Indians encouragement, an exalted opinion of themselves, and a firm belief in either the justice of their claims or in the ability to convert the government to their point of view.

Before the treaty of 1757, the Governor wrote to the Friendly Association and told them that the Proprietors had directed him not to allow them to participate in any treaty or to permit them to give presents to the Indians. He told them that since their activities had given offence to the ministers, they should not, as an organization, attend the forthcoming treaty.[16]

The reply to this demand of the Governor was a lengthy explanation of their activities and closed with a statement of their intention of going to Easton and an offer to augment the presents to be given to the Indians by the province.[17] They said:—"The business to be transacted there is of so much consequence to the lives, liberties, and properties of the people of this province, that should we omit to attend there – – – we should be deficient in our duty as Christians and Englishmen, denominations we hold more dear to us than any title or appelations whatsoever."

The effort of the Governor to stop the activities of the Quakers at the treaty of 1757 was so futile that no attempt was made to keep them from the treaty of 1758. At this conference the Friendly Association was represented by a large and active group.

The Penns and the Proprietary party were not the only ones who objected to the interference of the Friends in Indian affairs. The Quakers lived in the environs of Philadelphia in perfect safety, a safety made secure by the Scotch-Irish and the Germans who lived on the frontier. It was these pioneers who suffered from the depredations of the Indians. They felt that the Assembly, composed mostly of Friends, was the cause of the failure of the province to provide proper means of defense; and that the Friendly Association by supporting the Indians in their cause against the government prevented the speedy settlement of the Indian troubles.

It was the Germans and the Scotch-Irish, and not the Friends, who were killed in the Indian raids and it was their wives and their children who were murdered or carried off into captivity.

Pamphlets and articles in the newspapers were now published condemning the Quakers. Caricatures and verse were the popular methods used to express the opinion and anger of the "Presbyterians" as the Scotch-Irish and German protestant denominations were then sometimes called. Here is a doggerel verse published at the time:—[18]

> "Go on good Christians, never spare
> To give your Indians clothes to wear;
> Send 'em good beef and pork and bread,
> Guns, powder, flints, and stores of lead,
> To shoot your neighbor through the head.
> Encourage every friendly savage,
> To murder, burn, destroy and ravage.
> Of Scotch and Irish let them kill
> As many thousands as they will,
> That you may lord it o'er the land,
> And have the whole and sole command."

Some of the articles appearing in the newspapers were cruel and unjust. They imputed the affection of the Quakers for the Indians was entirely due to the charms of the Indian Sqaws. True the Indian women tried to enhance their beauty by the use of cosmetics, buying their red paint by the pound, yet not by the very wildest flight of the imagination could they be called 'glamour girls'.

* * *

The Moravians were also interested in the Indians. Like the Quakers they were a peace loving people who dressed plainly, led a simple life and were opposed to war. Their relations with the Indians were entirely unlike those of the Society of Friends. They had not come to America to escape persecution and to be free to worship God in their own way. They were missionaries and had crossed the Atlantic to convert the heathen aborigines. All of their activities were directed toward the accomplishment of that purpose. The Friends, on the other hand, as a religious organization, were not actively engaged in missionary work.

The Moravians did not participate in or even attend the Indian treaties. It is true that David Zeisberger, one of their missionaries, was present at the conferences held at Easton and was here in 1758,[19] but his attendance was purely a personal matter, and his object was to renew old acquaintances with the Indians, to keep the Christian Indian steadfast in his faith, to make new converts, and to reclaim those who had been baptized but had since fallen from grace.

Teedyuscung had been baptized on March 12, 1750, and given the name of Gideon.[20] What a prophetic name to give this redman! The Moravians had no way of knowing that in a few years their Gideon was to drive their invader from the land of his people as Gideon of Israel drove out the Midianites. That the King of the Delawares was not as successful as the leader of Israel does not affect this uncanny choice of a name. Bishop Cammerhoff, who performed the baptismal ceremony, called him the "chief among sinners." Teedyuscung was the outstanding savage who, failing to follow the teachings of the Moravian brethren, had fallen by the wayside a hopeless renegade. Indeed it is doubtful if he was ever a true convert to Christianity.

* * *

Benjamin Chew,[21] the Attorney General of the Province, and Mr. Mifflin, left Philadelphia some time after the Governor. They were accompanied by two youths, Andrew Allen, the son of William Allen, and James Peters, the nephew of Richard Peters. Immediately upon his arrival in Easton Mr. Chew called upon the Governor to pay his respects.

The Governor was in a very angry mood. He was having an argument with Mr. Growden, a member of his Council, relative to an order he was about to issue impressing wagons into the military service for the use of General Forbes. Benjamin Chew, in his capacity as Attorney General, informed the Governor that his order was illegal, unjustifiable, and would be attended with mischievous consequences which would reflect on his honor and reputation. With much heat, the Governor replied in a most sarcastic and insolent manner :—"Sir, you give me your opinion I suppose as a lawyer and I am very much obliged to you. As for

BENJAMIN CHEW

From "Benjamin Chew" by Alva Konkle. By permission of the publishers, the University of Pennsylvania Press.

my honor and reputation it is my business to take care of that, and as to the order I am determined to give it."

At this unfortunate moment Teedyuscung entered. He welcomed the Governor in the customary ceremonial manner. Denny, thoroughly beside himself, threw all formality aside and entered into conversation with the chief of the Delawares. He told him very plainly what he thought of the Indians and cautioned them to "take care", for they were in a bad way. He also threatened the Indianse in a manner which greatly displeased Teedyuscung. Mr. Peters, sizing up the situation, pacified the infuriated Indian by telling him that the Governor was not expressing his own sentiments but was merely repeating what some thoughtless and uninformed persons said.[22]

That evening Mr. Peters and Mr. Weiser agreed upon the ceremonies and ritual which the Governor would have to follow when the conference opened on the following day.

On Sunday, October 8 (1758) the Governor spoke to the Indians and carefully followed the instructions of Mr. Peters. In behalf of the Indians and with the passing of the traditional belts of wampum, Tagashata, the Seneca chief, arose and after an impressive pause, returned thanks, repeating the ceremonies used on such an occasion, and added that he was "very glad to find the road open to their brethren and should take care to preserve it so on their side.[23]

Many Quakers arrived in Easton on this Sunday.

That evening the Governor requested Mr. Chew and Mr. Weiser to write his speech for the next day.[24] Ghost writers are not a modern invention. The peevish Governor had instructed Mr. Peters that he wished to dine alone and that he would have no company except those whom he saw fit to invite. Seeing Andrew Allen and James Peters he turned upon Mr. Peters and ordered him to keep his nephew out of his sight, adding that "he was not a companion for boys."[25]

When Mr. Chew wrote his diary for that day's proceedings he closed with this remark about the Governor:—"What a strange, peevish, petulant creature it is."

Governor Bernard, who had arrived in Phillipsburg on Sunday, was ferried across the Delaware river at eleven o'clock Monday morning.[26] The soldiers, dressed in their bright scarlet uniforms, were drawn up on each side of the road leading to the ferry. As the flat boat reached the shore, Governor Denny, followed by his Council, the members of the Assembly, and the Commissioners, advanced and welcomed the Governor of the Jerseys to the Province of Pennsylvania.

The formalities having been attended to the two Governors were escorted to the Red Lion Inn. Following the flag of England came the drummers, then a company of Royal Grenadiers, preceding the two Governors who walked side by side. After the Governors and in order came Attorney General Chew, the members of the Council and of the Assembly, the Commissioners, members of the Friendly Association, citizens of the town and surrounding country, Indians, and children. The procession proceeded in as orderly and as dignified a manner as the dreadful conditions of the street would permit.

Governor Bernard desired to greet the Indians, but the chiefs sent word that they were in council and could not be disturbed. The other Indians were drunk. That evening the Governor of the Jerseys returned to Phillipsburg, where he maintained his headquarters.[27]

On Tuesday the redmen were still drunk or in council. In fact, the Indians secured so much liquor that much of the time they were unable to meet with the Governors and the proceedings bogged down, while the dignitaries of the two provinces fussed and fumed and found fault with the activities of the Quakers.

Governor Denny lodged at the Red Lion Inn at the northeast corner of Hamilton (now 4th) and Northampton Streets.

In the tap room of the inn, men from the city in broadcloth and bright colored waistcoats, carrying tasseled Malacca canes, rubbed elbows with the frontiersmen in drab homespun and leather jerkins, and swinging hickory cudgels.

Outside of the tap room, in small groups, gathered some sullen Indians, ever hopeful that they might secure more rum. On the tap room door was posted a proclamation by the Governor declaring it illegal to give or to sell liquor to the Indians.[28]

Diagonally across the street intersection was the home of Jasper Scull. From his blacksmith shop at the rear of his house was heard the ring of his anvil. Gathered by the open door were a number of Indian children and a few warriors, all watching the sparks fly as the hammer fell upon the red hot iron.

Some of the vacant town lots were under cultivation and in these the corn stood in shocks while between the shocks lay bright yellow pumpkins, as yet untouched by the frost. Here and there a lank hog rooted for a bare living. Along the streets or roads the cows grazed, keeping the grass and weeds from running rampant along the paths which edged each roadway.

The roads, by courtesy called streets, were but traveled paths made by the wagons. They twisted in and out to avoid stumps, mud holes, and ruts.

Now and then a cackling bevy of hens would scatter as a village housewife, with a magnificent gesture, threw out of the kitchen door a pan of dishwater.

In the Great Square there still stood a number of trees. The Court House had not as yet been built, but a shed had been erected in the northeast corner and under it the treaty was to be held.[29] About one hundred yards to the northeast of the shed stood the log school house which had been erected three years before.

On Wednesday morning while the Governor was holding a meeting with his Council word came that the Quakers and the Indians were holding a meeting in the school house. Attorney General Chew, accompanied by Messrs. Growden, Lardner, and Mifflin, left the meeting and sauntered down to the Great Square. They passed the treaty shed and continued on in the direction of the school house. From this little log building came the sounds of Indian oratory.

When it was apparent that Benjamin Chew, who had left his companions, was headed for the school, the speaking ceased. Chew approached and looked in through one of the open windows There he saw congregated about twenty-five white men and a larger number of red men. At the middle of a long table 'in great state' sat Israel Pemberton with a pipe in his mouth. On each side of him were seated prominent members of the Society of Friends. At the end of the long table stood Tom King, Chief of the Oneidas, who had just stopped talking.[30]

Pemberton invited Chew to come in and listen to the 'Roman oratory' about love and friendship. After some badinage Chew rejoined his companions and returned to the Governor's meeting, leaving the Quakers and the Indians to continue their discourse on brotherly love and affection.

Israel Pemberton was the aggressive member of the Friendly Association and in espousing the cause of the Indians became quite disagreeable and objectionable to the Governor's party. On one occasion Mr. Logan, a member of Council, threatened to knock him down.[31] Pemberton met Mr. Chew on the street one evening and the resulting discussion became very heated. Mr. Chew gave vent to his feelings in these words written in his diary:—"Indeed, I only wanted a fair opportunity to hit him a slap in the chops, and he saw it plainly, on which like a pitiful dog as he is, he became tame and complaisant."

George Croghan, Deputy Agent for Indian Affairs, was a fugitive from justice, but the Province of Pennsylvania passed a special act suspending his sentence for a period of ten years, [32] permitting him to attend the treaties without fear of arrest. The Quakers considered him a rascal and a villain and thought it a shame that he should have the management of the Indians.[33] They asked the Governor and the Council to interpose and to have him removed. While it does not appear that the Proprietary party were sympathetic with Croghan they were compelled to treat him civilly, as he was the official representative of Sir William Johnson and thus of the King.

Governor Denny and his party considered Charles Reed, the Secretary of the Jerseys, as the tool and creature of Israel Pemberton, or as they expressed it, Reed "was governed by the House of Israel."[34] They resolved to be on their guard against him.

The lack of harmony among the white men was matched by the discord among the red men.

Teedyuscung had come to Easton to establish himself as a "great man" and to prove that his tribe, the Delawares, had thrown off the yoke of subserviency to the Iroquois.

The Six Nations, knowing of Teedyuscung's ambitions, came to Easton to humble the Delaware Chief.

It would seem that in this maelstrom of incompetence, personal animosity, and cross purposes, the main object of the conference might become lost.

That the treaty did not get out of control was due to Richard Peters and Conrad Weiser, who faithfully and diligently, but quietly and unassumingly, worked through all the cross currents and succeeded in establishing friendly relations with the Indians.

* * *

The meetings of the authorities of Pennsylvania and of the Jerseys with the Indians were rather short and somewhat intermittent. The natives, every now and then, would go into council for an entire day and refuse to meet the Governors. If a question arose, the meeting was adjourned until the following day so that the correct answer might be decided upon. The ritual of the redmen had to be carefully followed and this required constant repetition of all statements. As a result the meetings extended from October 7th to November 26th.

Governor Denny opened the conferences by giving a brief account of the three previous treaties for the benefit of those who had not attended them. He also asked the redmen why they had taken up the hatchet against the English.

Thomas King, chief of the Oneidas, informed the Governors that the alienation of the Indians was chargeable to the English.[35] He recalled the capture, by the English, of some Shawnee Indians in North Carolina and at Greenbrier in Virginia. He demanded the return of these captives. Governor Denny readily promised to return them, if they could be found.

The chief of the Cayugas, Tahaaio, complained that the French "like a thief in the night" had stolen away and misled some of their own young men. The old chief expressed sorrow and promised that it would not happen again.[36]

Tagashata, chief of the Senecas, spoke at the request of Teedyuscung and stated that their nephews, the Delawares, living at Wyoming would never think of warring against the English in the future. He told how the Minisinks and three other tribes had listened to his advice and agreed to bury the hatchet. He also had sent word to the Delawares and members of his own tribe living on the Ohio to do likewise.[37]

The Indians had never been satisfied with the sale of land which they had made to the Province of Pennsylvania at Albany in 1754. They claimed that they had never been paid for much of this land. The Governor of Pennsylvania then agreed to deed back to the Indians all the northwestern part of the province west of the Susquehanna.[38] This transfer was carried out.

The Minisinks and Governor Bernard then negotiated the dispute in regard to certain lands in the Jerseys for which the Indians claimed they had never been paid. Bernard asked the Indians to name a price, but they modestly refused, feeling that they might mention too large a sum. They requested the Governor to set the figure. When the sum of eight hundred Spanish dollars was proposed they consulted with their uncles, the Six Nations, and replied that, considering their great number, they thought they should have one thousand dollars.[39] This amount proved satisfactory.

The Six Nations then promised to return all the English captives which they held. As an expression of good faith, they stated that "if any of them are gone down our throats, we will heave them up again." Tagashata ordered the Delawares to return all the captives which they had taken. This was agreed upon.

Some of the Indians having stolen a quantity of liquor from Nathaniel Vernon, a sentry was placed at the ferry house tavern. For some reason this precaution did not meet with the approval of the Quaker members of the Commission. They spoke in condemnation of this action by the Governor. Messrs. Rox and Galloway declaimed loud and long in the streets of the town and ranted about liberty and privilege and appeared determined to raise a riot. As to their motive, the Attorney General said:— "with what view except to make themselves popular, God knows."[40]

At one stage of the proceedings, Teedyuscung staggered into the conference and in a maudlin manner swore that he "was King of all the nations of the world and the Six Nations were fools."[41] He claimed that to secure attention and to be used well by the English, it was necessary to make war against them and to cut their throats. The other Indians, including the Delaware Chief's own councillors, were thoroughly disgusted with this drunken performance but at the time paid little attention to it.

After this outburst the Six Nations decided that the time had come to remove permanently the Delaware Chieftain from the exalted position into which he thought he had placed himself.

Shortly following Teedyuscung's drunken tirade, Nichas, the Chief of the Mohawks, addressed the meeting. He spoke at some length and with great passion and resentment. While he spoke to the Governor, during the most violent passages of his speech he turned and addressed Teedyuscung.

Many of the Indians could speak English but they considered it beneath their dignity to address the conference in any language but their own. So whatever was said by a redman had to be interpreted not only for the English, but for each of the other Indian tribes. Consequently, when Nichas delivered his denunciation of Teedyuscung there were very few, other than the Mohawks and the interpreters, who knew what he was saying. The interpreters refused to make public his speech.[42]

The following day the diatribe was interpreted to the Governor and the council. In the very best vituperative Indian manner Nichas had flayed the Delaware King. He charged him with assuming powers which he did not possess, and stated that he was only the leader of the Delawares, a tribe which the Iroquois had subjugated and on which they had placed petticoats.

When the Quakers heard this they became alarmed and publicly came to Teedyuscung's support, declaring that he was a "great man." They charged George Croghan with instigating the trouble. The Friends had not condoned the conduct of the Delaware King. In fact, they held a closed session with him and told him very plainly that he would have to mend his ways.

Following the interpretation of Nichas' speech, a conference was held with all the Indians except the Delawares. Nichas, Tagashata, Assarandonqua, Thomas King, and Tahaaio, all chieftains of the Six Nations, arose one at a time, and demanded to know who was it that made Teedyuscung a "great-man". They never knew that he was a "great-man."

Nichas' speech was then interpreted to Teedyuscung and the Delawares. They had nothing to say. Governor Denny then made a statement, pointedly directed to the Quakers, that he did not know who had made the Delaware a "great-man", certainly he had not. Governor Bernard then made a similar statement.

Some time after the Six Nations publicly refused to recognize Teedyuscung as more than a chief of a conquered tribe, they further humiliated this audacious Algonquin. At a conference the chastened Teedyuscung assured the Governors that he would do all that the Six Nations requested. The irrepressible Indian then took up his favorite theme of the land in the Forks of the Delaware and how it had been taken from him by fraud. As he addressed the Governor, each chieftain, in turn, quietly left the conference, so that when he finally turned to address them they had all departed, except old Tom King the Oneida and even he refused to listen. The humiliation of the Delaware chief was complete.

Teedyuscung was a tall, raw-boned, deep-chested Indian of over fifty years, an orator, a drunkard, a good tempered liar, but nobody's fool. He had come out of the fastness of the forest with the blood of the white settlers dripping from his hands to play the principal role at the wilderness dramas enacted at Easton in 1756 and 1757. He held the leading part in the treaty of 1758, but, at this conference, as we have seen, the Chiefs of the powerful Six Nations had removed all thoughts of grandeur from his mind and in the presence of the authorities of the province and all the principal Indians of New York and Pennsylvania had established the fact that he was merely the chief of a conquered tribe.

With humility Teedyuscung made one last appeal to the Iroquois. He requested that they give him a deed for the land at Wyoming where the Delawares had been sent when they were driven from the Forks. In a burst of eloquence he concluded:— "I sit there as a bird on a bough, I look about and do not know where to go; let me therefore come down upon the ground, and make that my own by a good deed, and I shall have a home for ever."[43] The Iroquois promised to consider the matter but the deed was never executed.

Several days before the close of the treaty one of the Seneca chiefs died.[44] The morning was devoted to tribal ceremonies.

The Governor and the other officials visited the Indians and expressed sympathy. The burial took place that morning and the deceased chief, dressed in his regalia, with his face and chest painted red, was carried to his grave on a stretcher.[45] The red warriors, with no sign of emotion and with heads erect, stood by as the body was lowered into the coffin which had previously been placed in the grave. The drum and fife corps sounded taps, the white men bowed their heads, and the squaws set up a loud lamentation. The chieftain's few belongings were placed in the coffin beside his body and as the grave was filled, the mourners turned away, all but a few women whose wailing was heard throughout the day.

In the summer of 1758, Governor Denny had sent Frederick Post, a German Moravian Missionary, to the Ohio country in an effort to persuade the western Indians to resume friendly relations with the English. Pisquetomen and Thomas Hickman, both Indians, who had accompanied Post on his perilous journey, now appeared at Easton and delivered a message from the Delawares and Shawnees living in the western part of the province.[46] This message stated that they longed for the peace and friendship which they formerly enjoyed and requested that it be sent to them with all possible dispatch.

After delivering the message, Pisquetomen produced three strings of wampum, giving one to Governor Denny, one to Teedyuscung and one to Israel Pemberton.[47] As Pemberton received his string, the Pennsylvania Governor said to those sitting beside him:—"I hope his will soon be favored with another string, which he richly merits."[48]

The answer to the message from the Ohio Indians was carefully prepared. It was approved by the Governors, the Council, the Assembly, the Quakers, and the Indians. Pisquetomen and a party of five or six, representatives of the various tribes, then left for the west. The message he carried welcomed the Ohio Indians back into the bonds of friendship. It told how all the eastern Indians were then gathered at Easton where they had re-established peace with the English. The message requested the western Indians to stay a long distance from Fort Duquesne, so that the warriors of the King of England would not by chance hurt them when they attacked the fort. It contained a cordial invitation to visit the Governor at Philadelphia who would warmly welcome his old friends whom he and the King of England had forgiven for their thoughtless relapse of friendship.[49]

Governor Denny, becoming impatient and irritable, returned to Philadelphia on October 23rd, leaving Mr. Logan and Mr. Peters in charge.[50]

The last few days were devoted to much repetition of what had been said, the preparation and execution of the land agreements, the expression of regrets for past misunderstandings, and the rejoicing at the happy conclusion of the treaty.

At the close of the conference the articles to be presented to the Indians were displayed and the following day was devoted to the proper distribution of these gifts. Most of the articles were fabrics and wearing apparel.[51] There were three gross of link sleeve buttons which no doubt puzzled the Indians. For the squaws who were domestically inclined there was one gross of thimbles. A few painted looking glasses were no doubt in much demand. For the men there were two dozen knives, several tobacco boxes and six gun locks. How an equitable distribution of these articles could be made among two hundred warriors must have been quite a problem.

Here and there a little discontent among the Indians could be noted. Wise old Tahaaio observed that he feared the English spoke only from their mouths and not from their hearts.[52] A truer word was never spoken. The lack of guns and ammunition from the gifts was noted by the Chieftain of the Oneidas who pertinently called attention to the fact that gun locks without guns were a useless article. However, all trivial irritations were forgotten in the general rejoicing.

With the exchange of many strings of wampum, numerous farewells were said. The address delivered by a member of the Pennsylvania Council faithfully followed the ceremonial ritual and the metaphorical phraseology of the Indian.[53] The speaker confirmed the ancient league of amity; he brightened the chain of friendship, and wiped the blood from the council benches; he condoled the Indian for the loss of their wise-men, their warriors, their women and children, and figuratively speaking he covered their graves in a decent manner according to their ancient custom. He dispersed the dark clouds which had hung over their heads, and he brought forth the sun so that they might again look upon each other with the same cheerfulness which they once enjoyed.

With the final expressions of good will, Governor Bernard and his party returned to the Jerseys and the Philadelphia contin‍gents left their inadequate and humble quarters in Easton and returned to Philadelphia.

Finally the Indians started their homeward journey, and, as quietly as they had come they now vanished into the somber shadows of the forests.

Teedyuscung, with his head held high, but with a heavy heart, started for Bethlehem. His dream of power had been shattered and his glory, like the glory of the autumn leaves, had faded.

The lobster backed grenadiers crossed the Lehigh and to the beat of drums wended their way southward over the hills of Williams township.

In the western part of the province, Pisquetomen delivered to the Ohio Indians the Easton message of peace. As a result these Indians refused to help the French in the defence of Fort Duquesne. Realizing their weakness without the support of the natives, and being short of supplies, the French burned the fort and fled. General Forbes took possession of the ruins without opposition, rebuilt the garrison and renamed it Fort Pitt.

The French and Indian War in the province of Pennsylvania was about over. Peace again reigned in the foothills of the Blue Mountains, and the struggling infant village at the Forks of the Delaware settled down to adjust itself to advancing civilization, a civilization which spelled the doom of the American Indian and drove the frontier from this broad land.

---

[1] Pennsylvania Colonial Records, Vol. VI, p. 683.
[2] Indian Treaties, Printed by Benjamin Franklin, p. LXIX.
[3] Pennsylvania Colonial Records, Vol. VII, p. 199.
[4] Pennsylvania Colonial Records, Vol. VII, p. 190.
Moravian Missions, Part II, p. 178.

[5]Pennsylvania Colonial Records, Vol. VII, p. 191.

[6]Pennsylvania Archives, First Series, Vol. II, p. 714.

[7]Pennsylvania Archives, First Series, Vol. II, p. 721.

[8]Indian Treaties, Printed by Benjamin Fraanklin, p. 216. Pennsylvania Archives, First Series, Vol. III, p. 558. Pennsylvania Colonial Records, Vol. VIII, p. 175.

[9]Pennsylvania Colonial Records, Vol. VIII, p. 170.

[10]Pennsylvania Colonial Records, Vol. VIII, p. 167.

[11]Pennsylvania Archives, First Series, Vol. III, p. 485.

[12]Pennsylvani a Colonial Records, Vol. VIII, p. 172.

[13]Ibid, p. 172.

[14]Indian Treaties, Printed by Benjamin Franklin, p. lxxxv.

[15]Pennsylvania Colonial Records, Vol. VII, p. 639.

[16]Pennsylvania Colonial Records, Vol. VII, p. 637.

[17]Ibid, p. 638.

[18]"Pennsylvania, Colony and Commonwealth," by Sydney George Fisher, 1897, p. 249.

[19]"Life and Times of David Zeisberger," by Edmund DeSchweinitz (1870), p. 245 to 251.

[20]"Memorials of the Moravian Church," Vol. I, p. 220.

[21]Benjamin Chew, Attorney General of the Province, kept a diary while in Easton during the treaty of 1758. A copy, in the handwriting of Richard Peters, is in the Historical Society of Pennsylvania. In 1938, this society published this diary in their publication "Indian Treaties, Published by Benjamin Franklin." This diary is entitled "Journal of a Journey to Easton, 1758." Much material used in this paper was secured from this source.

[22]Indian Treaties, Printed by Benjamin Franklin, p. 312.

[23]Pennsylvania Colonial Records, Vol. VIII, p. 177.

[24]Indian Treaties, Printed by Benjamin Franklin, p. 313.

[25]Ibid.

[26]Ibid.

[27]Ibid.

[28]Pennsylvania Colonial Records, Vol. VIII, p. 172.

[29]Indian Treaties, Printed by Benjamin Franklin, p. 313.

[30]Ibid, p. 313.

[31]Ibid, p. 314.

[32]Pennsylvania Archives, 8th Series, Vol. V. p. 4161 and p. 4165.

[33]Indian Treaties, p. 314. Pennsylvania Colonial Records, Vol. VII, p. 557.

[34]Ibid, p. 316.

[35]Ibid, p. 197.

[36]Ibid, p. 182.

[37]Pennsylvania Colonial Records, Vol. VIII, p. 181.

[38]Ibid, p. 204.

[39]Ibid, p. 209.

[40]Indian Treaties, Printed by Benjamin Franklin, p. 317.

41Ibid, p. 314.
42Pennsylvania Colonial Records, Vol. VIII, p. 190.
43Pennsylvania Colonial Records, Vol. VIII, p. 190.
44Ibid, p. 213.
45Moravian Missions, Part I, p. 119.
46Pennsylvania Colonial Records, Vol. VIII, p. 187.
47Ibid, p. 188.
48Indian Treaties, Printed by Benjamin Franklin, p. 315.
49Pennsylvania Colonial Records, Vol. VIII, p. 206.
50Pennsylvania Colonial Records, Vol. VIII, p. 217.
51Ibid, p. 214.
52Ibid, p. 212.
53Ibid, u. 219.

The Old Court House

The Old Court House

ON the afternoon of the 8th of May, 1752, William Parsons and Nicholas Scull dismounted from their horses on the top of the hill in Williams township, the hill which more than fifty years later was to be known as Mammy Morgan's Hill. They had spent the previous night at "The Sign of the Plow" in Gardenville, Bucks County,[1] and had stopped to rest their horses and to admire the magnificent view. Before them lay practically all of Northampton county north of the Lehigh River and south of the Blue or Endless Mountains.

It would be a mistake and an injustice to these two veteran weather-beaten surveyors to assume that they did not appreciate the beauties of the scene made additionally lovely by the vivid green of the new spring foliage. For Nicholas Scull was an amateur poet, and often wrote verse for Benjamin Franklin's Junto of which he was a member. Also William Parsons, in his later correspondence, occasionally dwelt upon the beauties of the hills surrounding Easton.[2]

One can, with a fair degree of accuracy, reconstruct the thoughts of these two town planners, who were about to descend upon a virgin territory to lay the foundation of a town which Thomas Penn had decreed should be the seat of government of the new county and for which he had selected the name of Easton.

It is doubtful if there was a sign of habitation visible in the entire territory over which they gazed. There were settlers in the region, but their cabins were small and mostly in the hollows or valleys along the streams, while Bethlehem was completely hidden from their point of observation.

Along the distant horizon rose the Blue Mountains, bluer than ever on this bright spring day. The notch to the north, through which the Delaware river flowed, brought to the mind of Nicholas Scull the trip which he made through that impressive defile on a similar day in May of 1740,[3] when, at the request of Governor Thomas he visited the Minisink to settle a difficulty which had arisen between a white man and an Indian.

The hill just south of the Lehigh shut out the view of a portion of the plateau between the two rivers, the plateau on which they had been instructed to lay out the town. The hills surrounding the proposed town site were all visible and William Parsons recalled how in 1736 he had surveyed this one thousand acre tract for the senior proprietor,[4] Thomas Penn, and how the Indians had sullenly watched the survey for they were embittered at the encroaching of the white man on their domain.

The two companions tried to locate, in the panorama before them the tavern of John Lefevre, for there they planned to make their headquarters. It is more than probable that they discussed the location of the proposed county seat. Both men were intensely loyal to the proprietaries, but they were practical men and must have realized the financial advantage which would accrue to the Penns. They also understood the great inconvenience to which the settlers would be put. The location was beautiful, and, insofar as the rivers were concerned, ideal, but it was far from the settled portions of the county and quite inaccessible. A wide belt of drylands, which was thought unfertil, adjoined the site on the north, northwest and west.

As the two companions remounted and slowly rode down the mountain side, the thoughts which ran through their minds must have been somewhat different. To Scull this was just another job in connection with his official position as surveyor general and he had no disturbing thoughts to mar his appreciation of the country. To William Parsons the situation was somewhat different. This was to be his home and he was responsible to the Proprietaries for the success or failure of the enterprise. Over a territory very much larger than they saw from the top of the hill he was to be the representative of the Proprietaries. In his saddle bags he carried commissions as prothonotary, as clerk of the orphans court, and as recorder of deeds, signed by the Governor only two days before. He was somewhat apprehensive of his success. He knew that he would have no pleasure or satisfaction in living among and trying to mould the opinion of the Germans, whom he despised, and of the Moravians, whom he hated.

On reaching the Lehigh they paid two shillings to be ferried across the river[5] and, having passed the time of day with the ferryman, proceeded five miles up the Lehicton creek to Lefevre's tavern. This tavern was located on the creek at the point where the present Wind Gap road crosses it in the Borough of Stockertown. Here they established their headquarters[6] and daily rode to and from their work of laying out the streets and lots in the embryonic town of Easton.

Before the work was completed Nicholas Scull returned to Philadelphia and the entire responsibility of changing the wilderness into a frontier village fell upon the shoulders of William Parsons. When the streets were cleared and the lot lines established, Parsons, assuming the duties of an auctioneer, held a public sale on May 25th and disposed of a number of lots.

*　*　*

Following the provisions of the act creating the county, the first court was held on June 15th (1752),[7] the Tuesday of the week following that in which Bucks County held court.

There is very little known about this session. Where was court held? There are three possibilities. It may have been held in the ferry-house; but this we know was very small. Again it may have been held in a shed constructed by William Parsons, as he had purchased boards to the amount of ten pounds[8] and these may have been used for this purpose. However it is more than likely that court was held out in the open, possibly in the great square, under a large tree, where the court crier's "Oyez! Oyez!", resounding through its branches, heralded the dawn of a new era and the passing of the virgin wilderness.

When this court was held there was not a house in Easton, excepting the small log ferry house and possibly a shed, which could have been built with the ten pounds worth of boads which had been purchased north of the Blue Mountains from John McMichael.

Exactly one week before court was held the Provincial Council, meeting in Philadelphia, named nine justices for the new county.[9] The following were appointed:—Thomas Craig, Daniel Brodhead, Timothy Horsfield, Hugh Wilson, John Vanetta, Aaron Depue, William Craig, James Martin, and William Parsons.

In a county where the Germans comprised eighty-five percent of the population, it is interesting to note that not one of that nationality was on the list of appointees. There were three Scotch-Irish, two Holland Dutch, and four English. True, Timothy Horsfield was a Moravian, but notwithstanding he was English and not German.

Just how many and which of these justices sat at Northampton county's first court is not known. William Parsons, who had been a justice in Lancaster county, no doubt acted as master of ceremonies and directed the other justices in the intricacies of court procedure, for at this time the judges or justices who presided at court were laymen and not learned in the law.

There is no complete record of the business of this primitive frontier court on the verge of civilization. We know that Lewis Gordon, formerly of Philadelphia but then of Easton, was granted permission to practice law before the courts of Northampton county and thus became the first member of the Northampton County Bar. There were other attorneys granted the same privilege, but they were residents of Philadelphia and therefore cannot be considered members of the local bar.

By statute all criminal and civil cases which had been started in Bucks county, before the division, were carried to completion before the Bucks county courts or officials even though the litigants lived within the limits of Northampton county after its erection.[10]

In the act of creating the county there were five men named to purchase land and erect a prison and a court house in Easton.[11] They were John Jones, Thomas Armstrong, James Martin, Thomas Craig, and Hugh Wilson. Three of these men were later named as justices. Again the absence of any German names is noted.

This commission was authorized to assess and levy as much money as might be necessary, provided the total sum did not exceed three hundred pounds.

A prison was built, but whether it was constructed by the commission is not known. By December 8th, 1752, the prison had been started and "covered in," [12] that is, under roof. On January 9th, 1753, Thomas Penn wrote to Richard Peters:[13]—"I observe what you said about the town of Easton and the prison which I thought would have been built of stone. We approve of your giving one hundred pounds for the building of it." We thus learn that the original prison was built of wood and that the Proprietaries paid for its construction.

A court house was not built at this time. Court was held in the large rooms of the various taverns. The rent for the use of the rooms, for the four sessions of court and for the elections, varied from three to seven pounds, which price included candles and fire-wood.

In the prerevolutionary war period, all elections were held in Easton. On election day the freeholders, the only persons allowed to vote, came to Easton to cast their ballot. Each township sent an inspector of election, who had been chosen by the township electorate. The inspector carried a list of all qualified voters in his district. As the voters cast their ballots they were identified by the inspector who then crossed their names from the list.[14]

The first election was held on October 1st, 1752, when James Burnside, an itinerant Moravian preacher, defeated William Parsons for the Assembly. The proprietaary party felt that it was quite necessary in the new county, to have their own representative in the Assembly rather than the representative of the people and had accordingly named William Parsons as their candidate. Parsons took his defeat in bad grace. The double humiliation of failing to meet the desire of the proprietary party and of being defeated by one of his hated Moravians made him bitter and he wrote a scathing letter to Richard Peters.

In this he maintained that Burnside had conducted his campaign in an unethical and undignified manner. He claimed that all the Moravian votes were illegal, because the Moravians would not take an oath but only an affirmation. He charged that all the inspectors were not freeholders and that one township, in which there was not one person qualified to vote, turned out en masse and voted.

Four years later (1756) William Allen was elected to the Assembly. Allen was a resident of Philadelphia and in the same election was elected by the people of Lancaster county to represent them. It was not necessary in electing a representative to choose a resident of the county which he was to represent. As Allen could not serve two masters and as he preferred Lancaster, Northampton county was without a representative and was compelled to hold another election.[15]   At this second election, William Plumstead, also of Philadelphia, was elected.

Immediately a petition was addressed to the Assembly charging that the election was illegal and praying that Plumstead be not seated. The petition was considered by the Assembly.[16]   Many hearings were held, many witnesses examined, and many postponements indulged in. Finally one year later the election was declared illegal.

Precedents were thus established early in the life of the county, not only for the great length of time it takes to dispose of these contests, but also for the unsuccessful candidate, in the disappointment and bitterness of defeat, to cry 'fraud' or to institute proceedings to have his successful rival unseated.

*   *   *

Before Northampton county was erected, some hardy pioneers had pushed through the Wind Gap and had settled in the valley of the Pohopoko creek. The present village of Gilbert, in Monroe county, is now the center of this fertile basin.

These people were industrious, of good German stock, and had carved a home in this Wilderness of St. Anthony, as that part of the province was then called. They were a happy and contented people. When in 1754, they addressed a petition to the court at Easton, asking that their part of the county might be established as a separate township, they used this title:—"The Petition of Sundry of the Inhabitants of Contented Valley."[17]

The very name, Contented Valley, is a story in itself, a prologue which intensifies the tragedy which was about to descend upon this vale of tranquility.

The court granted their request and authorized the establishment of a new township, the southeast corner of which should join Lower Smithfield at the Dry Gap. Later the township was named Chestnut Hill and the Dry Gap is now called the Wind Gap.

Hardly two years later, the Delaware Indians, in their hideous and terrifying war paint, descended into the valley of contentment and massacred many of the inhabitants. Those who escaped fled to the south over the Blue Mountains, leaving their homes, their barns, and their crops, to the mercies of the savage marauders, who burned everything before them.

After the French and Indian War, the survivors straggled back, reclaimed their land and rebuilt their homes. With the memory of the dreadful Indian raids ever before them, the name Contented Valley, seemed inappropriate, and in their great sorrow the name became forgotten and only now and then is found in some old paper.

* * *

A second jail was constructed in Easton to replace the earlier log structure. Just when it was built is not known, but the lot on which it was erected was purchased in 1762.[18] The jail may have been erected before title to the lot had been secured. It was built at the southeast corner of Pomfret, now Third Street, and an alley now called Pine Street. The three hundred pounds authorized[19] were spent on securing the lot and in building the jail and no funds remained to construct the court house. Therefore the county was compelled to rent rooms in the taverns for fourteen years.

As the population increased, so did the business of the court. It became more and more unsatisfactory to hold court in the taverns of the town where a bar room served as a lobby. The pleasures of the tap room interfered with the business of the county. The sound of singing, cursing and of brawls coming from the bar room disturbed the dignity and calm of the court.

On October 15th, 1762, the trustees petitioned the Assembly for funds to erect a court house,[20] stating that the amount originally authorized in 1752 had been required to build the jail. On February 17th, 1763, a bill was passed authorizing the trustees to raise four hundred and fifty pounds for the purpose requested.[21] A new board of five trustees was appointed at this time. Jones, Armstrong, and Martin were on the original board. The two new members were John Rinker and Henry Allshouse, both of Easton.

The board purchased a plot of ground, eighty by eighty feet, located in the center of the Great Square. The land was conveyed to the trustees on September 28th, 1763, and was held in trust by them for the erection and maintenance of a court house and for no other purpose. The yearly quit rent was to be one red rose.[22]

It is quite unlikely that the building was started before the early part of 1765. It is unfortunate that we do not know the name of the architect, for the building was well designed and most attractive. In plan it was a Greek cross, the roof forming gables at the ends of each arm. A well designed cupola or belfry capped the structure. It received much favorable comment. All the travellers who passed through Easton in the eighteenth century, and whose diaries have been found, invariably refer to the court house in complimentary terms. The citizens of the county, especially those who lived in Easton, must have felt a sense of civic pride, for in its surroundings, the building was an imposing structure. Without doubt it lent charm and dignity to the little village of small log and stone houses.

Our local historians state that the court house was copied from Carpenter's Hall in Philadelphia. This statement is most incorrect. The Easton building was completed in 1766 and the Philadelphia structure was not started until 1770. I suggest that the Philadelphia builders be charged with the plagiarism. It is conceivable that the same person designed both buildings. The general plans and outlines were the same, but the Philadelphia building, with greater funds available, and built in a sizable and sophisticated community, was more elaborate.

The trustees in erecting the court house spent the sum of nine hundred ninety-eight pounds or five hundred and forty-eight pounds more than the limit set by the act of 1763. To remedy this condition, the Assembly, upon petition from the trustees, authorized the raising of the additional amount needed. This supplemental act was passed September 30th, 1766,[23] six months after the first court was held in the new building, on March the 6th of that year.

* * *

Two years after the completion of the court house a bell was placed in the cupola. The bell had been cast on July 29th, 1768, by Mathias Tommerop, in the bell foundry of the Moravians at Bethlehem.[24] On August 9th, of that year, it was brought to Easton and put in place. Moravian Brother Arbo, carrying the bill, followed the bell to its destination. It is hardly an exaggeration to say, that as the first peal of the bell sounded from the belfry, Brother Arbo, perhaps to his surprise, certainly to his satisfaction, received his money. He returned to Bethlehem rejoicing.

* * *

Court week was quite an event in the simple life of the county seat. The merchants, the artisans, and the tavern keepers, reaped considerablie profit from the many persons who were drawn to the village. The Philadelphia attorneys came to represent their clients, the county officials were on hand to discharge their duties, the litigants presented themselves with fear and trepidation or hope and assurance, the politicians arrived to mingle with their constituents, and others came out of curiosity, to purchase supplies, or to satisfy some secret inhibition. All helped to liven up the village.

Old friends met and the county news and gossip were fairly well disseminated.

The taverns did a rushing business. In preparation for this periodical influx of people who had to be accommodated, the bed rooms were aired, the larder stocked, and the bar supplies replenished. The large rooms were dusted and put in shape for the evening's pleasure. Night clubs, cabarets, and floor shows were unknown, but the stamping of time and the calling of figures by the master of ceremonies as he fiddled away, could now and then be heard above the noise of the dancers.

At times these tavern dances became bacchanalian revelries. Consequently, in 1770, the court took notice of this situation and issued the following order:—"Whereas, great inconvenience have and do arise from the tavern keepers, innholders, and retailers of liquor of the town of Easton in suffering fiddling and dancing in their houses at the time of holding court to the great disturbance of the people who are obliged to attend to the business of the said court and, likewise tends to corrupt the morals of the people, it is ordered, etc. ‑ ‑" No attention was paid to the court order and the practice was not discontinued.

* * *

Even after the advent of the newspapers in the town of Easton, the mouth to mouth method of carrying and spreading news was so thorough that very little local news ever found its way into the papers. Deaths and marriages were generally published. The description of the weddings were most meagre and confined to the fact that the bride was "amiable and agreeable" or "virtuous and much admired". The virtues of the groom were not touched upon. In the early years of the nineteenth century a wave of poetry swept the country. During this period Easton's poet laureate made a specialty of wedding notices. Here is one taken at random from the local press:[25]—"Married, Mr. Peter Werst and Miss Elizabeth Tidd of Forks Township,"

> "May peace and comfort still be near,
> Their days be crowned with joy,
> And each revolving happy year,
> Bring them a girl or boy."

While on the subject of poetry, the following taken from a book published in 1809[26] is descriptive of the usual country court. The title is, "The Country Quarter Sessions".

"Three or four parsons, full of October
Three or four 'squires, between drunk and sober;
Three or four lawyers, three or four liars;
Three or four constables, three or four criers;
Three or four parishes, bringing appeals,
Three or four writings, three or four seals,
Three or four orators, three or four bores,
Tag, rag and bobtail, three or four scores;
Three or four statutes, misunderstood;
Three or four paupers, all praying for food;
Three or four roads, that never were mended;
Three or four scolds — and the session is ended."

* * *

One of the strange duties of the early courts was to establish the price of all liquor sold at retail as well as the price which the public stables should charge for provender for horses.[27] Four times a year the justices, at the close of each quarter session, put their judicial heads together and decided what the tavern keepers should charge for a glass of wine, a mug of beer, or a pot of ale. The court crier would then announce, in stentorian tones, so all within a wide radius could hear, the findings of the judiciary. So that those beyond the range of his voice could know, before entering a tavern, just how much and what he could drink for the few coins in his pocket, the schedule of prices was tacked to the court house door.

In 1779, George Grim, an innkeeper of Weisenberg township, was arrested and held in fifty pounds bail for his appearance at the next term of court to answer a charge of "keeping a dancing frollick on Pancake day."[28] The Century dictionary will tell you that Pancake Day was Shrove Tuesday.

* * *

In every profession, every calling, and every walk of life, there are always one or two who are unethical, unscrupulous, or even criminal. Nine years after the first court was held in Easton, David Henderson, an attorney, who had often represented William Parsons, and was one of the attorneys to prosecute Nathaniel Vernon, was disbarred from practice before the courts of Northampton county.[29] The order was signed by Lewis Gordon, perhaps with some satisfaction, for he often opposed Henderson. Thus our local bar, for the first time, purged itself of a practitioner who today would be classified as an ambulance chaser or a shyster.

Henderson, who formerly lived in Philadelphia, but at this time resided in Reading, had been disbarred from practice at the Berks county courts. He was charged with being rude and insolent to the justices and of repudiating his own handwriting. He was accused of malversation and barratry. Four years later we find him languishing in the Philadelphia jail where he occupied a debtor's cell.[30] In May of 1765 he petitioned the assembly to be released as he claimed to be dying and that continued confinement would hasten his death. The Assembly laid his petition on the table.

* * *

The same crimes were found in the early days of the county as we now have to contend with. The punishments were quite different.

The pioneers and settlers, who carried the frontier back into the hinterland in the colonial period and during the early years of the republic, were a hardy, rugged race of men. In the absence of policing, the arm of the law was both long and strong. There was no attempt at reprimanding, reforming, and paroling. A criminal was a blot on society and was promptly eliminated. Felonies, such as burglary, highway robbery, arson, rape, mayhem, treason, and murder, were punished by death. A person who was convicted of counterfeiting any gold or silver coin was sentenced to death, "without the benefit of clergy."

It might be well to explain just what the phrase, "without the benefit of clergy", means. In England, during the twelfth century, the ecclesiastical authorities claimed that the clergy should be exempt from the jurisdiction of the temporal courts and that all crimes committed by the clergy should be tried by the spiritual courts. A compromise was finally agreed upon whereby the courts abandoned the punishment of death when the person convicted was a clericus. The term clericus always included a large number of persons in the minor church orders. It therefore came about that, when a clericus was tried for a felony, the punishment for which was death, he could claim the benefit of clergy and the sentence was not imposed. In 1530 the privilege was extended to include secular as well as religious clerks. At that period the ability to read was a rare accomplishment, but one necessary for the duties of a clerk. Therefore the test of being a clerk was the ability to read a few lines from the Bible. As the man's life depended upon his ability to read the part selected, that particular verse, for obvious reasons, became known as the 'neck-verse'. Each prison had a different verse, although they were not bound to its exclusive use. The prison at Newgate used the first verse of the fifty-first psalm.

"Have mercy upon me, O God, according to thy loving kindness; according unto the multitude of thy tender mercies blot out my transgressions."

During the trial the bishop of the diocese stood by and if he felt so inclined he would say in Latin: "He reads like a clerk." Thus the transgression was blotted out. The offender was then burned on the brawn of the thumb. If the bishop failed to pronounce the saving phrase, the prisoner was put to death. The benefit of clergy was permitted only for those convicted for the first time. The branding on the thumb made it impossible again to claim this benefit.

As civilization advanced and education and learning became more common it was apparent that the ability to read was no extenuation of guilt but quite the reverse. If the punishment of death for a simple felony was too severe for those who had been liberally educated, it was much too severe for the ignorant. This antiquated form was therefore made the means of notifying the severity of the punishment. After a time the reading of the neck-verse was eliminated and every one was allowed the benefit of clergy for their first conviction.

While the penalty of death was too severe in most cases, the mere branding on the thumb was not punishment enough. Therefore secondary punishments were added to suit the heinousness of the crime. These punishments consisted in the paying of fines, standing in the pillory, public whippings, jail terms, and the disfigurement of the body.

When it was desired that the crime should actually be punished by death the statute called for the death penalty "without the benefit of clergy." This was the English law. Now the laws of the province were in large measure copied or patterned after the English statutes and the phrase "without the benefit of clergy" became part of the laws of the province of Pennsylvania. In branding the thumb, Pennsylvania used the letter "M" when the crime was murder and the letter "T" for all other felonies.

The punishment after the revolutionary war was just as severe as in the colonial period. The punishments which the law provided and the court decreed were designed not only to punish and humiliate the guilty but to serve as a dreadful warning which might deter the innocent and upright from leaving the paths of rectitude. The punishments were therefore made as public as possible.

The pillory and whipping post in Easton were located in the square between the court house and south Pomfret Street.[31] As these adjuncts of the jail were very necessary in punishing the criminals it is reasonable to assume that they were erected at the time the first jail was built. They were discontinued in 1790.[32]

* * *

The following account is from records recently found at the court house in Easton and covers a case of horse stealing.[33] The Grand Jury at the September session of court in 1786, found true bills against one John Judee for horse stealing. He had stolen a black mare from John Haupt of Weisenberg township and a sorrel gelding from Herman Mohr of the township of Macungy. John Judee no doubt felt that his case was hopeless and wishing to secure some leniency from the court, pleaded guilty. After hearing the sentence of the court you will be in a position to determine the amount of leniency which the judges meted out to horse thieves.

The judge prescribed the punishment called for by an act passed in 1780, in pronouncing the following sentence. "John Judee, hold up your hand. You stand convicted in your own confession of stealing one black mare of the price of twenty pounds, the property of John Haupt, for which offense the judgment of this court is that you restore the said mare to the owner or pay him the full value thereof and also pay him the sum of three pounds six shillings and six pence for his loss of time and charges in apprehending and prosecuting you. That you pay a fine of twenty pounds to the Honourable President and council of this state for the support of the government thereof and further that on Thursday the fifth of October between the hours of ten and twelve of the clock in the forenoon of that day you stand in the pillory in this town for the space of one hour and shall be publicly whipped on your bare back with thirty-nine lashes well laid on, and at the same time shall have your ears cut off and nailed to the pillory, that you pay the costs of prosecution and remain in the sheriff's custody till you have complied with this sentence."

The court immediately pronounced sentence for the second offense. This sentence paralleled the first in every way except in the lopping off of the ears. After the execution of the first sentence John Judee would have no ears to remove, so the worthy justices decreed that, after standing in the pillory, and receiving the thirty-nine lashes, he should be branded on the forehead with the letters HT.

Today the sentence for the second offense would likely be mitigated or held over the offender. Not so in the early days of the republic. Justice was swift and severe. If John Judee survived the ordeal, what future could he look forward to with both ears cut off, a forehead branded with the letters HT, notifying the world that he was a horse thief, and a back scarred with seventy-eight lashes given in two applications with but one day's interval between?

* * *

The law and the courts, insofar as punishment was concerned, made no distinction between the men and the women offenders.

Some time during the colonial period, a woman named Mary Nickum, was found guilty, by a Northampton county court, of stealing linen to the value of twenty-six shillings.[34] Any one who happened to be in the vicinity of the Square and South Pomfret Street, at the time the sentence was executed, would have seen the sheriff leading the unfortunate woman from the jail to the whipping post, where he stripped her to the waist, tied her hands to the post, and in pursuance of the court order, gave her twenty-one lashes on her bare back, each blow raising a welt, until finally the blood trickled from the cuts thus made.

The prisoner was then taken back to the jail, the spectators dispersed, satisfied that the dignity of the law had been upheld, the sentence of the court carried out, and that justice had triumphed. It was just another of those necessary but unfortunate happenings which must be taken in the day's stride. If they gave any further thought to the affair it was only to ponder on what a degraded woman the prisoner had been. In the eighteenth century, this was not an uncommon sight in Easton's quaint and attractive Square.

* * *

The poor we have with us always. This has been true on down through the centuries and in colonial Northampton county the overseers of the poor were busy officials, looking after the indolent, the weak-minded, the ill, and the unfortunate who were unable to support themselves and their families.

As the law branded the criminal so did it, in a manner, brand the pauper, not by a hot iron searing the flesh but by the letters "PN" worn on the right shoulder.[35] The letter P standing for pauper and the letter N for Northampton. In the case of a man with a family, his wife and his children were also required to wear the degrading letters. Neglect or refusal to wear this badge of poverty was punishable by a severe penalty. If the overseer of the poor did not enforce this law he was liable to a fine of twenty shillings.

In those early days only property owners could vote and as a pauper could not hold property he could not vote. Consequently he was of no political importance. In 1771 the act requiring the marking of paupers was repealed. From a humane point of view we have made remarkable progress.

* * *

In common with the rest of the province the people of Northampton county followed the prerevolutionary war acts of England, of Pennsylvania, and of the other colonies in America, with intetnse interest. None of the stamped paper issued in England, in conformity with the Stamp Act ever reached our county and our courts functioned in the usual manner.[36]

In December of 1774, as a result of a resolution passed by the Association of the Continental Congress, there was formed in the county a Committee of Observation and Inspection. From that time on through the war, this committee met in the court house and assumed many of the duties of the courts.

On July 8th, 1776, four days after the Declaration of Independence was adopted, it was read to the people of Northampton county from the steps of the court house.[37] A large crowd had gathered. The colonel and field officers of the 1st battalion were among the select group gathered about the entrance to the building. Just before the reading started, a company of light infantry marched down Northampton street, to the beating of drums and the playing of fifes. The ensign of the company, marching in the van, carried a flag, the forerunner of our national emblem. The story of this flag is too long to be told here. A Philadelphia paper,[38] published on July 11th, of that year, in describing the ceremonies in connection with the reading of the Declaration at Easton, mentions the flag in the following words:—"the standard, the device for which is the thirteen united colonies, - - was ordered displayed."

As the company of infantry was drawn up in front of the court house and the new flag held at attention, Robert Levers read the imperishable document to a large, attentive, and serious audience. At the close of the reading the bell in the cupola pealed forth the glad tidings of the birth of the Nation and the spectators "gave their hearty consent with three loud huzzas, and cried out 'May God long preserve and unite the Free and Independent States of America'."

The last court session, under the reign of King George III, was held on June 19th, 1777, and on the same day court held its first session under the United States of America.[38]

During the revolutionary war the center of activity for the county was the Great Square in Easton and in the very center of this Square stood the court house. The men going to war, those returning, the injured, the convalescent, the supplies for the army, the wagons which had been commandeered, General Lee's retreating army, the wounded on their way to Bethlehem, the Indians at the treaty of 1777, General Sullivan and his army, and the people of the town with nerves on edge trying to carry on in a normal manner, all milled about the court house. At times the building was used as barracks and again it was pressed into service as a hospital.

On June of 1779, Martha Washington, accompanied by a large escort of officers, drove through the square,[39] and past the court house. On July 26th, 1782, General Washington, on his way to Newburg, rode by the building. Within its portals the Committee of Observation met, the court held sessions, and men were tried for treason and lesser crimes. In the cupola the Moravian bell tolled the death of prominent citizens or joyfully summoned the citizens to hear of a victory. In 1783 it rang out the good news that peace had been declared and that America was a free and independent nation.

* * *

As the years rolled by the population of the county rapidly increased and the business of the courts and of the county outgrew the stone building. It became necessary either to increase the size of the building or to build an additional structure. The latter method was adopted and a new one story stone building was erected to house the county records. Later the prothonotary and the clerk of the orphans court moved into the structure. The courts continued to hold sessions in the court house in the center of the Square. The new building was called the County Records Building or the County Building and was erected on the south side of the Square, east of Pomfret street. The property was purchased from George Snyder on February 25th, 1793,[40] after several other sites had been offered the commissioners.[41]

William Nyce was the contractor and the amount of his contract was one thousand pounds. Martin Frey was the stone cutter, John Green furnished some of the lumber, Abraham Berlin supplied the iron work, and Samuel Sitgreaves was paid ten dollars for his advice in prosecuting the contractor for noncompliance with his contract.[42] The building must have been completed the latter part of 1795, for in November of that year the county paid twenty-six pounds, twelve shillings, and six pence for three stoves with which to heat it.[43]

* * *

Water for domestic consumption was a problem in the early days of Easton. There were a number of wells throughout the town. Some of these had been constructed within the limits of the public streets and were paid for jointly by several of the property owners in the immediate vicinity. At times, generally in the summer, the wells became dry or very low in water.

In the summer of 1801, a petition was presented to the court stating that the judges, jurors, witnesses, and litigants attending court were greatly inconvenienced for want of a good water supply near the court house,[44] that all the wells in the town were not only very low but at quite a distance away. The petition prayed for the construction of a well near the court house. There were many signers to this petition. Among the more prominent were George Wolf, who became Governor of Pennsylvania, and Samuel Sitgreaves, who was appointed a special commissioner by President Adams, and sent to London to adjust the differences which had grown out of the Jay Treaty. The petition was granted and the well constructed.

* * *

In 1800 the census taker reported that there were upwards of one thousand persons in the Borough of Easton. At that time there was a decided pastoral atmosphere in and about the Great Square. The cattle, the swine, and the sheep ran at large about the town, and like the citizens, congregated in the square. There was a low spot in the southwest corner and in rainy seasons and after storms that part of the square became a pond. In this body of water the pigs would wallow. On sunny days the sheep gathered in the shade of the court house. The stench at times was intolerable.

In August of 1803, a meeting of citizens was held in the court house to express their opinion on two ordinances then before the burgesses.[45] On the question "Shall the ordinance to prevent the running at large of swine be enacted?", the citizens decided in favor of the pigs. On the other ordinance the citizens voted to forbid the running at large of horses. The sheep seem to have been entirely overlooked.

* * *

Shortly after the Revolutionary War, Benjamin Franklin remarked that the war then ended was the war of the rebellion and that the war of independence was yet to be fought. Franklin was seldom wrong.

England failed to realize or admit that their recent rebellious subjects were now an independent nation. For many years she disregarded portions of the treaty of 1783. During the Napoleonic wars, England's navy numbered about one thousand ships. She considered herself the supreme mistress of the seas. To man her extensive fleet she used press gangs and boarded vessels of the United States merchant marine, taking the best able-bodied seamen to augment her depleted crews. This was done under the pretence that the men taken were deserters from the British navy. She did this on the high seas, within the three mile limit, and even in our harbors along the Atlantic coast.

Franklin was right. It was again necessary to fight England in a war for independence. This was called the War of 1812.

On September 13th, 1814, about three weeks after the British had burned the Capitol at Washington, two companies of volunteers, under Captain Abraham Horn and Captain Peter Nunges-ser, gathered in the Square in front of the court house. When the companies were drawn up at attention, Rosanna Beidleman, a girl of fourteen, presented a flag to Captain Horn's company with these words: "Under this flag march to glory." Ensign John Dingler, in his embarrassment and patriotic fervor replied, "I will, mam."[46] The men then marched to the Delaware River where they boarded ten Durham boats and with the flag flapping in the breeze started down the river, to help maintain the freedom of the seas. After three months in camp these soldiers returned home without seeing any active service. The war of 1812 was over. Again America had won a glorious victory.

This flag which had been presented to our local volunteers in the fall of 1814, may have been the same flag that was held at attention on July 8th, 1776, when the Declaration of Independence was read from the court house steps. It is now framed and hangs on the walls of the Easton Public Library. Its design has been adopted as the official flag of the City of Easton.

* * *

The Easton Lodge of Free and Accepted Masons, No. 152, was instituted in the court house on May 26th, 1817,[47] and for a number of years this organization held their meetings in the building. During this period Peter Ihrie annually paid to the county the sum of about forty-eight dollars. This amount was credited to Ihrie, on the report of the county treasurer, as a gift and a contribution. It hardly seems probable that Peter Ihrie worried over the small amount of taxes which he was compelled to pay and voluntarily increased his payments to the county. It is more than likely that these payments represent the rent which the Masonic Order paid for the use of the court house.

* * *

In September of 1826 the town council suggested the propriety of erecting a town clock in the belfry of the court house and issued a call for a town meeting.[48] On September 25th, the town meeting was held and passed an ordinance authorizing the Burgesses to assess and collect the sum of five hundred dollars for the purpose. Advertisements asking for proposals covering the furnishing and installing a clock brought three bids. Jedediah

Weiss of Bethlehem was the lowest bidder and he was awarded the contract at the sum of seven hundred dollars, conditional on raising the additional amount.

On January 27th, 1827, James Madison Porter, Chief Burgess, called upon the county commissioners and asked their consent to place the clock in the court house and requested them to contribute two hundred dollars. Permission to place the clock was granted but the commissioners refused to contribute toward its cost. On Tuesday, February 27th, a town meeting authorized the raising of an additional three hundred dollars.

For some reason the award of the contract to Mr. Weiss must have been cancelled, for on August 7th, 1827, a contract for a clock with hour and minute hands and four dials facing the cardinal points of the compass was awarded to Gottlieb Schultz of Philadelphia. The clock was installed by Mr. Schultz with the dials placed in the four gables of the building. On September 10th, Christian Bixler was requested to take charge of its maintenance at a salary of twenty-five dollars per year.

There is a remote possibility that a clock may have been placed in the court house long before this time. An engraving of the court house made in 1798 shows a clock in the west gable directly over the entrance. This may have been an artist's fancy, for no records of a clock at this early date have been found.

* * *

With the passing of the years the building began to show signs of age. The interior of the old stone walls became damp, the paint dingy, and the woodwork worn and decayed. The interior of the building was gloomy.

In 1844 some consideration was given to building a new court house, but the taxes were even then a burden and the county was content with making repairs and alterations.[49]

The following is from the Whig and Journal of July 3rd, 1844:—"The new arrangement spoken of for the court room will be a handsome improvement, and when the steeple and other wood work gets a few coats of paint and the weather beaten walls a rough cast or some other fixing up it will answer all purposes for which it was intended for twenty-five years to come - - and all at a cost of less than one thousand dollars, which will not add one cent to the present rate of taxes. People of old Northampton only think of it - - A new court house out of the old one at such a dog cheap rate; not much more than a fashionable tailor would charge to fit out a modern dandy. Why the very thought makes us feel proud; and with the splendid fitting up in prospect we wouldn't swap the old fabric for the ninety thousand dollar court house recently built by our extravagant neighbor of Berks."

On November 20th of that year the same paper said :—"Many of the citizens who have been attending our courts for the last half century appeared to be surprised on entering to find it painted, handsomely papered, and conveniently arranged with seats to which they were conducted with a constable's order of 'Hats off'. - - The exterior of the building is much improved with a neat portico at the west entrance and the whole surrounded with a fence enclosing the eighty feet of ground belonging to the county."

* * *

In May of 1846 Congress declared war against Mexico and President Polk called for fifty thousand volunteers.

On the evening of June the 15th (1846) a large town meeting was held in the court house and patriotic enthusiasm ran high. The Easton Fencibles volunteered their services. In December the Governor of Pennsylvania selected ten companies from various sections of the state to form a regiment but the Fencibles were not among the select.

Another company, the Easton Guards, drilled nightly and offered their services. The grand jury recommended to the county commissioners that they appropriate one thousand dollars for the use of this company in case they were called, but again the selection passed over Northampton county. Some of the more enthusiastic of our local citizens enrolled with the Stockton Artillerists of Mauch Chunk and the Wyoming Artillerists of Wilkes-Barre. No company or organized group of recruits ever left Northampton County for the Mexican War.

When those from Easton, who had enrolled with the Mauch Chunk and Wilkes-Barre companies returned, they were given a royal reception. The Easton Brass Band, the Phoenix Fire Company; and the greater part of the population of the borough met them at the railroad station. They were paraded through the principal streets to the booming of a cannon on Mt. Jefferson and the ringing of the bells in the town. The triumphal processions wound up at the court house, where local orators extolled their patriotism and their bravery and welcomed home the returning heroes.

* * *

The borough of Easton not only used the court house as a place in which to hold their town meetings but also as a meeting place for the burgesses. The borough corporation occupied county property in the rear of the County Records Building for a hose and engine house. For the use of the county property the borough paid no rent and on November 18th, 1846, the county commissioners notified the borough to vacate.

This action on the part of the commissioners was resented by the burgesses and they retaliated, when improving the Square, by laying out a circle in its center and around which they erected a fence. This circular fence was of sufficient diameter to include the property of the county which the commissioners had just fenced in. So some time in 1847 or 1848 the old court house was surrounded by two fences, the outer one erected by the borough forming a circle and the inner one forming a square erected by the county. The county commissioners vigorously opposed the erection of the borough fence but without avail.

While there was nothing unusual in a controversy between the borough and the county authorities it does seem strange that a spite fence, erected as a result of this disagreement, should have established our present day Circle.

* * *

The improvements made in 1844, which were presumed to last at least twenty-five years, were but ten years old when the question of a new court house was again raised. While various grand juries had considered the matter and refused to approve the erection of a new building, the county commissioners proceeded with certain improvements, chief of which was the cutting of a new door in the south side of the building. The old west entrance was then reserved for the judges, the lawyers, and others of the privileged class. The Easton Argus, which supported the movement of a new court house, refers to this improvement in its issue of January 21st, 1858, in the following manner:—"The new door will doubtless make the old shanty more comfortable to those who are compelled to go into the dirty place but it will present no new attractions to men who prefer cleanliness and pure air."

In a sarcastic article, the Free Press[50] calls attention to the fact that the county is enlarging the poor house to accommodate the "better citizens of foreign lands" but it can not afford to build a "temple of justice to try the sinners of our native soil."

* * *

Easton was never popular as a county seat and efforts were constantly being made to have the court house moved to a more central location. When Thomas and John Penn had decided, as early as 1736, that the land between the Delaware and Lehigh rivers was well suited for the location of a town, they did not foresee the possibility of its being a shiretown for a new county. However, when the agitation for the erection of a new county was started, they realized the great advantage of laying out a town at the Forks of the Delaware and having it selected as the county seat. It was entirely due to their instructions that Easton, a town which did not exist, was named the county seat when Northampton county was erected in 1752. It was a remarkable set up for a real-estate development.

There can be no question about the location being most undesirable from the point of view of the county inhabitants. With the exception of a few homes in Williams Township, the site was remote from the settled portions of the county and extremely hard to reach.

During the colonial period, Thomas Penn exercised sufficient control over the Assembly to prevent a change in the location of the county seat. After Penn's influence ceased to be a factor, the investment in the public buildings made it inexpedient to change.

Each time a new county was taken from Northampton, the

size of the county was reduced until it reached its present relative small area. This, with the changes in our civilization, and the great improvement in transportation has entirely changed the situation. Today, Easton is the logical location for the county seat.

After the construction of the court house was started, a petition was presented to the Assembly in May of 1765, praying that the court house be erected at some other point nearer the center of the county. The Petition stated, that for twelve years, they had experienced "great hardship and inconvenience" due to the location of "the seat of Judicature" in so remote a corner of the county. They claimed that there "could not have been devised a place more improper and inconvenient than Easton, environed on all sides with hills and rivers secluding it from the rest of the county." They admitted that to change the location of the court house would inconvenience a few of the residents of Easton, but they conceived, "that as in all good government a lesser evil is to be suffered in order to obtain a greater good to the community, so they hope, that, in this free government, a greater evil, though established by law, shall not prevail, only to obtain a lesser good." They trusted that the whole county should not "languish for ever" under a condition "which appears so grievious and burdensome." The Assembly gave the petition serious consideration but reffirmed the previous act.

Again in 1784 a petition was addressed to the Legislature of the commonwealth asking that the location of the county seat be changed, enumerating all the reasons given in 1765.

The next serious attempt to move the county offices and buildings was in 1858.[51] At that time it was evident that a new court house would be built. A movement was started to have the new court house erected at Nazareth. A monster mass meeting was held at Hecktown and a petition drawn up and sent to the legislature. A bill was introduced authorizing an election in the county to determine the choice of the people. This bill was eventually laid on the table and never brought up.

By this time the canal had been built and the railroads constructed so that Easton had become a commercial city of great importance in the county. The same arguments, which in the early days had been unsuccessfully used to show why the county seat should be moved from Easton, were now successfully used to show why it should not be moved.

The following is taken from the Easton Argus of March 4th, 1858 :—"- - when Easton can now be reached by railroads from almost every portion of the county in one hour's time, how ridiculous this whole proceeding appears. The citizens of Upper and Lower Mount Bethel, Saucon, Williams, Allen, Lehigh, Bethlehem Borough, Bethlehem township, Freemansburg, etc., can all come to Easton by railroad while they would have to go to Nazareth or Bath in their own conveyances. As a matter of consequence, a majority of the people would be greatly inconvenienced."

In March of 1854 the county commissioners resolved to build a new court house in the borough of Easton, provided the grand jury approved. It was not until December of 1859 that the grand jury sanctioned the erection of a new building and the abandonment of the old one.[52]

* * *

The doom of the court house had been signed and sealed but the execution had not been put into effect when on April 12th, 1861, a shot fired at Fort Sumter, from the quiet shores of Charlestown harbor, startled the nation into a realization that the differences which had arisen between the south and the north were about to be settled on the bloody field of battle. The Union which the old court house had helped to establish was about to be torn asunder.

On the Saturday evening following the attack on Fort Sumter, a monster mass meeting was held in the court house.[53] Notwithstanding the short notice and the fact that a heavy rain added to the gloom, the building was packed. The windows were opened so that the overflow crowd, standing in the rain, could participate. Judge H. D. Maxwell in a fine patriotic oration addressed the meeting which then adjourned until the following Monday evening. The Monday meeting was again packed and again the overflow crowd stood in a downpour of rain.

On this day President Lincoln issued a call for seventy-five thousand volunteer militiamen. Three days later, in answer to this call, one hundred and eighty volunteers gathered in the northwest corner of the Square. To the music of Pomp's Band they marched to the railroad station where they entrained for Harrisburg to be equipped and mustered into the army. Two days later the same scene was enacted with one hundred and seventy volunteers. From time to time, the choice sons of the county, offered their services. It was not until the court house had been abandoned that men were drafted for service in the army.

* * *

Very little consideration could be given to the abandonment of a court house in a community of suppressed excitement and patriotic fervor. With bands playing, the flags flying, and with the population now wildly cheering and now wiping away a tear as a loved one marched by, the mere fate of a court house secured but scant attention. The county authorities, however, proceeded with the recommendations of the grand jury.

The problem confronting the commissioners was the selection of a site for the new court house. They first decided to build on the site of the old building. Then they selected the location of the county records building. The final choice was the lot upon which our present court house stands.

In the early part of December, 1861,[54] the old court house was sold to John Maxwell for fifty-six dollars. He purchased it for its salvage value and agreed to have it removed by the 15th of May, 1862.

The Free Press, of December 26th, 1861, in reference to the tearing down of the court house, says: "That this ancient building should give way for one better calculated for the business of the county is not much to be regretted, had we a better one in its place. But when it is remembered that in its place we have only a miserable abortion, a monument of the folly of ignorant and stubborn county commissioners, then is the pulling down of the venerable old building to be regretted. But the fiat has gone forth, and soon, the old court house will have disappeared."

The building now took on a deserted appearance. The doors, the window frames and sash, and everything of value had been removed. The county commissioners had taken the bell to the new court house and the town burgesses had installed the clock in the steeple of the German Reformed Church.[55] The walls of the building were decorated with crude drawings by the youth of the town and adorned by the advance agent of a circus with posters calling attention to the coming colossal and stupendous extravaganza, with a waterproof pavilion accommodating three thousand persons and illuminated with a patented sylvic gas giving a light scarcely less brilliant than the noonday sun and free from all "nauseous affluvia."

On Monday, April 14th, 1862, Mr. Maxwell started to raze the empty shell and his wrecking crew fastening a rope to the cupola tugged away until the crowning glory of the old building toppled to the roof and then crashed to the ground.[56] The supports were taken from the roof causing that to sag and then collapse, and the undermined walls, with the circus murals of elephants, bears,[57] and other animals, fell into the ruins and became but heaps of stone.

* * *

The building, which had played its part in the struggles of the frontier, in the birth throes of the nation, the fight for the freedom of the seas, the political struggles of the province, the county, the state, and the nation, whose walls had resounded to the oratory of Lewis Gordon, Robert Traill, Samuel Sitgreaves, James Madison Porter, George Wolf, and Joel Jones, was torn down by the hands which had erected it, the citizens of Northampton County.

The old stone court house, which should have been kept and revered as a memorial to our forefathers, who suffered and endured, fought and conquered, that this nation might live, met an ignominious fate, and the colonial building which today should be our heritage, our pride, and our joy, on a cold and dreary day in May of 1862, lay in the center of our Great Square, a mere pile of rubbish.

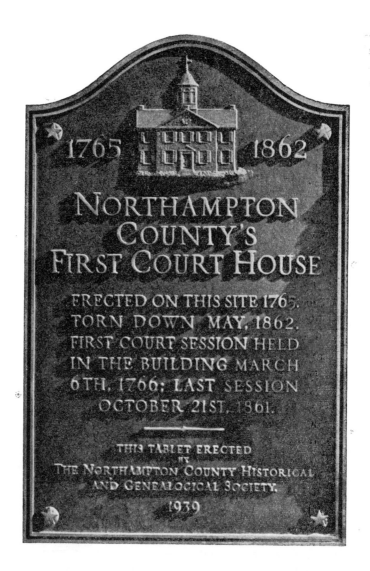

Marker, Designed by A. D. Chidsey, Jr., Mounted on Native Boulder in Centre Square, Easton, Pennsylvania.

The building is gone; its memory lingers.

The bronze tablet which has been erected to mark its site should cause us, and future generations, to pause in passing and visualize the pageant of history, which for nearly one hundred years, passed by and through its massive stone walls. May this marker instill in us a desire to learn more of the events of the past and of the deeds of our forefathers so that the history of our county and of our nation, yes, of our very liberty, may become a living tradition.

All the newspapers here mentioned are on file at the Easton (Pa.) Public Library.

[1]Pennsylvania Magazine of History, Vol. 38, p. 113. Expense account of William Parsons.
[2]Pennsylvania Historical Society, Northampton County Manuscript, Vol. 1729-1758, p. 141. William Parsons' letter to Richard Peters, Nov. 17, 1754.
[3]Pennsylvania Colonial Records, Vol. IV, p. 413-420.
[4]Pennsylvania Historical Society. Original fiield book of William Parsons showing 1736 survey of the Easton Tract.
[5]Pennsylvania Magazine of History, Vol. 38, p. 113.
[6]Ibid.
[7]The Statutes at Large of Pennsylvania, Vol. V, p. 140.
[8]Pennsylvania Magazine of History, Vol. 38, p. 113.
[9]Pennsylvania Colonial Records, Vol. V, p. 572.
[10]The Statutes at Large of Pennsylvania, Vol. V, p. 140.
[11]Ibid.
[12]Pennsylvania Archives, Vol. II, p. 98.
[13]Pennsylvania Historical Society. Richard Peters Manuscript. Vol. III, p. 63.
[14]The Statutes at Large of Pennsylvania.
[15]Pennsylvania Colonial Records. Vol. III, p. 291.
[16]Pennsylvania Archives, 8th Series, p. 4422.
[17]Pennsylvania Historical Society. Northampton County Manuscripts, Vol. 1727 to 1758, p. 147.
[18]Land Office, Harrisburg, Pa., Patent Book AA-4, p. 220.
[19]Pennsylvania Archives—8th Series, Vol. VI, p. 5370.
[20]Ibid.
[21]Ibid, p. 5402.
[22]Land Office, Harrisburg, Pa., Patent Book AA-6, p. 115.
[23]Pennsylvania Archives, 8th Series, Vol. VII, Sept. 30, 1766.
[24]Moravian Archives.
[25]"Historical Notes" Manuscript, by E. A. Weaver. Vol. 3, 1st Series, Easton (Pa.) Public Library.
[26]"The Cabinet of Momus"—1809. Pub. by R. Desilver, Phila., Pa.
[27]The Statutes at Large of Pennsylvania. Vol. III, p. 198.
[28]Original Manuscript. Archives Room, Court House, Easton, Pa.
[29]Office of Prothonotary, Court House, Easton, Pa., Continuance Docket, Vol. 6, p. 291.

[30]Pennsylvania Archives. 8th Series. Vol. VII, p. 5754.
[31]"Notes, relative to old Court House," by E. A. Weaver. Manuscript. Easton (Pa.) Public Library.
[32]The Statutes at Large of Pennsylvania.
[33]Original Manuscript. Archives Room, Court House, Easton, Pa.
[34]Ibid.
[35]The Statutes at Large of Pennsylvania. Vol. III, p. 224.
[36]All the available county records indicate that court sessions were held regularly during the period.
[37]American Archives, 1848, by Peter Force. 5th Series, Vol. I, p. 119.
[38]Ibid.
[39]Pennsylvania Magazine of History, Vol. 38, p. 110.
[40]Deed filed, Easton, Pa., Deed Book H, Vol. 8, p. 258.
[41]Conrad Ihrie, Dr. Andrew Ledlie, and Mordacai Peirsol offered their properties for various sums. Original manuscript. Archives Room, Court House, Easton, Pa.
[42]Original Manuscript. Archives Room, Court House, Easton, Pa.
[43]Ibid.
[44]Original petition. Archives Room, Court House, Easton, Pa.
[45]"Historical Notes." Manuscript by E. A. Weaver, Easton (Pa.) Public Library.
[46]Statement of S. Moore, a member of Captain Horn's Company. Northampton County (Pa.) Historical Society.
[47]"Old Masonic Lodges in Pennsylvania," Vol. II, p. 3 and 140; also "Historical Notes" Manuscript of E. A. Weaver, Easton (Pa.) Public Library.
[48]Minutes of the Borough, City Clerk's Office, Easton, Pa., Sept. 28, 1826, Sept. 25, 1826, Nov. 11, 1826, Jan. 27, 1827, Feb. 19, 1827, Feb. 27, 1827, Aug. 7, 1827, and Sept. 10, 1827.
[49]The Northampton Whig and Lehigh Journal, issues of July 3, 1884; Sept. 25, 1884; Oct. 23, 1844; and Nov. 20, 1844.
[50]"Easton Free Press," issue of January 28, 1858.
[51]"Easton Argus," issue of March 4, 1858.
[52]"Easton Free Press," issue of Dec. 1, 1859.
[53]"Easton Argus," issue of Arpil 18, 1861.
[54]In the local press, both Charles Dawes and John Maxwell are reported as having purchased the building. Easton Argus of Dec. 26, 1861; Northampton County Journal of Dec. 25, 1861. Annual report of County Treasurer gives item "Received of John Maxwell for old court house $55.00.' See Northampton County Journal of Feb. 10, 1862.
[55]"The Northampton County Journal," Nov. 6, 1861; "Easton Argus," Nov. 7, 1861; Apr. 17, 1862, and May 8, 1862.
[56]"Journal," April 16th and 30th, 1862.
[57]"Easton Argus," May 1, 1862.
[58]Prothonotary's Office, Easton, Pa.

Property Owners in Easton
in 1776

Property Owners in Easton in 1776

F OR twenty-four years the little town of Easton had grown under the rule of Great Britain. The frontier, in which it had been founded had reached far to the north and west. The local struggle to claim the wilderness had been won. The citizens of the town were now engaged in another struggle, a contest to throw off the yoke of England and establish a new and independent nation. They were willing and ready to give "their lives, their fortunes, and their sacred honor" in support of the nation born on July 4th, 1776. The rule of England had ended.

The locations of the buildings shown on the map were determined from warrants, surveys, patents, deeds, agreements, mortgages, wills, and partition proceedings. This information, except in rare instances, did not show the exact location of the building on the lot.

The notes herein given are not intended as briefs-of-title or as genealogical data of the families mentioned. Such information as came to hand in the compiling of the map has been set down with the hope that it may be of some interest.

There are sixty-nine houses shown on the map. Jacob Grotz, Sr., the assessor for 1776, lists but sixty-four. There were at least five houses, known to have been in existence, which, for some reason, are not included in the assessment. These five are the dwelling owned by George Taylor at the northeast corner of Northampton and Fermor Streets; the Moravian building on the southwest corner of Ferry and Pomfret Streets, the house at the northeast corner of the Great Square and Pomfret Street owned

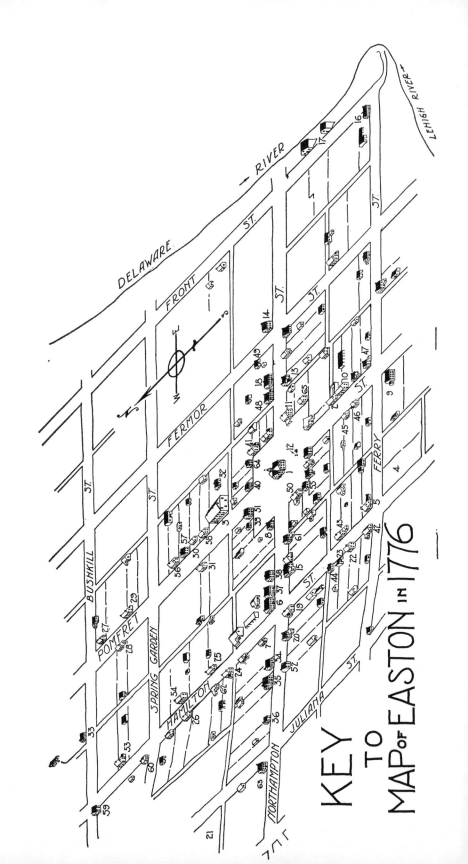

KEY
TO
MAP of EASTON IN 1776

Legend to Key Map

1. Court House
2. County Goal
3. Reformed-Lutheran Church
4. Burial Ground, Lutheran
5. Residence, built by Wm. Parsons
6. Red Lion Tavern
7. Residence, built by Wm. Parsons
8. Residence, Henry Alshouse
9. Moravian Building
10. Residence, Robert Levers
11. Michael Hart, Store & Residence
12. Whipping Post and Pillory
13. Residence, Leonard Smith
14. Property of George Taylor
15. Louis Gordon, Residence
16. Ferry House Tavern
17. Warehouses
18. Robert Traill, Residence
19. Adam Yohe, Innkeeper
20. Henry Shnyder, Residence
21. Burial Ground, Reformed
22. Abraham Berlin, Residence
23. Abraham Berlin, Blacksmith Shop
24. Michael Yohe, Residence
25. Ernest Becker, Baker
26. John Batt, Residence
27. John Dingler, Residence
28. Residence of John Nicholas
29. Conrad Rohn, Residence
30. Residence of Andrew Herster
31. Residence of John Rees, Tailor
32. Log School House, Built in 1755
33. Herman Schneider, Tanner
34. Frederick Schaus, Mason
35. Jeremiah Trexler, Residence
36. John Mush, Residence
37. Property of Casper Doll
38. Myer Hart, Residence
39. Shop of Moritz Bishoff
40. Property of Fred. Nungesser
41. Andrew Ledlie, Doctor
42. Elizabeth Streiber, Residence
43. Jacob Berlin, Residence
44. Residence of George Bush
45. Residence of John Spangenberg
46. Christian Holland, Residence
47. Henry Bush, Butcher
48. Henry Fullert, Sheriff
49. George Taylor, Stone Stable
50. Christian Nungesser, Shopkeeper
51. John Spering, Cordwainer
52. Residence, Christian Peiffer
53. John Deichman, Residence
54. Abraham Labar, Residence
55. John Simon, Hatter
56. Jacob Grotz, Sr., Residence
57. Christian Bittenbender, Residence
58. Jacob Grotz, Jr., Residence
59. Henry Barnet, Tanner
60. Frederick Reeger, Dyer
61. Parsonage, German Reformed
62. Andrew Eichelmeyer, Residence
63. Stone House
64. Arnold Everhard, Residence
65. Michael Lean, Residence

by the estate of Frederick Nungesser; the present home of the
D.A.R. at the northeast corner of Ferry and Fourth (then Hamilton) Streets; and Meyer Hart is assessed for but one house
when he owned two. There may have been others.

---

*NAMES AND OCCUPATIONS TAKEN FROM
THE ASSESSMENT OF JANUARY 2, 1776
FOR EASTON*

Jeremiah Traxler, Collector for Easton Township.
Jacob Grotz, Sen'r, Assessor for Easton Township.

Henry Allshouse, Joiner
Philip Achenbach, Shopkeeper
Henry Barnet, Tanner
Abraham Berlin, Smith
Henry Bush, Butcher
George Bush, Carpenter
Ernest Becker, Baker
John Batt, Skindresser
Christopher Bittenbender, Smith
George Bittenbender
Henry Brown, Taylor
John Coleman, Taverner
Jacob Dinkey
John Dingler, Laborer
John Deichman, Weaver
John Dunn, Taverner
Peter Ealer, Gaoler
Andrew Eikenmyer, Laborer
Arnold Evenhart, Laborer
Jacob Everet, Farmer
Henry Fullert, Sheriff
Nicholas Funston, Farmer
James Funston, Laborer

Lewis Gordon, Esq., Prothonotary
Jacob Grotz, Sen'r, Carpenter
Andrew Grotz, Carpenter
Jacob Grotz, Jr., Carpenter
Abel Gibbons
Myer Hart, Shopkeeper
Michael Hart, Shopkeeper
Stephen Horn, Mason
Andrew Harster, Laborer
Adam Hay Weaver
Christian Holland, Nailsmith
Peter Kachlein, Miller
Lewis Knows, Sadler
Peter Kachlein, Jr., Fuller
Abraham Labar, Taylor
Michael Lean, Laborer
Jacob Lickfelt, Laborer
Widow Lions, Shopkeeper
Matthias Miller, Taverner
John Musch, Shoemaker
Joseph Mimm, Taylor
Christina Nungesser, Taverner
John Nicholas, Laborer

Jacob Opp, Taverner

Michael Opp, Weaver

Christian Peiffer

John Rinker, Taverner

John Reese, Taylor

Frederick Reeger, Dyer

Ludwig Reeger, Mason

Conrad Rohn, Butcher

Adam Reeser, Laborer

John Repsher

Peter Richter, Cooper

Nicholas Ripple

Harman Shnyder, Tanner

Leonard Smith, Sadler

John Simon, Hatter

John Spering, Shoemaker

Ludwig Shaub, Joiner

Frederick Shouse, Mason

Henry Shnyder, Taverner

Isaac Sidman, Taverner

Widow Streiber

Jeremiah Trexler

Robert Traill, Scrivener

Nicholas Traxel, Shoemaker

Adam Yohe, Taverner

Michael Yohe, Shoemaker

Henry Young, Silversmith

David Wagner, Miller

Samuel Webber, Shoemaker

SINGLEMEN

Andrew Ledlie

William Funstone

Jacob Berlin

Peter Shnyder

Thomas Tyson

Number of Houses Listed 64

Number of Horses 29

Number of Horned Cattle 66

Number of Sheep 60

Bound Servants 3

Negroes and Mullattoes (Slaves) 4

The numbers at the head of the following paragraphs correspond with the numbers of the buildings as shown on the "Map of Easton, Pennsylvania, in 1776." (See Key Map).

NUMBER 1

The County Court House was built in 1765 by a board of trustees consisting of John Jones, Henry Armstrong, James Martin, John Rinker and Henry Allshouse. Rinker and Allshouse were of Easton, Jones was from Bethlehem, Armstrong lived in the Irish Settlement, and Martin came from up the Delaware River at what is now Martin's Creek. The total cost was Nine Hundred Ninety Eight pounds. It was undoubtedly the first building erected in Easton to be designed by a competent person. Its lines, including the belfry, were too pleasing to have been the result of any hit-or-miss construction. It was built of native blue limestone and was rough cast in 1844. The building became inadequate and was torn down in 1862.

* * *

Number 2

The stone county gaol, constructed about 1762, was the second one built in Easton and replaced an earlier log structure. In 1776 Peter Earler was gaoler. (Town Lot No. 96)

* * *

Number 3

The corner stone of the German Reformed Church was laid on June 8th, 1775 and the building was consecrated on November 17th, 1776. The entrance vestibule and the steeple were added in 1832-3. Rev. Ingold was pastor when the church was consecrated. The name of the architect is unknown. A pipe organ, built by Dannaker, was installed at the time the church was erected. The pipes, or reeds, of this organ are now in the possession of the Northampton County Historical and Genealogical Society. The Indian Treaty of 1777 was held in this building and the minutes of the meeting record that the treaty was opened by the shaking of hands and the drinking of rum as the organ was played. Historians tell us that the building was used as a hospital during the Revolutionary War. On Sunday, October 17, 1799, two days after General Sullivan and part of his army returned to Easton from their expedition into New York State, a thanksgiving sermon was delivered by Rev. Israel Evans, the chaplain of General Poore's brigade. General Sullivan and his officers and many of his men attended this service. (Town Lots Nos. 70 and 72.)

NUMBER 4

This was the Lutheran burial ground. Just when the first interment was made is not known. George Taylor, who died in 1781, was buried here. In 1802 the Penns gave a deed to the Lutheran and the Reformed congregations for this burial ground and for the one between Juliana and John Streets. This joint ownership did not work out well and in 1811 an agreement between the two congregations was entered into whereby the German Lutheran Evangelical Congregation of Easton secured the exclusive control of this cemetery. The 1802 deed from the Penns restricted the use of the property to burial only. In 1812 they gave a new deed to the Lutheran Congregation which permitted the erection of a church, a schoolhouse, and a parsonage in addition to using it as a burial ground. (Town Lots Nos. 179 and 180)

* * *

NUMBER 5

William Parsons constructed this house for his own use. He moved into the property in April of 1757. His enjoyment of his new home was brief for on December 17, of that year he died. In 1776 the property was owned by the estate of John Hughes. Hughes had died in 1772. George Taylor, signer of the Declaration of Independence, rented the property and moved in some time in April of 1770. He died in this house on February 23, 1781. Who occupied the property in 1776 is not known. The house is still standing and is the home of the George Taylor Chapter of the Daughters of the American Revolution. (Town Lot No. 176)

* * *

NUMBER 6

William Parsons, acting as agent for Paul Miller, stocking-weaver, purchased this corner property in 1754 and Miller erected thereon a stone building which he used as a dwelling and tavern. In September of 1757 this property was conveyed to Adam Yohe, who had previously occupied the premises as a tenant. Yohe conducted a tavern which he called the Red Lion. This was

Easton's principal hostelry during the French and Indian War. Yohe disposed of the property in 1760 to George Cungware who still owned it in 1772. Later Jacob Opp became owner and continued to operate the tavern. Just when Opp secured possession is not known but as the 1776 assessment list refers to him as a tavern keeper owning a house it is assumed that he lived here during the war. In 1806 the Orphans Court adjudges the property to Elizabeth, the daughter of Jacob Opp, and the wife of Abraham Horn. Eve, the eldest daughter of Opp, married Daniel Wagner. Opp's daughter Catharine married Christian Bixler. The first well in Easton was located in Northampton Street in front of this tavern. This well was somewhat of a public utility, for the cost of construction was borne by a number of the residents of the town and by the Proprietaries. The well was constructed in 1752. (Town Lot No. 165)

* * *

NUMBER 7

This was probably the first house built in Easton after the erection of Northampton County in 1752. A ferry house at the 'point' had been built previous to this date. William Parsons, who laid out the town, selected this site for the location of his residence which he constructed immediately after his arrival. He failed to secure a deed from the Penns and it was not until after his death that his executor secured title from the Proprietaries. This was in the year 1759. In 1760 Myer Hart purchased the property, which included two lots, for one hundred and thirty-one pounds. Hart held title until 1787 when Peter Schnyder, tanner, of Easton, became the owner. While Hart owned the property in 1776 it is not known whether he lived in the dwelling at that time. (Town Lots Nos. 217 and 218)

* * *

NUMBER 8

Henry Allshouse was, according to the early records, a "joyner" or house carpenter. He was one of the original settlers who spent the winter of 1752-3 at Easton. He was appointed one of five trustees to raise the money and build the court house. He lived at the northwest corner of Northampton Street and the Great Square, although he had previously owned and perhaps occupied other property in the village. His wife was named Susannah and he had three sons, Henry, Jacob and John. He also had two daughters, Susannah, who married Henry Kern, and Catharine, who remained a spinster and was called 'Caty'. Henry Allshouse died sometime between 1803 and 1809. (Parts of Town Lots No. 134, 135, 136, and 137)

* * *

NUMBER 9

In the year 1776 this property, purchased by John Okely for the Moravians in 1757, belonged to the heirs of Frederick Nungesser. The title to the property from Okely to Nungesser passed as follows:—In 1762 Nathaniel Seidel purchased it for four hundred and fifty pounds. In 1765 Conrad Streuber, a tanner, paid four hundred pounds for it. Streuber died and his widow, Elizabeth Margaret, sold it later in the same year to David Barringer for seven hundred pounds. Barringer became involved in financial difficulties and the sheriff, Peter Kachlein, sold the house and two lots to Frederick Nungesser in 1773. During the time that Okely held title to the property the Moravians constructed a large stone building which they intended to use as a place of worship but never did. There are some references to a purchase by the Lutheran Congregation who intended to use the building as a church. The recorded deeds indicate that any plan for the purchase of the property by the Lutherans was never carried out. It should, however, be pointed out that Conrad Streuber was a member of that denomination. Barringer kept a store in the building at the time of his failure and Isaac Sidman was a clerk in his employ. After the sheriff disposed of the property, Sidman became a merchant and may have conducted his store in this building and also lived there. This theory is strengthened by the fact that he married Elizabeth, the daughter of Frederick Nungesser, about seven months after Nungesser acquired the property. Whether Sidman lived in this house during the Revolutionary War may never be definitely determined. (Town Lots 121 and 122)

* * *

Number 10

Henry Rinker secured a patent for this lot on February 11, 1761. He erected thereon, perhaps before he secured title, a stone building which served as his residence and also as a hotel. In 1766 the sheriff sold the property to Henry Keppele, a merchant of Philadelphia, who held it for eight years, selling it on May 27th, 1774 to Jacob Meyer, a blacksmith of Bethlehem Township. On December 5th, of that year, Conrad Ihrie purchased the property. During the Revolutionary War he leased it to Robert Levers who used it as a residence during the war. It was in this house that Levers kept the valuable papers which had been sent from Philadelphia for safe keeping during the British occupation of that city. In 1778 Conrad Ihrie notified Levers to vacate. There must have been a shortage of houses in Easton at that time, for Levers states that he could not secure another house and asked permission of the Council to move to Allentown and take the state papers with him. His request was granted, but Levers, in consideration of the great inconvenience of living in Allentown and transacting business in Easton, the county seat, decided not to move and finally made arrangements to stay at Ihrie's house. Levers had been paying thirteen pounds per year rent. Ihrie now demanded and secured a rent beyond all reason. Levers writes: "I esteem it my duty - - - to close with my landlord, notwithstanding his extortionate demand, and engaged his house for a year at one hundred pounds." (Town Lot 98)

* * *

Number 11

At the March term of court in the year 1755, Samuel Henry, a merchant of Trenton, Province of New Jersey, secured a judgment, amounting to a little over two hundred fifty pounds, against Andrew McFarlin, who was then in possession of this property. These lots were seized by Nicholas Scull, Jr., High Sheriff, and sold by him on September 16, 1755, to Lewis Gordon. It is impossible to tell whether a dwelling had been erected on this property at the time Gordon acquired it. If not, Lewis Gordon built a stone house thereon, in which he lived until 1773, when he purchased a house on the south side of Northampton Street just east of Hamilton Street . (No. 15 of Map) On June 4th, 1778, he sold this stone dwelling to Michael Hart, who here conducted a store. At the time Hart secured the property John Murp'ly held it under a lease which had about one year to run. Murphy was a clockmaker and was still in Easton in 1779. It is likely that he occupied this property in 1776. He eventually moved to Allentown. (Town Lots Nos. 88 and 89.)

* * *

NUMBER 12

The pillory and whipping post were located in the Great Square and were likely constructed when the county was erected in 1752. They served the county for thirty-eight years and were legally abolished in 1790.

* * *

NUMBER 13

A warrant of survey for this lot was issued in favor of William Craig on April 2nd, 1753, by which time he had built a stone dwelling on the lot. By various conveyances the title became vested in Frederick Nungesser, who on June 8, 1771, sold the lot to Leonard Smith for the sum of two hundred pounds. Smith, a saddler, was Nungesser's son-in-law, having married his daughter, Christina. Smith and his wife disposed of the property in 1779 for fifteen hundred pounds. The increase in purchase price was largely due to the low value of the continental money. (Town Lot No. 87)

NUMBER 14

John Bachman (Baughman) secured a deed for this lot on November 17th, 1754 and erected a stone dwelling thereon. John Potts secured a judgment against Bachman and the sheriff seized the property and sold it to George Taylor. The deed to Taylor was dated December 24th, 1761. Taylor owned the property in 1776 but did not live in it. In 1779 Taylor, then living in Greenwich Township, New Jersey, sold the property to Theophilus Shannon, who is referred to as a merchant and as an innkeeper.

George Taylor was a signer of the Declaration of Independence. (Town Lot No. 24)

* * *

NUMBER 15

This is the house in which Lewis Gordon lived in from 1773 to the time of his death in 1778. It is referred to in some of the deeds as a "good stone dwelling house, two stories high". In 1754 John Meiner, cordwainer, secured a patent for this lot and built the house. Meiner sold it to Bartholomew Kelsey for ninety pounds, Kelsey sold it in 1757 to Ann Dougherty, of Philadelphia, for one hundred and fifty pounds. In 1767 she sold it to William Ledlie, merchant of Easton, for the same consideration. Ledlie sold it to Lewis Gordon on October 7, 1773, for two hundred fifty pounds. In 1776 Gordon secured a deed from the Penns for the vacant lot adjoining and at the southwest corner of Northampton and Hamilton Streets. It was in this house that Gordon lived while under arrest, but on parole. Several British officers, also under arrest and on parole, lived here with him. (Town Lots Nos. 171 and 172)

NUMBER 16

Just when this Ferry Tavern was erected is not known but it was likely between the years 1761 and 1765. In 1776 the Ferry and the Tavern were owned by Richard Penn and leased to Lewis Gordon. The operation of the ferry was the most lucrative business in Easton and had been in continuous operation since 1741 when the Penns granted the exclusive ferry privilege to David Martin, a prominent citizen of Trenton, New Jersey. The first ferry house was constructed prior to or during the year 1750, for in that year Dr. Thomas Graeme in a letter to Thomas Penn mentions the ferry house at this point. The ferry was of great importance during the Revolutionary War. (Town Lot No. 1)

*   *   *

NUMBER 17

Warehouses were erected along the banks of the Delaware and Lehigh Rivers some time previous to 1776. The two shown on the map are still standing but have been converted to other uses. Merchandise was stored in these buildings waiting transportation to Philadelphia by Durham boats. These boats were loaded at wharves adjoining the buildings. Vast quantity of supplies for the army were stored in and passed through these buildings during the Revolutionary War. These buildings are not given on the 1776 assessment list.

*   *   *

NUMBER 18

Robert Traill owned this property and lived here in 1776. It is not known if he built the house. In the year 1765 the lot was vacant. Traill was actively engaged in the cause of the American colonies, although for some time he refused to take the oath of allegiance. He was secretary of the Committee of Observation of Northampton County. In 1777 he was elected Major of the Fifth Battalion of the county and in 1779 was assistant deputy quartermaster general. He was a member of the State Assembly and in 1782 was sheriff of the county. On March 3, 1774 he married Elizabeth, the daughter of Jacob and Elizabeth Grotz. Elizabeth's father was a carpenter and lived on North Pomfret Street. (No. 56 of the Map) Robert Traill was a scrivener and was then admitted to practice law before the county courts. He lived in this house as late as 1787. (Town Lot No. 75)

* * *

NUMBER 19

In 1772 Adam Yohe purchased this property from the estate of John Fricker. This consideration was one hundred pounds. Fricker in his will refers to the property as "my house and lot". The deed carried the "right" in a draw well in front of the tavern at the northeast corner of Northampton and Hamilton Streets. A house was built on this lot by Jasper Scull in 1752 or 1753. Scull was a blacksmith and had contributed to the construction of the well, so this property carried a right to its use. Scull was the son of Nicholas Scull, who succeeded William Parsons as Surveyor General of the Province. Yohe evidently removed the buildings and built a stone dwelling and a stone stable which, in 1783, he sold to his son Adam Yohe Jr. for the sum of eight hundred pounds. In 1776 Adam Yohe conducted an inn in this building. On February 3, 1794 Adam Yohe Jr. conveyed title to Robert Traill. (Town Lot No. 216)

* * *

NUMBER 20

This property was occupied by Henry Shnyder, who in 1772 is listed as a shoemaker. In 1774, under the name of Henry Schneider, he is listed as an innkeeper. In 1776 he owned this house and lot. He died about 1778 and left a widow and the following children:—Henry, who acquired title to this property in 1793; Elizabeth, who married Christopher Meixsell; Margaret,

the wife of John Herster; Juliana, and Catharine. His widow
married a neighbor, John Shook. (Town Lot No. 215)*

* * *

NUMBER 21

William Parsons was buried in this burial ground in December of 1757. His grave, properly marked, is in front of the
Easton Public Library, which was erected on this, the first burial
ground in Easton. While this land was early set aside for burial
purposes it was not until 1802 that the Lutheran and Reformed
Congregations secured a deed from the Penns for the ground.
This joint ownership proved unsatisfactory and, in 1811, an agreement between the two denominations was entered into whereby
the German Reformed Congregation secured exclusive use of this
plot of ground. When the Easton School Board took over the
grounds for the use of the Public Library the remains of those
who had been buried here were removed to the Easton Cemetery.
Lewis Gordon was buried here in 1778, but the early records
showing the location of his grave have never been found and his
grave remained unidentified.

* * *

NUMBER 22

Abraham Berlin was one of Easton's eleven pioneers. He
was a blacksmith and a most respected citizen. When the school
house (No. 32 of Map) was constructed in 1755 he contributed
four days of labor. He built the windlass for the first well constructed in Easton. This well was located in front of the Red
Lion Inn at the northeast corner of Northampton and Hamilton Streets. It was dug in 1752. On July 15th, 1760, Berlin pur-

chased this dwelling from Frederick Nuncaster (Nungesser) and lived here until 1786 when the property was sold by the sheriff to satisfy a judgment which had been secured against him. Where he lived previous to 1760 is not known. In 1776 he succeeded Lewis Gordon as Chairman of the Committee of Observation for the county. On August 6, 1777, he was appointed one of the justices for the county. (Town Lot No. 203)

* * *

Number 23

Abraham Berlin acquired this lot adjoining the lot on which his residence was located and erected thereon a stone blacksmith shop. It is probable that in this shop most of the hardware for the court house was made, for it is safe to assume that Berlin furnished the greater part, if not all, of this material. His son Jacob, also a blacksmith, bought this shop when it was sold by the sheriff in 1786. (Town Lot No. 202)

* * *

Number 24

Michael Yohe was a shoemaker and had married Mary, the daughter of Frederick Shouse, a stone mason. It was here that they lived and Michael kept his shop. Just when the residence was built is not known, but Michael Yohe established his title to the lot by securing a deed from the Penns in 1789. He sold the property on April 13, 1795 to Michael Traxel, a house carpenter. The consideration was three hundred pounds. On January 13, 1802, Michael Yohe requested the court to relieve him of the duties as administrator of the estate of Henry Bush, stating that he had moved three hundred miles from Easton. (Town Lot No. 225)

* * *

Number 25

George Ernst Becker was a baker and one of the eleven original citizens who came to Easton in 1752. When he arrived there were but three houses in the village. He and his family lived in a tent in the Great Square for several days while, with the help of those who had preceded him to the town, he built a small house on North Hamilton Street. In a survey for town lot No. 162, made in 1764, the statement is made that Ernst Becker was in possession of lot No. 163. Becker died on December 21st, 1788. He married twice, his second wife was named Helena. Children by his first wife were Gertraut, Elizabeth, Bastian, Jacob, and George. His son George was a potter who died in 1768. A daughter named Ann Margaret married Nicholas Traxell. Ernst Becker never perfected title to his lot which he left to his daughter Ann Margaret. After Becker's death Ann Margaret and her husband Nicholas Traxell secured a deed from the Penns. This deed is dated December 4th, 1789. (Town Lot No. 163)

* * *

Number 26

John Batt is listed as a laborer in the tax list of 1772. His name on this list is given as John Bad. In the tax list of 1774, under the name of Johannes Batt, his occupation is recorded as tanner. Beside this property he owned outlots numbers 77 and 94. He secured title from the Penns in 1789 and in this deed he is referred to as a skindresser. From these facts it is assumed that his trade was that of skindresser and that he was not the owner of a tannery. The property was sold in 1808 by Peter Batt, a son, who was the executor of his father's estate. No mention is made of a wife in his will which he wrote on July 7, 1806. He mentions a married daughter, Catharine and the following other children: Peter, Susanna, Margaret, Jacob, Sarah, Elizabeth, and John. (Town Lot No. 233)

* * *

Number 27

On March 29, 1759, John Dingler (or Dengler) and his wife Anna Margaret were appointed administrators of the estate of Martin Adam, deceased. Anna Margaret was the widow of Adam at the time she married Dingler. It was likely this fact which accounts for their appointment. In the inventory of the estate of Martin Adam his house in Easton is valued at six pounds.

(About $15.00) Even at that time this was an extremely low figure and the dwelling must have been a poor structure. As the house became the property of widow Adam, it is assumed that this is the Adam house and that John Dingler when he married the widow, moved into her property. John Dingler was a laborer and a member of the German Reformed Congregation. He was paid one pound, ten shillings, in continental money for digging the grave of Lewis Gordon. This was equivalent to seven shillings and six pence in specie. There is some confusion between John Dingler the father and John George Dingler the son. The son was a cordwainer. The father or his wife owned this property in 1776 and the son secured a deed from the Penns in 1789. (Town Lots Nos. 50 and 52)

* * *

NUMBER 28
John Nicholas Jr. perfected title to this lot on December 4, 1789, when he secured a deed from the Penns. In 1825 John Nicholas Jr. and his wife Sarah, sold this lot with the "log messuage" to John Carey Jr. Nicholas' name does not appear on the tax list of 1772. He is listed in 1774, 1776, and 1779, but in none of these lists is his occupation given. In his deed to Carey he states that he was an innkeeper. It is likely that he had some other occupation. (Town Lot No. 150)

* * *

NUMBER 29
Conrad Rohn and his wife Elizabeth lived in this property as early as 1774, but he did not secure a deed from the Penns until January 10, 1794. In 1772 he is referred to as a laborer. In the year 1797 he sold the property to Samuel Sitgreaves. The present Y.M.C.A. building occupies part of this lot. (Town Lot No. 56)

* * *

NUMBER 30
Andrew Herster owned this property in 1776. On December 4, 1789 his son Daniel received a deed from the Penns cover-

ing the lot. Andrew Herster is listed as a laborer and his son Daniel as a cordwainer. Daniel with his wife Catharine sold the house and lot together with the rights to a well in Pomfret Street to the four associated Protestant Religious Societies known by the name of the German Reformed Evangelical Societies. The date of this deed is April 4, 1794 and the property was to be used for a "Parsonage Mansion" for the minister or pastor of that denomination. The well which had never been fiilled was uncovered in the spring of 1939. It was located in the sidewalk in front of the present (1940) Porter property on north Third (then Pomfret) Street. (Town Lot No. 66)

* * *

NUMBER 31

John Rees purchased this property in 1765 from John Wagle, who had secured the lot from the Penns in 1754. William Parsons made the original survey in 1754. Rees paid fifty-six pounds for the house and lot. In 1775 Rees secured a deed from the Penns for the lot on the northwest corner of Pomfret Street and a twenty feet wide alley now called Church Street. Rees was a tailor. In the records the name is spelled in various ways, i. e., Riss, Ries, Reese, and Rees. (Town Lot No. 143)

* * *

NUMBER 32

This was the first public building of any kind built in Easton. It was a log school house and was built in 1775 by local contributions of money, materials, and labor, helped by a gift of thirty pounds received from the trustees of a fund established in Europe for educational purposes in the American colonies. William Parsons was appointed chairman of the local trustees to manage the school. He might therefore be called the first president of Easton's first Board of Education. The building was at times used as a place of worship by the Reformed, the Lutherans, and the Moravians. (Town Lots Nos. 70 and 72)

NUMBER 33

Herman Shnyder is listed as a tanner owning a house and lot in Easton in the years 1772 and 1776. This property was surveyed for his use on March 1st, 1771. The name Shnyder is spelled in many ways. On a map of Easton, dated 1857, this entire block, with the exception of one small lot, is shown as belonging to P. Shnyder and the tannery is still shown on the banks of the Bushkill Creek. (Town Lots Nos. 266 and 267)

* * *

NUMBER 34

The father of Frederick Shouse was Adam Schaus who migrated to Pennsylvania from Albsheim in the Lower Palatinate about the year 1735. His wife Barbara and two sons, Philip and Frederick, came with him. He was a wheelwright by occupation and settled at Falkner's Swamp. In the spring of 1743 Adam Schaus settled in Bethlehem, where he and his son Philip helped Mr. Antes erect a grist mill. In 1745 Adam Schaus was ferryman for the Moravians and operated the ferry across the Lehigh River at Bethlehem. In 1760 we find him and his son Frederick in Easton. The father was an innkeeper and the son a mason in charge of the erection of the Moravian Building on south Pomfret Street (No. 9 of the Map). It is likely that Frederick Shouse succeeded his father as an innkeeper. However the assessment lists of 1774 and 1776 list him as a mason. The executor of his estate refers to him as a mason. It is probable that he helped in the construction of the Court House. Frederick Shouse erected his own house on the north side of Northampton Street west of Hamilton. He wrote his will on February 18, 1788 and mentions the following children: Mary, the wife of Michael Yohe, Christian, Henry, Jacob, and John. On May 18, 1790 Michael Yohe, his son-in-law, and the executor of his estate, sold this property to Christian Meixsell, shopkeeper, for the consideration of two hundred and fifty pounds. (Town Lot No. 219)

NUMBER 35

Jeremiah Trexler purchased this property from the Proprietaries on March 12, 1754. He and his wife Catharine lived here, in the stone house which he had built, until August 4, 1779, when they sold the property to John Shuck, an innkeeper, for the sum of one hundred and fifty pounds. Jeremiah Trexler was one of the trustees of the little log school house built in 1755. (Town Lot No. 220)

* * *

NUMBER 36

John Mush was another of Easton's many shoemakers. He lived on this lot in 1772, perhaps before that date. His wife's name was Elizabeth. In 1803 they sold the western half of the lot, which was then vacant, to Peter Miller for five hundred dollars. In 1807 they sold the eastern half, on which had been erected a small log house, for one thousand dollars. John Mush (spelled Musch) was county treasurer from 1776 to 1781 during most of the Revolutionary War. (Town Lot No. 223)

* * *

NUMBER 37

This property was originally built and owned by Paul Miller. He was a stocking weaver and was licensed to sell liquor "by small measure". In September of 1757 he sold the property to Anthony Esser who is listed as a 'vitualler'. Six years after he acquired title Esser sold the property to George Gangware. In September of 1765 Gangware conveyed the house and lot to Peter Schneider, who strengthened his title by securing a deed from Sheriff Peter Kachlein when the goods and real estate of Gangware were sold by order of the court to satisfy a judgment. The date of the sheriff's deed is December 16, 1766. Casper Doll, one of the executors of the estate of Peter Shnyder (note change in spelling) on June 13, 1776 joined in conveying the house and lot to Peter Kachlein. On June 29, of that same year, Kachlein gave a deed for the property to Casper Doll. So in the year 1776 there were three individual owners of this house and lot, i. e., Peter

Shnyder Estate, Peter Kachlein, and Casper Doll. Who lived in the house at this time is not known. Peter Kachlein evidently did not, as he held title for only two weeks. It is not likely that Casper Doll lived here, for he was a resident of Plainfield Township. Doll had a daughter named Maria who married John Young. In his will, dated June 13, 1793, Casper Doll bequeathed the property to his daughter Maria Young. Maria outlived her husband and by her will dated June 29, 1813, she left the western half of the lot to her son Peter. On April 5, 1814, Peter Young as executor of his mother's estate, sold the eastern half with the house to Jacob Wagener. (Town Lot No. 166)

* * *

NUMBER 38

On December 30, 1771, Myer Hart, merchant, purchased this property from James Taylor, a son of George Taylor. The house had been built by Nicholas Scull Jr. about 1754 when he secured title to the lots from the Penns. Nicholas Scull, the surveyor general of the province, had two sons living in Easton. Nicholas Jr., herein mentioned, and Jasper, a blacksmith, who lived at the southwest corner of Northampton and Hamilton Streets. In 1795 the assignees of Myer Hart sold the property to Mordecai Peirsol. The dwelling was constructed of native blue limestone. Scull, while in possession of the property, used it as an inn and accommodated some of the Philadelphians who attended the various Indian Treaties. No record has been found of Scull's having a license to sell liquor either "by small measure" or wholesale. (Town Lot No. 167)

* * *

NUMBER 39

There is some uncertainty as to whether this building had been erected as early as 1776. In 1771 the lot was vacant. On February 6, 1781, Moritz Bishoff, a clockmaker, married, "with the consent of her parents", Christina Bush. They had at least two children, Johannes and Anna Maria. On May 31, 1791, Christina Bishoff, widow and administrator of Moritz Bishoff, deceased, sold the lot of ground and the stone shop erected thereon to Christian Winters. Winters was also a clock maker. In 1776, John Murphy, another clock maker, lived at the southeast corner of the Great Square and Northampton Street. Easton's best known clockmaker, Christian Bixler, did not settle in Easton until some time after the Revolutionary War. (Town Lot No. 139)

* * *

NUMBER 40

John Stillwagon of Philadelphia purchased this lot from the Proprietaries in 1760 and erected thereon a small dwelling. In 1772 he sold it to Frederick Nungesser, who died about a year later. The property remained in the estate until 1801 when it was sold to Absolom Reeder, who had married Christina Smith, a granddaughter of Nungesser. Absolom Reeder was the father of Andrew H. Reeder, who became the governor of the territory of Kansas. Who lived in the dwelling in 1776 is not known, but it is probable that one of the children of Frederick Nungesser occupied this residence. (Town Lot No. 83)

* * *

NUMBER 41

Andrew Ledlie, practitioner of physic, purchased this property from Thomas Miller, of Bucks County, on June 8, 1776. Ledlie was in possession of the property at the time he bought it. The lot had been purchased from the Penns by John Jones of Bethlehem township in 1755. Andrew Ledlie seems to have been quite active in his profession but his reputation is somewhat clouded by his relations with his house-keeper. The reference to them, in the minutes of the Committee of Safety, is in such plain harsh terms that the State of Pennsylvania, when they published these minutes in 1852, omitted part of the descriptive matter. (Town Lot No. 79)

* * *

NUMBER 42

Joseph Growf (Graff) purchased this lot from the Proprietors as early as 1754. He was a blacksmith and came from

Lower Saucon Township. He held title for three years and on March 15, 1757 sold it to David Barringer, a shoemaker from Upper Milford township. Barringer became a merchant after he moved to Easton. He became financially involved and the sheriff, Peter Kachlein, sold the property, in the year 1773, to Elizabeth the widow of Conrad Streuber, a tanner. Elizabeth Streuber lived in this property during the period of the Revolutionary War and in 1784 conveyed title to Christopher Hertzel, a saddle maker. The house could not have amounted to much for it brought the following prices:—in 1757, fifty-three pounds; in 1773, one hundred pounds; and in 1784 only eighty pounds. (Town Lot No. 204)

* * *

Number 43

Jacob Berlin, a son of Abraham Berlin, purchased this lot with the house, stable, and garden from Melchoir Hay on June 29, 1776. Jacob was a blacksmith, having served his apprenticeship under his father. Melchoir Hay secured title from the Penns on February 4, 1762. (Town Lot No. 174)

* * *

Number 44

George Bush, a carpenter, is assessed with a house and lot on the assessment list of 1776. No deed has been found for any lot conveyed to George Bush, but in some of the early deeds for the lot to the south of this property the statement is made that this lot was in his tenure. (Town Lot No. 201)

* * *

Number 45

Michael Butz of Forks township acquired this property at sheriff's sale on March 23, 1768. He held it until June 10, 1778 when he and his wife Elizabeth sold it to John Spengenbergh who at the time of the sale was living in Easton and who in the deed is referred to as "schoolmaster". As Spengenbergh is not listed as owning a house in 1776 and Michael Butz was a resident of

Forks township it is assumed that Spengenbergh, the schoolmaster, was a tenant occupying this dwelling during the Revolution. There is some evidence to indicate that Adam Hay lived in this house in 1776. Further evidence may clear up this uncertainty. (Town Lot No. 125)

* * *

NUMBER 46

In 1776 Christian Holland was assessed with a house and lot. This must have been his residence in that year. No records have been found showing how he secured title, but on July 12, 1785, he conveyed this property to Adam Dennis. Dennis was a twiner. Conrad Ihrie, Jun., secured title to this property and on December 4, 1789, he secured a deed from the Penns.

Christian Holland was a nailsmith. (Town Lot No. 124)

* * *

NUMBER 47

Henry Busch (Bush) lived in this house from 1757 to 1790. In 1777 he made application for a liquor license which was granted. The tax list of 1772 gives his occupation as laborer, while the lists of 1774 and 1776 call him a butcher. In 1789 he secured a deed from the Penns and in this conveyance he is referred to as a yeoman. In 1790 he and his wife Eve sold the property to Jacob Sickman. Henry Busch had a daughter Mary who married Jacob Good. They may have had other children. (Town Lot No. 102)

* * *

NUMBER 48

In the year 1752, John Lefevre, the tavern keeper on the Wind Gap road at a point now in the Borough of Stockertown, secured a warrant for this lot. Adam Yohe purchased Lefevre's interest in this lot and a deed or patent was issued to him on October 30, 1765. On June 13, 1775, Yohe and his wife Christina sold the messuage and lot of ground to Henry Fullert. Fullert lived here until his death when Abraham Berlin, the administrator of his estate, sold the lot to Adam Dreisbach. The date of this deed was November 15, 1782. Henry Fullert was under-sheriff in 1772 and high-sheriff from 1774 to 1777. (Town Lot No. 76)

* * *

NUMBER 49

In 1776 George Taylor owned this lot. On it he had erected a stone stable. The stable was used in connection with the house which he then owned at the northeast corner of Northampton and Fermor Streets. He sold the lot and stable to Theophilus Shannon on August 24, 1779. (Town Lot No. 73)

* * *

NUMBER 50

Frederick Nungesser is listed as a storekeeper and as a tavern keeper. The fact that he had been granted a license to sell liquor and that he also ran a general store accounts for this dual classification. He died on May 3, 1774 and his widow Christina was appointed administratrix of the estate. She continued the business for a number of years. Frederick secured that portion of the lot on which the house stands from the Penns in 1765. Although he evidently had a warrant or some kind of a claim on the corner portion of this lot and on which he had built his stable, it was not until 1789 that the Penns gave his widow a deed to this part of the property. In 1795, John Nungesser, a son of Frederick, in whom the title was then vested, sold the property to Adam Yohe, Innkeeper. It is more than likely that the Widow Nungesser lived in this house in 1776. (Town Lots Nos. 132 and 133)

* * *

NUMBER 51

John Spering was a cordwainer and a native of England. On November 19, 1771, he purchased this frame house and lot from Melchoir Hay. On November the 20, 1771, he gave a mortgage, covering this property, to Peter Ealer. Spering paid the mortgage money in full to the assignees of Peter Ealer on March 29, 1777. In 1775 he was a post-rider between Easton and Philadelphia.

Some time in March of 1778 he abandoned his wife Katharine and his children, passed through the enemy lines, and sailed for England. Summons were issued requiring him to appear before a Justice of the county on a charge of high treason. Failing to appear he was attainted a traitor and his property confiscated.

John Spering left his family in sore financial straights. The daughter Jane, then over fourteen years of age, was bound out as a servant to Jacob Arndt. The daughter Elizabeth, under fourteen years of age, was bound out to Andrew Kachline.

A son, Henry, on behalf of himself and his brother, John, a soldier in the army of the United States, and his two sisters, petitioned the Assembly to restore their father's property to them. On November 22, 1782, an act was passed vesting the title to the house and lot to the four children. Henry subsequently became the sole owner and in order to perfect his title secured a deed from the Penns, which deed was dated September 27, 1791.

Henry Spering was sheriff from 1797 to 1800. (Town Lot No. 140)

* * *

NUMBER 52

Christian Peiffer (Pipher), yeoman, of Forks Township, purchased this lot in 1774 from Mayer Hart who had owned it for a period of ten years. Hart was a merchant and may have conducted his store at this location. The purchase price was forty pounds. Peiffer evidently moved into the village and established himself as a store keeper, for thus we find him classified in the assessment lists. In his will dated February 19, 1785, he bequeathed this lot and house, wherein he then dwelt, to his son John. A daughter named Catharina married John Deichman (Dickman). The property sold in 1812 for thirty-one hundred dollars. (Town Lot No. 213)

* * *

NUMBER 53

John Deichman was a weaver and in 1776 was assessed with a house and lot. No conveyance to Deichman for this or any

other lot has been found. In a deed from the Penns to Andrew
Strasberger reference is made to this lot as belonging to John
Dickman. It therefore appears that this is the lot and house
where John Deichman lived in 1776. In 1794 the title became
vested in Mathias Eyerman, who secured a deed from the Penns.
In 1812 the property was sold for four hundred dollars. (Town
Lot No. 155)

* * *

NUMBER 54

On December 18, 1777, Abraham Labar, a tailor, wrote his
will and bequeathed this house and lot to his wife Rosina. This
man and his wife evidently lived here in 1776. After Abraham
Labar died, his widow married a man by the name of Rothrock.
(Town Lot No. 160)

* * *

NUMBER 55

John Simon was a hatter and lived in Easton, possibly in this
house, as early as June 12, 1763. On that date his son was baptized at the school house by the minister of the German Reformed
Church. In 1779 he became an elder of the church. After living
here for many years he perfected title to this property by securing
a deed from the Penns. This was dated November 9, 1789. The
consideration was fifty-six pounds and fourteen shillings. The lot
was L shaped. In 1814 his son Michael, who was also a hatter,
and Daniel Herster were appointed administrators of the estate
of John Simon, deceased. (Town Lots Nos. 130 and 131)

* * *

NUMBER 56

In 1772, a carpenter named Jacob Grotz Sr., secured title to
this lot from the Penns. Here he lived until his death which
occurred about 1803. On December 2, 1803 his heirs sold the
property to Samuel Sitgreaves for nine hundred forty-three dollars and thirty-three cents. His wife's maiden name was Elizabeth Shaffbuch. His son Jacob was also a carpenter and lived

in the same block. His daughter Elizabeth married Robert Traill. Jacob Grotz Sr. was the assessor for Easton who prepared the 1776 assessment list from which much of the information contained in these notes was secured. (Town Lot No. 62)

* * *

NUMBER 57

In 1765 Christopher Bittenbender, a blacksmith, secured a deed for this lot from the Penns. He died in 1804 or 1805, leaving a widow named Mary Elizabeth. The property was sold by his estate in 1816 to John Horn, the consideration being seventeen hundred and sixty-five dollars. Christopher Bittenbender had two brothers named Jacob and Conrad. (Town Lot No. 64)

* * *

NUMBER 58

Jacob Grotz, Jr., served his apprenticeship under his father and became a carpenter. He married Maria, the daughter of Conrad Hess of Williams Township. Just when he built this dwelling is not known, but he is listed as the owner of a house and lot in 1776. In common with many of the residents of Easton he secured a deed from the Penns on November 9, 1789. (Town Lot No. 68)

* * *

NUMBER 59

In the list of 1776, Henry Barnet, tanner, is assessed with a house, two horned cattle, and two horses. The house was of stone and was located at the southwest corner of Hamilton and Bushkill Streets. He died intestate about 1801 and left a widow and the following children: John, William, Elizabeth, and Susanna. A daughter named Mary, who preceded him in death, had married Adam Yohe. Elizabeth became the wife of Conrad Bittenbender and Susanna married Jacob Yohe. At the time of the death of Henry Barnet his real estate consisted of the stone house, six acres of land, a tanyard, and two lots in the Borough of Easton. In the distribution of the real estate, Conrad Bittenbender, on behalf of his wife Elizabeth, accepted the stone house and lot. This was on August 22, 1806. The stone house stood until 1939, when, due to old age and neglect, it was torn down. (Town Lot No. 269)

* * *

NUMBER 60

Jacob Reeger purchased this lot from the Penns on December 4, 1789. Jacob was the son of Frederick Reeger, who is listed on the tax lists of 1774, 1776, and 1779 as a dyer and the owner of a house. A Frederick Ricker, a laborer, is listed in 1772 and he may have been the same as the Frederick mentioned above.

Frederick Reeger died in the spring of 1780, leaving a widow named Barbara and three children: Frederick, Ann, and Jacob. Frederick married Margaret, the daughter of Michael Lean (Lehn). Jacob secured possession of his father's interest in the property and perfected title by securing a deed from the Penns as above recited. Jacob Reeger and his wife Ann sold the northern half of this lot to Conrad Bittenbender on September 5, 1792.

In 1772 a Ludwig Richer is listed as "poor". In 1774 Ludwig Rieger is taxed as a dyer and in 1776 Ludwig Reeger appears on the tax list as a mason owning a house. In 1779 a Lewis Reiger's name appears.

It is more than likely that Frederick Reeger (Sr.) occupied this property in 1776. (Town Lot No. 268)

* * *

NUMBER 61

This lot was deeded to John Rinker in 1765. Before that date Rinker had erected a house on the lot. To satisfy a judgment which George Taylor had secured against John Rinker, Peter Kachlein, sheriff, sold the house and lot to Jacob Arndt of Forks Township. This was on December 18, 1766. Three weeks later Arndt sold the property to trustees who purchased it as a parsonage for the minister of the German Reformed Church. This minister was to serve Easton and vicinity as well as Greenwich Township in the Province of New Jersey. Rinker built the house before the Indian Treaties and conducted it as a tavern or inn.

During the treaties a number of citizens from Philadelphia roomed here. In 1776 the house was the parsonage of the German Reformed Church and was frequently referred to as the "Presbyterian Parsonage". (Town Lot No. 169)

* * *

NUMBER 62

No deed or other conveyance appears on record covering a house and lot belonging to Andrew Eichelmeyer. However, in 1776 he is assessed with a house, a town lot, and an outlot and is listed as a laborer. In 1794 Absolom Reeder secured title from the Penns for this lot. The deed conveyed the lot subject to the rights of Andrew Eichelmeyer. In May of 1802 Eichelmeyer, then of Lower Mount Bethel Township, gave a release to Absolom Reeder covering all his rights in the property. The release states that Daniel Reichert had a lease on the property which did not expire until April 1, 1803. From these facts it is assumed that Andrew Eichelmeyer lived here in 1776. (Town Lot No. 227)

* * *

NUMBER 63

In April of 1777, Robert Lettis Hooper, Jr. (the third of that name) lived in Saucon Township about five miles south of Bethlehem. He later moved to Easton and was living in this stone house in April of 1779. He lived here some time previous to and some time after this date. His wife Margaret died in this building.

Colonel Robert Lettis Hooper, Jr., was Deputy Quartermaster General during the Revolutionary War and was one of the three superintendents having charge of the magazines for the Continental Army. He was also Assistant Commissary of Purchases and Deputy Commissary of Transportation for General Sullivan's expedition against the Six Nations.

The house is now standing but who built it or lived in it in 1776 is not known. (Town Lot No. 239)

* * *

NUMBER 64

In 1789 Margaret Everhart (Everhard, Everhardt), widow of Arnold Everhart, was in possession of this property. Arnold

Everhart's name appears on the tax lists of 1774 and 1776 as the owner of a house and lot. He is recorded as a weaver in 1774 and as a laborer in 1776. His will, written on February 1, 1782, bequeathed his property to his widow during her widowhood. On the death of Margaret the property became vested in her son Frederick.

On October 2, 1810, Frederick Everhard made an assignment of the property to William White. Here White conducted Easton's best hostelry which soon became known as "Chippy White's Hotel". It is quite likely that White erected a new building for his hotel. It was in the "back-room" of this hotel that Lafayette College was conceived.

It seems probable that Arnold Everhart and his family lived here when the Declaration of Independence was read from the Court House steps on July 8, 1776. (Town Lot No. 81)

* * *

NUMBER 65

Michael Lean (Lehn) wrote his will on March 13, 1781. It was probated April 24, 1784. He mentions his house and lot in Easton wherein he dwelt. He names a son Adam and a daughter Margaret who married Frederick Reeger. He also mentions his step-son Michael Yohe. Adam Lean, the son of Michael, secured a deed from the Penns for this property. Michael Lean was in possession of this lot in 1767 and the tax lists of 1763, 1772, 1774, and 1776 list him as a laborer. The conclusion is that Michael Lean lived in this property in 1776. (Town Lot No. 90)

Index to

A FRONTIER VILLAGE

by

A. D. CHIDSEY, Jr.

Compiled by

WILLIAM W. CARLING

and

RICHARD I. SHELLING

1950

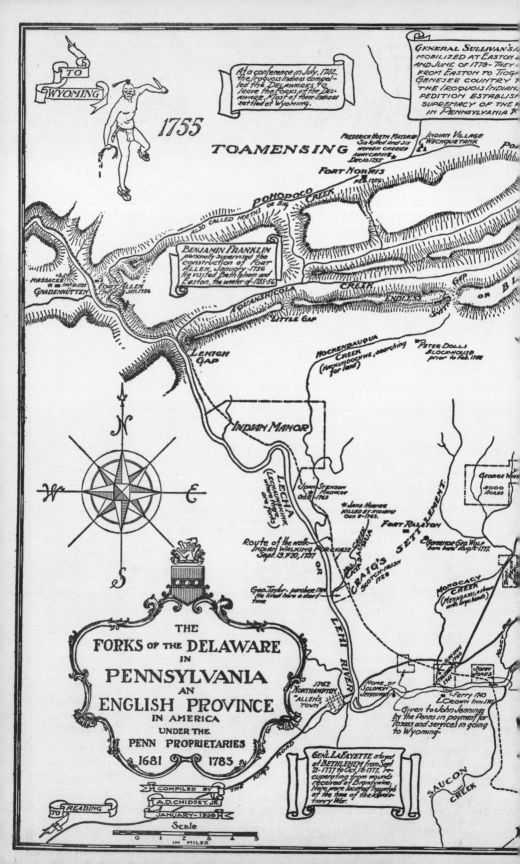

TO WYOMING

1755

TOAMENSING

At a conference in July, 1742, the Iroquois Indians compelled the Delawares to leave the forks of the Delaware. Most of their Indians settled at Wyoming.

GENERAL SULLIVAN'S A... MOBILIZED AT EASTON ... AND JUNE OF 1779. THEY ... FROM EASTON TO TIOGA ... GENESEE COUNTRY T... THE IROQUOIS INDIAN... PEDITION ESTABLISH... SUPREMACY OF THE M... IN PENNSYLVANIA

FREDERICK HOETH MASSACRE Six killed and six women carried away captive Dec. 10. 1755.

INDIAN VILLAGE WECHQUETANK

Po...

FORT NORRIS FEB. 1756

POHOPOCO CREEK or Big

also called HOETHS

BENJAMIN FRANKLIN personally supervised the construction of FORT ALLEN, January. 1756. He visited Bethlehem and Easton, the winter of 1755-56.

CREEK

ENDLESS

GAP or BL...

MASSACRE 1755 GNADENHÜTTEN

FORT ALLEN JAN. 1756

AQUANSHICOLA

LITTLE GAP

SOUTH

LEHIGH GAP

HOCKENDAUQUA CREEK (Hachkundochwe, searching for land)

PETER DOLLS BLOCKHOUSE prior to Feb. 1756.

N

INDIAN MANOR

LECHIA (Lechaurokink where the forks are)

JOHN STENSON Oct. 8. 1763.

JANE HORNER KILLED BY INDIANS Oct 8. 1763.

GEORGE WHI... 5000 ACRES

FORT RALSTON

W E

Route of the walk INDIAN WALKING PURCHASE Sept. 19 & 20, 1737.

CATASAUQUA CREEK OR

CRAIG'S SCOTCH-IRISH 1728

SETTLEMENT

GOVERNOR GEO. WOLF born here Aug. 12. 1777.

S

Geo. Taylor purchased 1768. He lived here a short time.

LEHI RIVER

MONOCACY CREEK (Menagassi, a stream with large bends)

THE FORKS OF THE DELAWARE IN PENNSYLVANIA AN ENGLISH PROVINCE IN AMERICA UNDER THE PENN PROPRIETARIES 1681 1783

1762 NORTHAMPTON ALLEN'S TOWN

HOME OF SOLOMON JENNINGS

JOHN JONES

Ferry 1743 CROWN INN Given to John Jennings by the Penns in payment for losses and services in going to Wyoming.

COMPILED BY A. D. CHIDSEY, JR. JANUARY-1936

TO READING

GEN'L LAFAYETTE stayed at BETHLEHEM from Sept. 21-1777 to Oct. 18-1777. recuperating from wounds received at Brandywine. Here were located hospitals of the time of the Revolutionary War.

THE KING'S ROAD

SAUCON CREEK

Scale
0 1 2 3 4 5
IN MILES